Thoughts on Preaching

Thoughts on Preaching

Being contributions to homiletics

JAMES W. ALEXANDER

THE BANNER OF TRUTH TRUST

THE BANNER OF TRUTH TRUST

3 Murrayfield Road, Edinburgh EH12 6EL
P.O. Box 652, Carlisle, Pennsylvania 17013, U.S.A.

*

First published 1864
First Banner of Truth reprint 1975

*

ISBN 0 85151 210 0

PREFACE.

IT had long been the cherished wish of Dr Alexander to prepare a volume on Homiletics, for the use of young ministers and students; and with this object in view, he was in the habit of jotting down, in his private journals, in the form of paragraphs, such thoughts as occurred to him on the subject. In one of his later journals I find the following entry: "If the Lord should spare me below, it will be well for me some day to look over all my dailies, and collect what I have written from time to time on Ministerial Work. It is already enough for a volume. It might do good when I am gone." But death defeated his plans.

To carry out his purpose as far as it is now possible, I have collected these paragraphs, and print them just as they occur in his journals, without any attempt to arrange them in the order of subjects. I have also added to them several articles on the same subject, contributed by him to the Princeton Review, and a series of letters to young ministers, published in the Presbyterian, thus giving to the public, in a permanent form, all that he has written upon these important topics. In addition to these I have introduced some paragraphs on miscellaneous subjects from the same journals, most of them bearing upon ministerial life and experience. Although deeply sensible of the inadequacy of this work to convey fully the matured experience of the author, I am not prepared to withhold its publication; believing that incomplete as it is, it may yet be of advantage to all who are looking forward to the sacred office.

In such a collection there must necessarily be some repetition of thoughts, and some opinions which were afterwards modified by the author; but I have concluded to give the whole as it stands, rather than attempt an elimination which might weaken rather than give strength to the subject.

S. D. A.

CONTENTS.

———0———

HOMILETICAL PARAGRAPHS.

LETTERS TO YOUNG MINISTERS.

LETTER I.

LETTER VI.

LETTER VII.

LETTER VIII.

LETTER IX.

LETTER X.

STUDIES AND DISCIPLINE OF THE PREACHER.

THE MATTER OF PREACHING.

EXPOSITORY PREACHING.

THE PULPIT IN ANCIENT AND MODERN TIMES.

ELOQUENCE OF THE FRENCH PULPIT.

THOUGHTS ON PREACHING.

HOMILETICAL PARAGRAPHS.

FROM THE AUTHOR'S PRIVATE JOURNALS.

§ 1. *Formalism of Sermons.*—Without flattering myself with the notion that I was ever eloquent, I am persuaded that the most effective discourses I ever delivered, were those for which I had made the least regular preparation. I wish I could make sermons as if I had never heard or read how they are made by other people. The formalism of regular divisions and applications is deadly. And as to written sermons, what is written with weariness is heard with weariness.

§ 2. *Avoid Abstractions.*—If you would keep up attention, avoid abstractions in your sermons, except those of mere argument. Come down from generals to specifications, and especially to individual cases. Whenever possible, give name and place, and intersperse anecdote. By this means the Puritans, even when they were prolix, were vivacious. They subsidized every event of Old Testament history, and talked of David and of Judas, instead of royalty and treason.

§ 3. *Memoriter Discourse.*—When Pompey the Great was going from the vessel to be murdered, he spent his time in the little Egyptian boat, in reading a little book in which he had written a Greek oration, which he had intended to speak to Ptolemy. Vol. 13, p. 257.

§ 4. *Suggested by my Last Sermon.*—Unless a sermon is amazingly long, one must not write an analysis, or brief, of many members. You will find that on each you have hardly more than a couple of pages, in which short space you cannot get a-going on any of the topics.

Again: There is a greater force and condensation in the rapid first draughts which I write as a basis, than in the sermons which I make on them: Why? Because in writing the second time I try to expand each of the points. How shall the weakness consequent on this be avoided? By writing a rapid, warm, percussive, cordial *basis*, at a glow—and then doing little more than to put this into shape; turning the hints into propositions.

§ 5. *Diction.*—The great fastidiousness of the House of Commons is often mentioned, but it is nothing to that of the Greek Demos. The standard which Aristotle assumes, and which was evidently that of the times, was so severe as to exclude from oratory every thing in the diction which betrayed the slightest artifice. Read particularly on this subject what is written, Chap. 2, Book iii. of the Rhet., especially § 10.

The third chapter of the third book, about Frigid diction, is capital. The four sources of the Frigid are flowing perpetually among our Americans. He speaks admirably of the tendency to make prose run into poetry.

§ 6. *Reading the Scriptures.*—To-day I took up my Greek Testament, and, as I walked about the floor, read the 2d Epistle to Timothy, pausing in thought on certain striking places. I saw many new excellencies—had some new rays of light—and was more than ever convinced of the excellency of this way of Scripture study. Especially when, after a number of *rapid* perusals, one goes over the ground with more and more ease every time.

§ 7. *On Composing Sermons.*—*Notes on Conversations with J. A. A.*—My father says a man should not begin with making a plan. Should not wait until he is in the vein. Begin, however you feel; and write until you get into the vein—however long it be. 'Tis thus men do in mining. You may throw away all the beginnings. Men who write with ease think best pen in hand. This applies to sermons, and also to books. It might be well to write a sermon *currente calamo*, and then begin again and write afresh (not copying, or even looking at the other, but), using all the lights struck out in the former exercise.

§ 8. *Preaching.*—The sermon I have last written, on Gen. 49, 4, is the least evangelical I ever made; yet this did not once enter into my head until I had finished. Let me learn to be careful how I censure others. Further, let me learn the importance of making *all* my written sermons discussions of some important point of doctrine. The times need this, and my mind needs it, both in regard of theological knowledge and ratiocinative discipline. Treat doctrines practically, and experience argumentatively. Avoid technicalities, avoid heaping up of texts, like stones without mortar.

§ 9. *Dwell on Good Thoughts.*—Very important. This seems something more than what is hackneyed. Think it out. If it occur in reading, pause, raise your eyes from the book, and follow it out. Thoughts which come up first are naturally trite. This is especially so of illustration. If one occurs, pursue it, follow it into the particular parts of the resemblance. If a metaphor or similitude, carry it forth in all its lesser resemblances. If it seem hackneyed, take some analogous one—take several. All these processes of thought will be useful at some other time, for our good trains of thought are seldom entirely lost. No man could ever speak extempore, if every thing he said was literally the fruit of the moment. No; in many instances by some association, a whole train of thoughts which had been forgotten for years will be brought up.

§ 10. *On Sermon-writing.* (*Concio ad meipsum.*)—The last Lord's day of the year has arrived, and, on reviewing your labours, you must feel that you have not stirred up the gift that is in you. Your talent, *qualiscunque sit*, has been too much laid up in the napkin. Especially in the matter of writing you have been delinquent. Many things you have written, and even printed ; but few sermons. You have bestowed your time and labour on secondary and inferior things. One thing is needful.

You have been favoured by Providence with a degree of acceptance as a writer which you had not dared to expect, and for which you cannot be too thankful; but the same little attractions might have been cast around the great things of the kingdom. Consider these hints.

1. If your life be spared, you will never see a time in which, better than now, you can lay up a store of sermons. Eyesight, manual dexterity, memory, and vivacity must necessarily be on the wane.

2. Consider in what manner you have produced those things which have gained a little popularity. They have all been written *currente calamo ;* especially those which have most life in them were so written. Not so most of your sermons. Turn over a new leaf. Do not lay out new plans too carefully. Write while you are warm. Do not be avaricious of your best thoughts, nor reserve warm ideas for the last. This is like flooding the stomach of guests with soups, before dinner. Much of Jay's excellence arises from this. Try your father's recommendation of writing with great rapidity what first occurs to you. This you may methodize afterwards.

3. You study much of the Scriptures, and sometimes warm over the sacred page. Avail yourself of these moments, and let your discoveries and suggestions flow into the channel of a sermon.

4. Be willing to write even part of a sermon. Perhaps you will do the whole. If not, remember how few of these fragments have ever been lost to you; is there one, the time spent on which you regret ?

5. You have prayed to have your tastes, feelings, and pursuits

more concentrated on divine things ; and, for a short time past, you have felt as if this grace had in some degree been granted to you. Cherish this feeling, and make it available towards pulpit exercises.

6. God has granted you better health. Be tenderly thankful for such a benefit, and keep your harness always bright, that you may be ready, as soon as God shall cause the trumpet to sound, to go out into the regular ranks.

7. You have a text-book. Use it. Spend more time on it. Collect your scattered fragments. Mortify that procrastination which keeps so many plans *in petto*.

§ 11. *Offhand Writing.*—If I have ever written any thing acceptably, it has been with a free pen, and from the full heart ; not from compiled stores, though I have done much of the latter also. One who has preached in so many fields, and exactly surveyed so few, had well confine himself to this sort of offhand and discursive composition. What is the reason that, having plainly shown a turn for a lively, superficial, easy kind of chat, enlivened by a few out-of-the-way stories, &c., &c., I have never perpetrated any thing like a book of this kind, save the two books for the working-folks, which were mere strung beads? And why have I, contrary to my natural turn, always preached in the commonplace humdrum manner, instead of giving free vent to the things that come into my head? I have been gathering long enough ; it is time for me to write more, and to write something which may attract attention to the things of God, and do good to people who will not read heavy, learned books. I have penned a great deal, but mostly under some constraint, which has pent me up and hampered me. It is high time that I followed nature, and let out the stream without constraint. Sometimes I have written for children, and this was of course a great restraint ; at other times for newspapers, where I had to be very short, or very careful not to offend ; and in the case of the Sunday-School Journal, for which I have done a good deal, I have had to avoid every thing sectarian. When I wrote for the Review, which pieces have been most laboured, I have necessarily tied myself up to the formal paces demanded in such affairs. And as I said, my sermons have never got clear of the formality with which I unfortunately began to write. I am conscious of a great desire to use my poor, and almost single talent of writing for the people, in some way which may recommend religion more than I have ever done yet.

§ 12. *Earnest Preaching.*—I have been reading an article on the *Eloquence of the Pulpit* in the Montauban " Revue Theologique " for the present month, written by Adolphe Monod. It is one of the best things I ever read on the subject. He makes elocution to depend on the inward conception and feeling. The work must begin from within.

The great reason why we have so little good preaching is that we have so little piety. To be eloquent one must be in earnest; he must not only act as if he were in earnest, or try to be in earnest, but be in earnest, or he cannot be effective.

We have loud and vehement, we have smooth and graceful, we have splendid and elaborate preaching, but very little that is earnest. One man who so feels for the souls of his hearers as to be ready to weep over them—will assuredly make himself felt. This is what makes——effective; he really feels what he says. This made Cookman eloquent. This especially was the charm of Summerfield, above all men I ever heard. We must aim therefore at high degrees of warmth in our religious exercises, if we would produce an impression upon the public mind. Two or three such preachers in our Old School Church as—— is, would make themselves felt throughout the country. O ! that we had them ! O ! that those we had were inspired with greater zeal !

Without any increase of our numbers, the very men we now have, if actuated with burning zeal for God, might work a mighty reformation in our country.

§ 13. *New Sermons.*—Philip Henry used to love to preach sermons which were " newly studied." It is a crying sin of mine that I am so ready to go to my old store. Even when I preach to the blacks, I ought, for my own sake, no less than for theirs, to prepare a plan, and study it out. If I daily had on hand some sermon on an important passage, I should be daily learning more Scripture and more theology.

§ 14. *Great Subjects.*—Again I am impressed with what I have already mentioned in this book, viz., the importance of choosing *great subjects* for sermons; such as Creation, the Deluge, the Atonement, the Last Things. This is the more important considering that I preach only occasionally, and write seldom.* These discourses ought to be highly elaborated. I have no sermons such as I ought to preach, and such as I think I have preached extempore. Humphrey's remarks on easy engraving have given me new thoughts on easy writing. I have often intended to write out a discourse which I have preached with some sense of doing better than common; but as far as I remember, I have never yet done it.

§ 15. *Themes for Preaching.*—They should be great themes— *the* great themes. These are many. Evil of dwelling on the smaller themes. They are such as move the feelings. The great questions which have agitated the world—which agitate our own bosoms—which we should like to have settled before we die—which we should ask an Apostle about if he were here. These are to general Scripture truth, what great mountains are in Geography. Some, anxious to avoid hackneyed topics, omit the greatest. Just as if we should, describe Switzerland and omit the Alps.

Some ministers preach twenty years, and yet never preach on Judgment, Hell, the Crucifixion, the essence of saving faith— nor on those great themes which in all ages affect children, and effect the common mind, such as the Deluge, the sacrifice intended of Isaac, the death of Absalom, the parable of Lazarus. The Methodists consequently pick out these striking themes, and herein they gain a just advantage over us.

A man should begin early to grapple with great subjects.

* He was at this time Professor in the College of New Jersey.

An athleta (2 Tim. 2, 5) gains might only by great exertions. So that a man does not overstrain his powers, the more he wrestles the better, but he *must* wrestle, and not merely take a great subject, and dream over it or play with it.

Evil of seeking new and recondite subjects. All the great subjects are old and often treated. False refinement and wire-drawing. Analogy of the great sculptors and painters. Many took the same themes. Greek tragedians. No two men will treat the same subject alike, unless they borrow from one another.

§ 16. *Sermon-writing.*—As I consider sermonizing a great art, and one of the chief employments of a minister, I think it good from time to time, to set down the results of my experience ; though I have a painful consciousness of my own want of proficiency.

In the early part of my ministry there were two methods of preparation which I highly valued, both of which I now reject.

1. It was my manner to take some doctrinal head, such as Justification, and carefully to read the best authors on it, such as Calvin, Witsius, Markius, Dwight, making notes as I went along, and then endeavouring, when I wrote, to introduce the best things I could remember from these authors. I had not then learned, that the only way to profit from such authors, is to let their matter digest in the mind, and then to write freely, with a total forgetfulness of them. Only in this way, does it become our own. Only in this way does it take a natural method, and have a natural liveliness. It is difficult to reject the things remembered, and the effort at recollection is itself an incumbrance. I would advise a preacher, in preparation, to take no notes. I would advise him to take no schedule of arrangement from another. If one thinks at all for himself, his train of thoughts will be his own, and this will suggest its own arrangement. There is something unreasonable in setting out with a preadjusted method. It is to attempt a classification, before we have that which is to be classified. It produces a stiffness, hardness, and want of continuity, which are great faults. The

true way is, be full of the subject, and then write with perfect freedom, beginning at any corner of the subject.

2. Another method which I pursued, was to choose a text, and then having written out in full all the parallel passages, to classify them, and found my divisions on this classification. Then to correct all these passages, interweaving them with my own remarks. I flattered myself that this was a happy method, because it made my sermon scriptural. It did so indeed, but it had great disadvantages. The *nexus* between the texts was factitious; often refined and recondite; and always more obvious to the writer than it could be to the reader. It prevented the flow of thought in a natural channel. It was like a number of lakes connected by artificial canals, as compared with a flowing natural stream. The discourse was disjointed, and overladen with texts, and uninteresting. I am convinced that those passages of Scripture which suggest themselves unsought, in rapid writing or speaking, are the most effective; nay, that one such is worth a hundred lugged in *collo obtorto*. To be Scriptural in preaching, we must be familiar with the Bible at common times. Hence one of the great advantages of preaching without notes, even in regard to method. Such is the sympathy between soul and soul, that a connection of thoughts which is easy, agreeable, and awakening to the hearer, will always be found to be that which has been natural and unconstrained in the mind of the preacher. The best way is, to study the parallel places exegetically, perhaps as they lie in the Scripture, and then to let them come in or not, as they may suggest themselves during preparation.

§ 17. *The Power of the Pulpit.*—I fear none of us apprehend as we ought to do the value of the preacher's office. Our young men do not gird themselves for it with the spirit of those who are on the eve of a great conflict; nor do they prepare as those who are to lay their hands upon the springs of the mightiest passions, and stir up to their depths the ocean of human feelings. Where this estimate of the work prevails, men even of inferior training accomplish much; such as Summerfield, and even ——.

The pulpit will still remain the grand means of effecting the mass of men. It is God's own method, and he will honour it. The work done by Wesley and by Whitfield, and by Christmas Evans in Wales, could not have been accomplished by any other human agency—the press, for instance. In every age, great reformers have been great preachers ; and even in the corrupt Roman Church, the most wonderful effects have been produced by preaching. Bourdaloue and Massillon were successively brought to Paris from the Provinces; and when the former, late in life, most pathetically entreated that he might go into retirement, and at first was gratified, his Jesuit superiors used means with the Pope to have him restored to the metropolis.

To be a great preacher a man must be nothing else. The daily exercises of Demosthenes and Cicero may give us a hint of the devotion which is necessary. The analogy of all other arts and sciences may instruct. There are among us preachers who may be considered good, and in a certain sense great ones, who spend their principal strength during the week upon other pursuits. They write essays, systems, and commentaries. It may be observed of them all, that however useful they may be, these are not the men who move, and warm, and melt, and mould the public masses. Indeed, I think, to be a great preacher, a man must lay his account to forego that reputation which comes from erudition and literature. The channel must be narrowed, that the stream may flow in a rapid current, and fall with mighty impression. Even the learning of the schools must undergo a great process of transmutation and assimilation, before it is suitable to be produced in the pulpit. Great is the difference, though little apprehended, between a theological dissertation and a sermon, on the same subject. The crude matter falls heavily upon the popular ear. Only the last exquisite results of mental action are proper for public address. Not that the truth of doctrine is to be neglected; this is the very substance of all good sermons, and of every sentence of them, even in their most impassioned parts ; but it must have undergone a great change in the mind of the preacher, and present itself in a more popular form, with more of colour of imagination and warmth of passion, before it can reach the deep places of the heart with due effect.

The power of the preacher is not to be attained by rhetorical studies. These have their place, but it is an inferior and subsidiary one; and the result of undue attention to them is beautiful debility and cold polish. Let the imbecile elegancies of Blair be an everlasting beacon to the student of homiletics. It has been observed, that the age of elegant criticism follows that of poetry and eloquence. It would seem that the creative and critical spirit cannot coexist. The scruple and hesitation of rhetorical criticism are deadly foes to passion, the true source of effective discourse. To be powerful in pulpit address the preacher must be full to overflowing of his theme, affected in due measure by every truth he handles, and in full view, during all his preparation and all his discourse, of the minds which he has to reach.

§ 18. *Self-repetition in Preaching.*—It has been often observed, that preachers who rely on their extemporaneous powers, are very apt to fall into a great sameness. They repeat the same thoughts and the same trains of thought, and at length almost the same sermons : and this they do without being conscious of it. The same thing occurs to them which happens to some story-tellers : who remember the anecdote perfectly, but forget that they have told it before. Mere writing is not a certain preventive of this evil, but it has an excellent tendency to prevent it; as insuring an excellent amount of fresh study, and by keeping the mind, for longer periods and with greater deliberation, in view of the truth.

The evil is so disastrous, that there should be a constant effort to avoid it. Without this struggle, the preacher, on arriving at certain topics, which are familiar, will, by the simple influence of association, hitch into the old rut, and treat them exactly as he has treated them before. We observe this in extemporaneous prayers, which with some good men become as stereotyped as if they had been committed to memory : as, indeed, though unconsciously, they have been. We observe the same thing in that part of sermons, on which least of new meditation has been bestowed, namely, the conclusion. This accounts for the familiar fact, that some very fluent extemporaneous preachers are quite popular abroad, while at home, among their own flocks, they have lost all power, and seem to the people to be preaching the same discourse over and over.

The only remedy for this evil is the obvious one of devoting the mind to the origination of new trains of thought, which may vary, complete, or supersede the old ones. There may be superficial reflection and even superficial writing; but the meditation which is intended must go deeply into thorough investigation, and follow out the thoughts into new relations. It must be the habit of the preacher to be continually opening new veins, and deeply considering subjects allied to those on which he is to preach. This habit is greatly aided by judicious reading on theological topics. A man will be as his books. But of all means, none is so effectual as the perpetual study of the Scriptures. Let a man be interested in them day and night, continually labouring in this mine, and whether he write or not, he will be effectually secured against self-repetition. There is such profundity, comprehensiveness and variety in the Word of God, that it is a library of itself. There is such a freshness in its mode of presenting truth, that he who is perpetually conversant with it can scarcely be dull.

The liveliest preachers are those who are most familiar with the Bible, without note or comment; and we frequently find them among men who have had no education better than that of the common school. It was this which gave such animation to the vivid books and discourses of the Puritans. As there is no poetry so rich and bold as that of the Bible, so he who daily makes this his study, will even on human principles be awakened, and acquire a striking manner of conveying his thoughts. The sacred books are full of fact, example, and illustration, which with copiousness and variety will cluster around the truths which the man of God derives from the same source. One preacher gives us naked heads of theology; they are true, Scriptural, and important, but they are uninteresting, especially when reiterated for the thousandth time in the same naked manner. Another gives us the same truths, but each of them brings in its train a retinue of Scriptural example, history, a figure by way of illustration; and a variety hence arises which is perpetually becoming richer as the preacher goes more deeply into the mine of Scripture. There are some great preachers, who, like Whitfield, do not appear to bestow great labour on the preparation of particular discourses; but it may be observed, that these are always persons whose life is a study of the Word. Each sermon is an outflowing from a fountain which is constantly full. The Bible is, after all, the one book of the preacher. He who is most familiar with it, will become most like it; and this in respect to every one of its wonderful qualities; and will bring forth from its treasury things *new* and old.

§ 19. *Scripture Citation in Preaching.*—Do not cite many Scripture references in your notes. You often find them less available than those which occur *inter loquendum*. The best way of preparing for prompt quotation, is to be daily conversant with Scripture, and to commit large portions to memory. I regret more than I can express, my neglect of this in former years. The next best way, and a means of getting the facility just mentioned, is, in preparing for a given preformance, to read attentively and with meditation all the pertinent Scriptures, committing as many as possible to memory, but not referring them to particular places, or determining to use this or that without fail; it is enough to imbue the mind with them, and leave the use of any or all to be prompted by the impulse of the moment. The best effect of many Scripture texts on a sermon is often that which does not lead to a direct rehearsal of them. They suggest new thoughts and illustrations, and afford the very best preventive of that sameness and routine, into which most extempore preachers fall. The tendency in all, is to be contented with a narrow stock of texts. Take almost any extemporaneous preacher, whom you hear often, and observe how seldom he quotes a new text, one which you have not heard him quote before. How many noble incidents in the Old Testament history, touching emblems in the Levitical ritual, and poetic strains of the Prophets, are never introduced into the pulpit! All which commends the daily interested study of the Bible.

§ 20. *Uninvited Trains of Thought.*—The thoughts which come to us unasked, and the trains which float in the twilight of our careless hours, are often those which are most precious, longest remembered, and most deep in their influence on future life. They are sometimes the result of long studies pursued at irregular intervals during previous years, the distillation from many gathered flowers, and therefore they cannot be looked for as daily visitations. As they will not come for being called, so they will not stay for being courted. And when they give the first intimations of their approach, we should lay aside lesser employments and joys; as we open our windows when the fragrance of orchards is wafted on the breeze. Yet there is a posture of soul, better fitted than all others for the reception of these revelations; and there are pursuits and habits so alien to them as to be almost prohibitions.

We must not look for them in the crowd of mammon-mongers, or amidst the clangour of political array, or the mining drudgery of technical study. They steal over us rather when we close the eye at nightfall, listening to the drowsy music of the autumnal insect-tribe; when we walk alone in the sight of mountains, or on the sea-shore; or when we kneel before the open Bible, and meditate on the oriental usages of inspiration. Enthusiasts of various sects have taken these goodly visions for direct revelations of new truths: and mystics have deemed themselves inspired. But they are, after all, only higher manifestations of the Reason which is common to us all. We deny not that a Divine agent is sometimes at work, but the operation follows the laws of our rational humanity, and conforms itself to the conditions of all influence from above upon free creatures. The mind though elevated is not overborne. The free-thinking principle is the same as before, though raised to a loftier point of observation. God, who speaks in this silence, speaks by the word which was recorded hundreds of years ago; and though chapter or verse or textual phrase may not always be recognized, the truths which ring in the ear are echoes from Sinai or from Zion. That word of the Lord which abideth forever, has an infinite variety in its combinations and suggestions. It is a well whose sources are hidden in infinite wisdom, and whose flow is fresh and abundant and sparkling to everlasting periods.

We place ourselves in the way of such favoured contemplations, when we linger long and often over the holy pages, and imbue our thoughts with the lessons of Apostles and Prophets, to be inspired like them, we may not pray for, in this world, but we may catch a kindred glow from their heavenly rapture, sympathize with their affections, carry out the trains which they have begun, harmonize the scattered propositions which they have announced, and live over again in our experience the divine happiness of their sanctification. Though our circumstances may be unlike theirs, in the proportion in which the new world is unlike the old, our faith and love may be essentially the same, and may at some favoured moments realize to us glories of religious awe or fruition, which, after many years of Scriptural study, shall still be new and unwonted. It is thus that Christian experience is a book, of which the page we are turning over to-day, is unlike all that have filled the volume before.

To gain these results, a man must in some degree live apart. He must leave the beaten track, and converse less with earth than heaven. There are meditations which the common talk and worldly reading of our busy day do not prompt and cannot represent. They are beyond the scope of science, and unwhispered in the halls of letters, and the galleries of art. But as little should we seek them in the cell of the ascetic. True love and true humility, which are the nurses of such a progeny, are closely connected with familiar converse with our kind. Best thoughts are those which spring up under the shower of tears that falls over the ills of distressed fellow-creatures. Jesus Christ is still present by his Spirit where broken hearts are to be bound up. The house of mourning and the house of prayer are the places where the heart is made better.

§ 21. *Preaching, Remarks struck out in Talk with J. A. A.*—1. Almost all extemporaneous preachers have this fault; they talk about the *way* in which they are preaching—Thus : " After a few preliminary remarks, I shall proceed to," &c. ; or " What I lay down shall take the form of general principles." " I come with hesitation," &c. " I shall be more brief on this point." " You will observe that in this discussion I do so and so." Avoid all such observations.—More generally still, avoid all that brings the speaker's personality before the hearer. A better model than our honoured father in this there could not be.

2. Whenever I write down heads, from which to preach extempore, I always find myself disappointed, by not having as much to say under each as I thought, but whenever I premeditate a subject, and take my pen to write on it, I always find myself disappointed in a way exactly opposite.

3. Addison says truly, there is this difference between him and me. I am more warm and ornate when I do not write ; he, when he does.

4. As men who strut in walking, sometimes find it difficult to get out of it, and step in the ordinary way, so in writing men get into a measured, rhythmical, ornamental flow of diction, and find it hard, even when the subject demands it, to come down to the pedestrian style. Hence a great argument for simplicity. What a wonderful simplicity in Goethe ! It is his characteristic in regard to style. Even Voltaire, simple as his structure of sentence always lies, has a mannerism : so has Macaulay. The reader comes to look for a certain pungent apodosis. In Goethe, nothing leads you to expect any particular bringing up of the period, or antithesis of the thought.

§ 22. *Overhaul Sermons.*—It strikes me as a great neglect that I have scarcely ever looked over my pulpit MSS. except when I was going to preach. There is much work to be done in this field at other times.

§ 23. *On Writing down One's Thoughts.*—I mean such writing as I put in this book.

1. Writing does good to one's thinking.

2. It has the same effect in part as animated conversation.

3. Many good thoughts are lost that might have been preserved in this way.

4. Many good trains are carried to a greater length by this means.

5. Style is improved, especially by promptness and facility. Earnestness and impressiveness in writing grow as one advances.

6. Write till you feel a glow.

7. Write *when* you feel a glow. You will otherwise loose the very best things that ever occur to you. Remember Pascal (vid. Bib. Rep. Ap. 1845).

8. This is one of the chief exercises of mind; therefore embrace every occasion.

9. Choose topics which will excite you in the greatest degree. Choose the most important subjects, difficulties but not niceties, fundamentals, cardinal and central points, those which touch the heart of systems.

10. *Often give full scope to freedom of thought and style.* Thought creates style. If you write down to your readers, you lose this particular advantage of writing, as exercising thought.

Even in *sermons* to intelligent audiences there will be much of this, necessarily. It is desirable, therefore, to have some outlet for thoughts more free and unobstructed. The reflex influence of perfectly free composition is very great. What we so write, even in fragments, is remembered by us, goes to establish opinions, lays up arguments, gives matter for extemporaneous discourse, and moulds the character.

11. Devotional writing and prayer are of the highest moment.

12. It matters comparatively little whether you ever read over what you have written or not.

§ 24. *Mode of making Brief.*—I follow a brief penned at my table during a short interval. I made it thus: mere catchwords—took a general thought to start with, let the next come of itself, then the next, and so on without effort. It served well. The thing to be noted is, that in a few moments, *by letting the mind flow*, and not interfering with the flow, one may jot down materials for a long discourse. It was not merely *heads :* these are barren, they are disconnected; it was concatenation, it was *genesis.*

I consider this a little new, but Nevins showed me something like it for Sabbath lectures; I have done too much in the way of naked skeleton. I wish I could embody my thoughts in a formula; try it thus :

1. Write rapid sketch, the faster the better.

2. In first draught omit all partition, and do not force your mind to method.

3. Let thought generate thought.

4. Do not dwell on particulars; leave all amplification for the pulpit.

5. Keep the mind in a glow.

6. Come to it with a full mind.

7. Forget all care of language.

8. Forget all previous cramming, research, quotation, and study.

9. In delivery, learn to know when to dwell on a point; let the enlargement be, not where you *determined* in your closet it should be ; but where you feel the spring flowing as you speak *let it gush.* Let contemplation have place *while you speak.*

For this, *pauses* are all important. Thus Rob. Hall preached. Thus my beloved honoured father, above all men I ever heard ; his eye kindled, his face was radiant; he forgot the people; and as he was wrapt in contemplation, *he thought aloud.*

All this is connected with the subject of *gifts* in preaching ; and the operation of the Holy Spirit aiding the speaker. Holy emotions are indispensable. Hence the best sermons can never be exactly reproduced—much less written. The best written discourse of my father is no more to his best preaching, than a black candle is to a burning flame.

§ 25. *Extempore Preaching.*—This afternoon I made another trial of the method mentioned above. I found it good as far as tried. The fault was, that I used an old skeleton, and used my method only in the application.

Nota bene. It would be all the better if I made my brief early in the week.

§ 26. *Sermonizing.*—I have just finished a sermon on Isa. 59, ult. I am not pleased. I was " hampered" throughout, by a preconcerted *skeleton.* Thus it worked. Things would arise in my mind, and flow into my pen just at the right place, but I could not use them, *because they belonged to another head.* The result was, the articulation was broken, the flow was interrupted; the work became a mosaic. I perceive my father was right, when he advised me to write my first draught *currente calamo*, without any plan, with absolute abandon; giving free scope in every direction whenever a vein was struck, and reserving the particulars for the copy.

N.B. The best time for noticing emendations in a sermon, is just when you are done. They should be jotted down, even if you have no time to rewrite.

§ 27. *Sermons.*—I sometimes think I never acted out my inner man in a sermon. The nearest approach has been extempore. Causes which prevent:—fear of being too learned; fear of being too sentimental; fear of being too decorative; fear of being obscure; fear of being too vehement: all this is fear of being *myself*.

I consider some of my conclusions about simplicity; and doubt, more than doubt, whether a man may not aim at over-perspicuity. The thought makes the language. High thoughts will make high language.

Some men of study and research are called upon to preach in a strain above the common level, even if some do not understand them. There are enough who cannot rise above average minds. A man's best and loftiest meditations should go out of him in the shape of sermons.

I love to write, yet I have a repugnance to write sermons. This arises partly from constitutional trammels—skeletons—

plans—traditionary modes. Why do I not break out? I read
Vinet or Howe, and feel "Io ancheson pittore!"

§ 28. *Eloquence.*—In physics there are forces which operate
not mechanically, but dynamically; not by the conveyance of
new matter, but by the production of a new state or contact.
Such is now believed to be the mode of producing vision in the
human organ.

Something analogous to this occurs in operation of mind on
mind. *Over and above the truth conveyed,* I believe there may be
an operation. When I go to see a poor widow, and take her by
the hand, the words which I speak to her are for the most part
such as she has known before ; and yet she is comforted. The
same truths uttered from the pulpit by different men, or by the
same man in different states of feeling, will produce very different
effects. Some of these are far beyond what the bare conviction
of the truth so uttered would ordinarily produce. The whole
mass of truth, by the sudden passion of the speaker, is made
red-hot and burns its way. Passion is eloquence. Hence the
great value of extempore discourse.

Demosthenes' discourses read coldly sometimes ; but who can
restore on paper the whirlwind and earthquake power of the
passion with which they were delivered! No man can be a
great preacher, without great feeling. Hence the value of
devotional preparation. You should seize, for writing, moments
of great feeling. Record the outflow of these, and you will
perhaps have some measure of them in delivery.

§ 29. *Dividing Sermons.*—My opinion has changed a little
within a few months, about formality of *Division.* I mean I
incline more to Fenelon's judgment after having been very much
the other way.

I am perhaps in more favourable circumstances for a judgment than I was, because I am constantly experimenting.

The principle from which I set out, is one which grows in
my esteem every day, as a canon of composition : it is this—*In
writing or speaking throw off all restraint.*

Technical divisions are a restraint. I am familiar with their effect in trammelling the thoughts. Writing from a precomposed skeleton is eminently so. It forces one to parcel out his matter in a forced, Procustean way. There is a feeling like this: "I must have five pages for this branch, and five for that." The current is often thus stopped, at the very moment when it begins to gush.

The ideal of a discourse is that of a flow from first to last. The writing should begin when the mind is full. If then a division suggests itself, it may be followed; it may even be written down; but great care should be taken to prevent the mechanical partition of matter, so much here and so much there. Let the thoughts go on.

——, a veteran and able sermonizer, has formed the habit of casting every subject into a certain mould; two or three principal heads, followed by a series of reflections. The result is stiffness and sameness. I am not opposed to the strictest method, nor to the enunciation of it; but to the laying down beforehand of arbitrary arrangement. The matter to be arranged must precede legitimate arrangement.

In a sermon on Sanctification, I proceeded well till the application; when I went astray by making several topics of inference, which divided the stream instead of enlarging and quickening it.

It is impossible to close a sermon well, that is warmly, unless the train of thought has been so conducted as to bring the heart into a glow, which increases to the end. Having chosen a subject, it is well to think it over deeply, day and night, and to read on it carefully before putting pen to paper. Take few notes, but as far as may be let the matter digest itself in the mind. The result will be facility, fluency, close contexture, natural articulation of parts, vivacity, abundance of material, and as much originality as belongs to the author's genius. In this way, sermons will each have a separate, individual physiognomy, and sameness will be avoided.

I do not see why a sermon should not have all the freedom and fulness and progress of an oration. Consult in regard to this Demosthenes and Cicero. Though Augustine's sermons are very faulty as models, and abound in the false point of his time, they have their excellency. It belongs, moreover, to Fenelon, Howe, Chalmers, and Foster. Incomparable as Robert Hall is, in regard to argument, greatness and devotion, I am sensible in reading him, that he was clogged by the conventional manner of partition.

Be not prevented from indulging a flow which opens, even though it makes the sermon or any particular part of it, too long. You need not preach all that you have written; and the matter may be available for another occasion. This applies particularly to perorations, in which thoughts often overflow.

In a pathetic part, never write *invitâ Minervâ*. Never spin out coldly, or force the language of emotion. Rather be content with a single sentence: it may find enlargement in the delivery.

§ 30. *Application of Sermons.*—I still find myself trammelled, whenever I undertake to go in any of the regular harness of sermonizers. To be worth much, a sermon must begin like a river, and flow, and widen, and roughen, and deepen, until the end; and when it reaches this end, it is hurt by every syllable that is added.

Ordinary ' Applications' mar the unity of a discourse. They are often doctrinal corollaries; often commonplaces; often generalities, which equally fit a score of topics. When three or four heads of application are appended, the mind is first drawn one way and then another, and frequently altogether away from the body of the discourse. Every sermon tends *in some direction :* let it take that direction; it is the proper ending.

The superstitious reverence for an application of several points, cuts up this part of our sermons, short enough at best, and does not allow time to rise upon the wing, or to kindle with a flame.

It would be well, if we could grow hotter and hotter without intermission, from beginning to end.

The true way is to have an object and be full of it. Grace does more than rules.

§ 31. *Fresh Writing.*—There is a certain kind of writing on religion which greatly affects me, but which I find it hard to describe.

It is fresh, unscholastic, and awakening. It has little to do with quotation or erudition.

It proceeds from a mind full of thought and of feeling, and strikes as original even while the subject is familiar.

Examples : Pascal and Foster. Such an author reads the Bible, as if no one had ever read it before. It has a fresh impression. He meditates deeply, even on the smallest particular, and sees what has escaped others. He deduces reflections, which are at once natural and new. Nothing can produce such writing, but a constant and profound study of the original documents. And for this there must be a certain exclusion of other books and reading.

§ 32. *Genesis of Thought.* — Reading Mozart's life. What wonderful precocity ! wonderful genius ! Yet such a life seems frivolous, and his death was sad ; no religion. What most strikes me is the spontaniety of his genius. His compositions *came to him*, unsought, whether he would or no. The parts filled his mind, not successively, but all at once. Having bestowed much time on music, I see the wonder of this. I am totally destitute of the slightest musical conception of this kind. I believe, however, in exactly such a genesis of thought and feelings. We are more passive than is thought in our trains of thinking. Often have I been forced to say, " My best sermons make themselves." I fully believe in this kind of poetry. It is plain that Ovid wrote so : he says so somewhere in a verse, of which I only remember the last words,

——" Versus erat."

What dependent beings we are ! How awful the thought, that we may be sometimes guided by spiritual agency above our own.

Waiting upon God is often the most we can do. If the experiment were more believingly made, we should doubtless have more results. To fix *attention* is often all we can do, if, indeed, we can do this. Look in a given direction, and the train of thought will have a certain character. Look towards God, and the effect will sometimes be wonderful.

§ 33. *Massillon* introduced a new method of not citing so many passages verbatim from the Scriptures and the fathers. In preparations I am constantly violating my own rules, and perplexing myself lest I should not remember to use all the texts which I have looked out; and this even when it is not a subject requiring proof.

§ 34. *Preaching.*—Sermons should be written on subjects which thoroughly interest the mind of the writer. Those are seldom such, which he takes up by a sort of constraint, in a series, or *invitâ Minervâ;* nor those on which he is unprepared, and for which he has to make collection. Sometimes, though rarely, it happens, that during the process of collation a view is opened, in which the mind goes on *con amore*.

For an approximation to the right kind of study, one must have a permanent theological and religious interest. Something on these topics must always be uppermost. It must be the natural tendency of the mind when left to itself.

Here opens to our view a new value in the Scriptures. He who constantly reads them will be constantly awakened to trains of new thought. The best sermons are so suggested. No man can be uniformly a good preacher, who is not habitually perusing the Scriptures as his book of delights. There is no special preparation for the pulpit which can take the place of this general preparation. No man can lack subjects who is thus commonly employed.

The best subject is commonly that which comes of itself. I never could understand what is meant by making a sermon on a prescribed text.

The right text is the one which comes of itself during reading and meditation ; which accompanies you in walks, goes to bed with you, and rises with you. On such a text, thoughts swarm and cluster, like bees upon a branch. The sermon ferments for hours and days, and at length, after patient waiting, and almost spontaneous working, the subject clarifies itself, and the true method of treatment presents itself in a shape which cannot be rejected.

Those texts of Scripture which comes up, of themselves, or by the laws of mental suggestion, are the right ones, and are very different from those which are sought out. But observe, in order that this should take place largely and fully, and that the citations should be rich and pertinent, the mind must have a large stock of Scripture reading. Hence again the great value of close, enlarged, perpetual Bible-reading; reading with delight. There are various models of Scripture quotation. Some search out the texts with a concordance or similar helps. These are often the greatest quoters. But their citations are like strangers and foreigners. Or they may be likened to stones put together loosely with mortar. Others seldom go beyond a certain routine of stock texts; a hundred such writers shall give you the same texts on a given topic. They are so many dead branches on a living tree. The excerpted verse deadens the discussion instead of enlivening it. But one whose mind is full of a subject, will have abundance of passages flowing in, without opening the volume; they will be his own, suggested by peculiarities of his own thinking; so that nothing in his discourse will have more the air of originality, than the familiar passages of Scripture which he quotes. The jewel will shine with double lustre from its setting. The word fitly spoken will be " as apples of gold in pictures of silver." Striking instances may be found in Robt. Hall, and especially in Jay.

§ 35. *Theological Preaching.*—Better far to take a theological topic, and popularize it, then the reverse, namely, to take a hortatory topic and thicken it by doctrine. Argument made red-hot, is what interests people. Generally speaking, nothing interests so much as argument. People are accustomed to argument, in such a country as ours. Argument admits of great vehemence and fire. Argument may be made plain. Argument may be made ornate. Argument may be beaten out and thinned down to any degree of perspicuity.

It is a shame for a minister not to be acquainted with all the heads of theology, all the great schools of opinion, and all the famous distinctions : and he will not learn them well unless he preaches upon them.

Theological study brings along with it other important and interesting branches ; as doctrine, history, church history, symbolical history, dogmatics, metaphysics, ethics, homiletics. All these are of high value. They are all best approached from the side of theology.

Theology is superior, because it is the grand result. That is greatest, which is nearest the end. Exegesis is only a means to that end. Theology includes all the other things.

Theology, as inferring close and logical reasoning, is suited to the strength of middle life. As age advances, imagination and memory decay : not so the reasoning faculty. It may be going on and increasing in vigour to the latest day of life.

The stimulus to this pursuit will be best kept up if a man accustom himself to give a doctrinal tinge to all his preaching. Then he will read on these subjects. It is a great matter for a preacher to have the habit of deriving his entertainment day by day from the perusal of argumentative theology. Let him continually advance into new fields, and attack new adversaries. Let him continually revolve the terms of former controversies.

§ 36. *Dr Channing.*—" Gradual change of tone in Dr Channing's address . . . it was constantly becoming less *ministerial and more manly.*" (Biography.) I think I know what this means—coming out of the homiletic tortoise-shell—not leaving humanity at the foot of the pulpit stairs—talking like other men—as any profoundly thinking thoroughly, agitated *man* would talk on a great subject to a casual group of waiting persons also deeply interested. Effect of such a σχεσις on style, divisions, quotations, &c.

A little before, the biographer tells of Dr Channing's leaving off much ceremonious dignity in the pulpit. This, also, I know.

I am getting to feel the evils of the academic manner-primness, &c.—Also meditate on the tendency of clergy to be much with the rich and the lettered, instead of being lights to the world. I should have understood this less, if I had remained at Princeton. The Democracy must be reached—people must be made to feel that the heart of the minister is with them. Common people require this. Age requires it. Young men require it.

§ 37. *Preaching on Great Things.*—Differing as I do from Channing, and protesting as I do against him, I can never cease to honour and admire him for this; that he always wrote and preached on those things *which he considered the great things.* Let me explain my thought. I have written a good deal and published some; it has been too much off at one side. I have not seized hold of the main things. All topics which I treat are regarded by me more historically than philosophically; more with reference to books and authors than reasons. How different my father—Dr Hodge—Vinet—and (in error) Channing.

Yet I am constantly *meditating* on the great points. Is it that I never come to any results? Do I prove nothing? Attain nothing? Am I ever to be retailing what this man says, and that man says?

§ 38. *Theological Sermons.*—Dr Thornwell appears to me to show some greatness in devoting his preaching powers to the *making of great theological sermons.* Those who do this successfully leave their mark on their generation. It is not the turn of the age however. The young ministers who are coming out seem to me to preach sentimental, rather than argumentative sermons.

I have written a whole sermon to-day, the first of two on 1 John iv. 18. I am less and less in favour in quotation in sermons. My tendency used to be very much that way. As my manner becomes warmer, directer, and more practical, I let these brilliant patches alone.

§ 39. *Be yourself.*—In the making of sermons I have never so well succeeded as when I have forgotten all models, and consented to be myself. Every man has his own way, in which he is better than in all others. Those sermons have turned out the best in which I have turned the matter over in my mind several times, and then written without predetermined skeleton.

§ 40. *Collect Texts.*—There are particular times in which a man is better disposed and better able than at others, to seek out texts, and arrange plans of sermons. Such moments should be embraced ; and if the result should be an accumulation of texts and plans, it will be well ; for often the great difficulty is to get a text : as soon as one is lighted on, the matter goes easily on.

It has occurred to me as useful, to sit down and plan a series of discourses, not in any theological order, but with reference to some given effect on the people ; as for example, to promote a true revival of religion.

§ 41. *Free Writing.*—It seems to me that some of the best writings are those which men have made for themselves ; * that is, without having other people in view; without any end but to discharge the mind of its thoughts. In this posture the mind works most naturally and simple, and hence more strongly. Voltaire somewhere says the reverse, for he thinks the writer should always have both judge and audience in view; for such writing as Voltaire's, this is doubtless the best way. But there is always some interruption, some diversion, and some cramping of the thoughts in this mode. It is true, when a writer seeks only this natural overflow of his thoughts, that he is apt to be destitute of that method which prevails in the schools. The numerical partitions of discourse are sometimes forced, and when they are read, they partake more of aggregation than of growth. There is as real an order in the evolution of parts in a tree as in the successive additions which build a house : and if a discourse proceeds by an inward law which disregards symmetrical plans, it may have more coherence and vitality than

* See Vinet in his account of Vannargues.

could be produced by rule and square. The noble master-pieces of the ancients possess this easy flow, which often defiles the analysis of the commentator; but they are not therefore less pleasing or so less great.

To write by a plan, is in some degree to bind the thoughts to a given track. He is most likely to arrive at what is original and new who like the river " wanders at his own sweet will."

It is constraining and so injurious to thought, where one has some end constantly before him other than the prosecution of the trains on which he has entered. These ends may be various and some of them may be very good; they may even be necessary: but so far as the full and independent unfolding of the mind is concerned, they are injurious. The writer may seek the entertainment or profit of a particular class of readers. He may seek fame or emolument, or the elevation of sect or party. He may write as an exercise for proof of his powers or to strengthen them. So doing he may produce much that is excellent; but he does this in a less degree than when he gives full scope to the inward prompting. Hence the ill effect of writing for the public only; never encouraging those expatiating processes which take no note of readers and critics. Free writings of the kind just mentioned, are after all those which most interest the reader, and produce least weariness, even where the subject is a trifling one, as is exemplified by Montaigne. On higher subjects the same holds true, as in the case of Pascal's Thoughts.

A singular elevation is given to writings which are devotional in such a sense as to be addressed to God. Such are the confessions of St Augustine. There are also discourses, which in form are addressed to an audience, but which nevertheless have this character of meditational flow; such as the writings of Leighton and Scougal. The inspired books of the sacred canon, though they cannot properly be brought into comparison, have this quality of unconstrained flow and ample digression, which makes it hard to parcel them into regular divisions. This is true equally of the Psalms, the Prophecies, and the Epistles.

§ 42. The pulpit is too sacred to be turned into a place for exchanging clerical civilities, or into a space for cermonious etiquette.

§ 43. *Study of the Scripture.*—Constant perusal and re-perusal of Scripture is the great preparation for preaching. You get good even when you know it not. This is one of the most observable differences between old and young theologians.

" Give attendance to reading."

§ 44. *Preaching on Politics.*—A minister may well be absolved from preaching, or even forming opinions on politics. He has the common right of all citizens so to do ; but his proper work is enough for all his time and powers. The great themes of religious truth are enough to occupy more than he can get. Statemanship is a science by itself. If a preacher excels in it, he must do so by sacrificing some of his sacred hours.

§ 45. *Excess of Manner.*—Every excess of manner over matter·hinders the effect of delivery, on all wise judges. Where there is more voice, more emphasis, or more gesture, than there is feeling, there is waste, and worse ; powder beyond the shot.

§ 46. *Feeling.*—Feeling is the prime mover in eloquence ; but feeling cannot be produced to order ; and the affectation of it, however elegant, is powerless.

§ 47. *Animation.*—Every man may be said to have his *quantum* of animation, beyond which he cannot go without forcework and affectation. Hence, to exhort a young man to be more animated, is to mislead and perhaps spoil him, unless you mean to inculcate the cultivation of inward emotion. It is better therefore to let nature work, even though for the time the delivery is tame, than to generate a manner only rhetorically and artificially warm, which is hypocrisy.

§ 48. Uttering a chain of reasoning with the mock tones of

passion, is the crying sin of second-rate Southern orators. The true orators of the South are really eloquent, from natural inward heat.

§ 49. Reading good authors aloud, after full mastery of the sense by careful study, is a better exercise than declaiming one's own compositions from memory.

§. 50. No good preacher was ever made such by exercise in oratory.

§ 51. Eloquence, as a ministerial accomplishment, may be overrated. Only one man in a million can be eloquent. Now it is evident, Christ could not have intended that a work so universal should be dependent on a means so rare.

§ 52. Some of the greatest effects have been produced by men who had no external graces of style and elocution.

§ 53. There is a certain type of thought, diction, and delivery, which is proper to each individual; and he accomplishes most who hits on this. But all straining, all artifice, and all imitation, tend to prevent the attainment of this manner.

§ 54. The "utterance" which the Apostle Paul craved, and which is often mentioned in the New Testament, is very different from worldly eloquence, being a spiritual gift.

§ 55. The attraction of the modern pulpit is something altogether different from any spiritual quality. It indicates a sickly mind in the Christian public. Under such preaching a morbid state is produced.

§ 56. If Apostolical preaching could reappear, while it would be mighty in its effects upon the assembly and on multitudes, it would probably answer no demands of the schools or the stage ;

but would be unartificial, expository, simple, paternal, brief, natural, varied, gushing, and eminently spiritual.

§ 57. The day was when churches were much more concerned than we, about the truths conveyed, and much less about the garb of the truths.

Doctrine, rather than speaking, was what drew the audience.

§ 58. Let every preacher despair of delivering that discourse with true, natural, and effective warmth, which he has prepared with leisurely coldness.

§ 59. No rhetorical appliance can make a cold passage truly warm. If, for any cause, an inanimate sermon must needs be uttered, it ought to be delivered with no more emotion, than its contents engender in the speaker's soul. Everything beyond this is pretence; and here is the source of all mock-passion, which is the fixed habit of many speakers.

§ 60. There can be no high eloquence without inward feeling, naturally expressed. Hence he who begins his discourse on an ordinary topic, with the elevated voice and manner of great emotion, convinces every just critic that he is acting a part.

§ 61. *A Thought for Expansion.*—Occupy your mind, since life is so short, on the following, viz. :

1. *True rather than False.*—Truth always good—food—safe—consistent—propagative.

Falsehood, even when conversed with for good ends, is perturbing, paining, defiling, misleading, and wasteful of time.

2. *Positive rather than Negative.*—Not negation—not refutation—not mere defence.

3. *Great rather than Small.*—Great truths—great subjects—the most important—comprehensive of the lesser—elevating—discipline the understanding—not minutiæ—not trifles.

4. *Divine rather than Human.*—Revealed, not found out—inspired—the Bible above all.

He that should observe these rules for the conduct of his understanding, would save much time and escape many troubles.

§ 62. I find it hard to mingle doctrine and practice in due proportion in my preaching. Latterly I fear there has been too much exclusion of doctrinal discussion. The following hints will not be out of place :

1. To open some point of doctrine, or some portion of Scripture needing explanation, at least in one discourse of each week.

2. To select for this purpose, very frequently, those doctrines which are most vital; those which concern the salvation of the soul; those about which an inquirer or believer would seek information.

3. To treat these doctrinal points warmly, with a perpetual reference to Christian experience.

§ 63. *Preaching.*—My morning sermon was written and preached with more flow and animation than usual. I ascribe this to my having meditated somewhat on the history, and then written straight on, without the slightest reference to a logical analysis or programme, though I had actually formed such a one. I am persuaded, that as much as a discourse gains in method and articulation, by such a plan, so much it loses in rapidity, richness, and animation. I also found comfort in my method of preparing notes for an expository lecture, thus : 1. Study the exegesis. 2. Write rapid and pretty full notes on the successive parts, numerically, as so many *observations*. It is not always necessary to take them up in the order of the text.

§ 64. *The Bible.*—As the Bible is the best of books, so the *next best* is that which is most like it, that which teaches the same thing—or explains the Bible. Instead of studying and writing about Austin and Luther, do what Austin and Luther did, namely, tell what the Bible teaches. Go straight to the Law and the Testimony, instead of all subordinates and substitutes.

§ 65. In every age people have gone astray, by going away from the Bible. The statements of Scripture are positive truths, given on divine authority, and faith is as necessary as obedience ; for it is as much our duty to believe what God says, as to do what he commands.   If we received in its true meaning every proposition in the Bible, we should have a sufficient body of divine truth. But this is far from being the case. Some receive more and some less, but none receive the whole. One reason of this is, that we preposterously mingle our own reasonings with the conclusions of revelations.   Having accepted as true a certain number of the plain declarations of Scripture, we use those as so many premises with which to connect trains of reasoning. We do not wait to see whether the conclusions at which we would thus arrive are not asserted or denied in other plain Scriptural declarations.   Sometimes we arrive at conclusions from positive Scriptural declarations.   This is an inevitable result of the weakness of human reason ; and as there is nothing to which we have a more overweening attachment than the fruits of our ratiocination, we cling to these erroneous conclusions.   In order to do this with any show of reverence for inspiration, we find it hereupon necessary to explain away those plain declarations of the Word, which are opposed to our conclusions.   Thus our perverse deduction, even from Bible truths, leads to corrupt interpretation of the Word of God. It is analogous to overhasty generalization in natural philosophy, from a narrow basis of facts or phenomena.

The practical rule to be derived from these remarks is, *to go to the Bible as a fund, not so much of premises as of conclusions ;* to enlarge as far as possible the field of positive assertions ; to prefer the plain sense of the record ; to distrust our own reasonings from Scripture, in the way of logical interference ; and to discuss every conclusion which wars with clear Scripture definitions.

Hence also the importance of being much engaged in the simplest study of the Word, in its plainest sense ; heaping up this golden ore just as it comes out of the mine

§ 66. *My Father.*—My dear and honoured father has some

excellencies as a writer, which I did not value at a proper rate when I was younger. He goes always for the thought rather than the word; and is never led along by the bait of fine language or the course of figures. I am led to think that a man must early in life make his election between these two kinds of writing, and that I have fallen into the inferior one; though I am regarded among my friends as a simple writer.

Another remarkable quality of my father, is his going for truth and reason, rather then for authority. This is the more remarkable, as he has been one of the greatest and most miscellaneous readers I ever knew; has had the most extensive knowledge of books, and the most wonderful memory of their contents, so that I have often known him to give a clear account of works which he had not seen for forty years; and yet how seldom does he make citation! The train of his thoughts is all his own, with a thorough digestion in his own mind, and reference of all things to their principles. Hence he is original in the best sense; which superficial readers would not admit, because his style had no salient points, or overbold expressions.

I attribute this in some degree to the fact that almost every day of his life, known to me, it was his habit to sit alone, in silence, generally in the twilight, or musing over the fire, in deep and seemingly pleasurable thought. At such times he was doubtless maturing those trains of reasoning, which he brought out in his discourses; and this may account for his extraordinary readiness at almost any time, to rise in extemporaneous address.

§ 67. Some ministers seem to be familiar only with such and such passages and parts of Scripture.

The Puritans derived much of their liveliness from their minute acquaintance with the Old Testament, and their apposite citation of it. Another kind of familiarity with the Word is apparent in such a writer as Hengstenberg. It amazes me. What extensive and at the same time profound knowledge of the original.

At times it is useful simply to turn over the pages of the Scriptures, touching here and there, as a man walks among the rows of his vineyard, receiving general impressions, or learning where to go again.

§ 68. Cut off superfluous studies. Come back to the Bible. This rings in my ears as years go on. Consider all past studies as so much discipline, to fit you for this great study. Make Scripture the interpreter of Scripture. Seek practical wisdom, rather than learning, and as tending to holiness and eternal happiness. Make the Bible your book of prayer.

§ 69. My greatest acquisitions in Scripture come from no commentaries or expositors. The perusals of many former years turned over in the meditations, left to brew in the mind, yield their ripe results in new readings, and often make that clear which was formerly dark, and that fruitful which was once dry.

§ 70. *Bible Study.*—As Bible study is the best study, so I find it the most delightful. It is a good way to read large portions, and with much repetition, but always avoiding weariness. Having lately read over the Epistle to the Hebrews in Greek, I read it over this evening in the English version. Occasionally I looked out the Old Testament quotations ; I compared the Greek, whenever I had a suspicion about the English; and here and there looked in a lexicon, or another version ; but my chief view was to the scope and connection; and on this I found greater lights than common. Some verses held me long, and I walked up and down the floor meditating upon them. I omitted some separable parenthetic passages, reserving them for another perusal. By this means I got an unusual view of the lucid unity of the book. No method of Scriptural study gives me so much satisfaction. It unites reading with meditation. It is the best preparation for preaching. It scatters a thousand doubts. It familiarises the English text, no inconsiderable part of a preacher's furniture. Doctrines so derived are more firmly grasped, than when received from the ablest systems. Texts so learnt are better understood and more available, than such as are gathered from a concordance or marginal bible. They are taken into the system and assimilated. They become constitutional parts of one's mind. Even a human composition, when valuable, is an organized whole, united by a pervading principle, and with every part in its right place. Still more true is this of an inspired composition. Each proposition is not only truth, but truth in the right place, and in sacred connection with what goes before and follows after. In this divine connection, truth is best learned. And he who learns it thus, has a knowledge of it superior to that of one who learns even the same propositions, rent asunder, or forced into the technical connection and arrangement of a system; as far superior, as the knowledge of the human frame derived from examining a subject, over that which is acquired by a tabular view of all the chemical elements which go to constitute the vital fabric, however fully and accurately they may be stated. It is, therefore, all important to study the Bible in its due connection; and, for this end, to read over large portions, and even whole books, carefully and repeatedly.

§ 71. *Bible Study.*—I cannot revert to this subject too often. Reading what I wrote at the beginning of this book, has revived my interest in it. Experience shows me more and more the value of studying the pure text. Reading the account of the Scottish mission to Palestine has had the same effect. The mere hearing of a husband and wife, devoting themselves to the Scripture, without comment, has also been awakening. Recurrence to my morning task, of committing a few verses to memory, has kept up my interest. This evening I read the book of Ruth in Hebrew, which confirmed my resolution. Late preaching experiments corroborate my opinion, that the very best preparation for extempore discourses is textual knowledge. Luther says truly, *Bonus texnarius est bonus theologus.* What can I set before me more obligatory, useful or pleasant, than to spend my life in making the blessed word plain to others? If I were able to have a charge, how entirely might I give myself to the Word of God, and prayer, by the aid and impulse of the Holy Spirit. Twenty years ago, I had a great ambition to be extensively acquainted with the classics. I have, in rather an irregular way, acquired more of that knowledge than is perhaps common with our clergy, but I can truly say, I account it but stubble and dross in comparison with the Bible. *The study of the text* is the thing I mean. I have pored over many commentators, but life is too short for this circuitous method. If an hour is to be spent, either in reading and collating more of the text, or in reading human comments, surely the former is the way which gives more light. What is acquired in this way makes a peculiar impression, and is more truly one's own. It also carries with it a savour of divine authority. Sometimes going slowly over verse by verse, and meditating on each—a delightful employment—I learn more than by turning over volumes. Especially is this useful as a preparation for preaching. I can say with dying Salmasius, I wish I had devoted myself more to the study of the Scriptures !

N.B. Regular times are indispensable to proficiency in these researches.

§ 72. The Christian, and above all the minister, is bound to devote all his powers to the glory of God, in the good of mankind.

This is a work which requires great diligence and earnestness, and may well occcupy the whole man all his life.

Man may be called to labour in different spheres, but always with the same devotion and singleness of purpose.

The studies and authorship of a Christian are to be directed to this end.

Science and literature may be used as among the greatest in this work ; but they are not to be used so as to usurp the time and heart of the Christian scholar as to make him distinctly a man of science or letters. The same remarks apply still more clearly to other pursuits, such as art, politics, agriculture, and trade. Instances : Swift, Sterne, Robertson, Howe, many English university scholars.

An exception is to be made in favour of those pursuits, or even publications which are for recreation, in intervals of labour. Lord Bacon has said that every man owes a debt to his profession. A clergyman's work should be governed by this rule. It is seemly that a man's pen should utter the abundance of his heart, and that his books should bear the impress of that which is most in his thoughts.

It is unseemly for a minister of Christ to be known chiefly by works beyond the line of his calling, however valuable in themselves. Especially unfortunate is it, when his strength is dispersed among petty learned elegancies. No works of the pen are more honourable than those which evince a profound interest in the good of one's generation, church, and country. These betoken earnestness, patriotism, and a public spirit, and are far higher in the scale than even great treatises on scientific theology. Even though from their nature they have an interest that does not extend to coming generations, and thus do not become part of universal literature, they are of great value ; sometimes in the very proportion in which they are confined to time and place.

§ 73. Any man is excusable, to say no more, for employing himself about the great questions of the age and country.

It is just a reproach to any man to be indifferent to that which concerns the welfare of his people, and, while their interests are at stake, to spend his days in delicate trifles. Such was the fault of Goethe. How different the case of Milton, though he was wrong in many points. Be earnest. Be up and doing. Rust is worse than work. There is an excitement which is bad, ruinous ; there is also an excitement which is good, healthful, and corroborative. To be really in earnest is consistent with great care of health and strength. Husband your faculties, your acquisitions, your time. Husband them ! Therefore give yourself more to great topics, especially to Christian topics ; national topics ; topics that promise good to the world. After a man has been a great reader for many years, he ought to repose. He ought to distil his accumulations. He ought to write from his own mind. True, much of what he does so write will be the result of his previous reading, but

it will be without rehearsal or quotation. If he belongs to the
better order of minds he will quote little, except in those cases
in which the very matter of the argument lies in the very words
of another. He will think for himself. He will give the results of his learning rather than the learning itself. He will
advise himself thus :

"Why should you be so careful to remember what others have
said ? Of all you have read much has slipped. Well, most of
such thoughts are of no value. It were a pity to retain all. The
mind acts not as a coffer, but partly as a sieve, and more as an
alembic. Your book-knowledge, even if not increased, would
furnish abundance for many works. Do not give way to the
error of being afraid of saying plain and simple things, so they
are true, reasonable, and logically knit. Consider Daniel Webster. The greatest and most useful sayings are simple. Your
thoughts seem more commonplace to others than to yourself, for
an obvious reason.

"Try every day to repeat to yourself some solid truth, if
possible some new one. But true rather than novel. Fix the
truth in your mind, as something really attained and immovable.
Deduce from it other truths, but with caution. Shun haste and
paradox. Go to the highest principles. Be not so much concerned about the laws of thought as about truths, the matters of
knowledge.

"Avoid vexing, plaguing cogitations. Those are often the
best thoughts which have been wrung out with the knit brow.
There is a spontaneity in thinking. We do not so much create
the stream as watch it, and to a certain extent direct it. This
is the reason why great thinkers do not always draw themselves
out; rather the contrary. Placid, easy philosophising brings
the abundant fruit: Let the thread sometimes drop ; you will
find it again and at the right moment. In this meditation differs
from book-learning, which is necessarily wearing.

"The Scriptures furnish the best materials for thought. They
stimulate the soil. They secure the right posture of mind for
calm judgment and even for discovery. They correct error.
They give positive conclusions. They promote holy states which

are favourable to truth. They prevent trifling reasonings, by keeping the mind constantly in the presence of the greatest subjects."

§ 74. *To do good to men*, is the great work of life; to make them true Christians is the greatest good we can do them. Every investigation brings us round to this point. Begin here, and you are like one who strikes water from a rock on the summits of the mountains; it flows down over all the intervening tracts to the very base. If we could make each man love his neighbour, we should make a happy world. The true method is to begin with ourselves, and so to extend the circle to all around us. It should be perpetually in our minds.

§ 75. *Beneficence.*—There are two great classes of philanthropists, namely, those who *devise* plans of beneficence, and those who *execute* them. If we cannot be among the latter, perhaps we may be among the former. Invention is more creative than execution. Watt has done more for mechanics than a thousand steam-engine makers. The devisers of good may again be divided into those who devise particular plans, such as this or that association or mode of operation, and those who discover and make known great principles. The latter are the rarer and the most important. Hence a man who never stirs out of his study may be a great philanthropist, if he employs himself in discovering from the study of the Scriptures and the study of human nature, those laws which originate and condition all effectual endeavours for human good.

§ 76. *Byron.*—I have been looking into a dreadful book, Moore's life of Byron,—the life of one debauchee written by another. It is instructive, amidst all its impiety. It is the most forcible comment I ever read on that divine word, " The way of transgressors is hard." Voluptuary as he was, ever sighing after some new pleasure, and drinking to its depth the cup of worldly and sensual enjoyment, Byron seems to have endured little less than a hell upon earth. Here I read in awful colours the tormenting power of uncontrolled selfishness. Here I see abject ignorance of all religion in one of the greatest human minds. Remorse without repentance, and self-contempt without amendment, are dreadful scourges. From country to country he fled, but he carried the scorpion with him. His later works are only the disgorging of tumultuous thoughts and cruel passions, lust, mortified pride, and malignity; as if he would outrage the world, even at the expense of every pang in his own bosom. Happy the poorest, weakest sufferer, that believes in Christ!

§ 77. *God in Nature.*—Sweet showers about sunrise. How refreshing! Methinks we have not books enow which connect the exercises of religion with the delights of external scenery. Though an infidel said it, I assent to it as true, that I have found no temple so inspiring as the open vault of heaven and the green earth. Everything around me breathes of divine benignity. The sparrow has laid her young in a rose-tree just beside my door-sill, another has built in the vine by the woodhouse. The bluebirds seem to be tenanting the house I prepared for them over the arbour, and I am looking for the return of my wrens to their lodge above the swing. The indigo bird, and some unknown pied bird appear among my young elms. I also have seen a dark bird with a dash of crimson on the back. The catbird sings almost all day in the large cherry-tree by our icehouse; and in the orchard just beyond, bobo'lincoln indulges in his caprices, morning, noon, and night. But no song so affects me as the plaintive note of the robin, heard at a distance in the evening. It tells of solitude and care. It is such a strain as, were I a bird, I could not choose but sing myself. All these praise God. To attend to them, and note their proceedings on the Lord's day, need not trouble the strictest Sabbatarian; it is but to paraphrase and illustrate the 104th psalm. I am no Pantheist, but I love to honour a God in nature, in whom all that is has life, and not only life, but being. " The meanest flower that blows has power to raise thoughts in me that lie too deep for tears." Pansies have called forth such thoughts to-day. Blessed be God for summer, and for the thousand, thousand varied manifestations of life in the animal and vegetable world.

§ 78. *See God in Nature.*—When the prospects of the heavens or the verdant summer earth look most beautiful to me, I most think of God. But let us be careful how we see God in nature. The Pantheist sees the visible phenomena as a *part of God.* This is a sort of Atheism. The poet sees *beauty, order,* the *picturesque,* or the *sublime,* and this he makes his God. The Christian sees in the glories of nature not merely the effect of God's hand, but its presence; not only God's work, but God working. He not only created that landscape of field, wood, and orchard which I see from my window, but he upholds it, he gives it its existence, he causes every change, at every moment—at every moment there is a coming forth of his attributes into action. And these innumerable acts are each of them a display of some perfection; each is divine. I behold God in his works, I do not merely see a mark that the Creator *has been* there, but a token that he *is* there. Just as when I hear the footstep of my dearest friend in his chamber, I know that he is there present.

§ 79. *On the late cloudy Weather.*

> Clouds on clouds have long been here,
>   Overhanging all our sky;
> Scarce a sunny hour did peer
>   Through the mantle spread on high.
>
> Yet we know the sun is still
>   Reigning in his bridegroom power,
> And the happy instant will
>   Pour his radiance through the shower.
>
> Then the tinted promise-bow,
>   Spanning woods and meads, shall smile,
> Then the cornfields brilliant glow,
>   If meek patience wait a while.
>
> Nature is the type of grace—
>   Spirits have their cloudy time;
> 'Tis, alas! our present case,
>   While we wait the dawn sublime.

Yet in darkness we will hope,
  He is coming who is Light,
Though we may disheartened grope
  For a season—as in night—

He is coming; lo! his beam
  Gilds already yonder hill,
Streaks of opening clearness seem
  The horizon's edge to fill.

Come, expected brightness, come,
  We are panting for thy ray,
Let not hopeless grief benumb
  Souls that do thy word obey.

Weeping may a night endure,
  Yet the morning shall be joy;
Trust the promise—it is sure,
  Hopeful toil be thine employ.

He who loves me makes my day,
  Clouds but minister his will;
Christ is waiting to display
  Charms that every wish shall fill.

§ 80. *Converse with God.*—It is not enough to know of God *that* he is, or even *what* he is, unless in the latter we include that he is conversable with us, that we have access to him, that we may commune with him. On this most interesting and momentous point, see Howe's "Living Temple." The persuasion that we can really hold converse with God, as a friend with a friend, or even as a slave with a sovereign, is one of the most delightful which can reveal itself to a human soul. How would Socrates, Plato, Tully, or Seneca have received the annunciation! A great part of religion consists in seeking and maintaining this converse.

§ 81. *God is the Portion*, the *one* portion. In him is rest. Read on this à Kempis, Leighton, and Fenelon. I have been thinking a good deal lately of the sin and folly of seeking happiness in anything but God. Every other object we must seek *for the sake* of something else, but God for the sake of himself.

§ 82. *Writing Books.*—In writing a book, as much as anything in the world, it is important for a man to be *himself*, to be un-shackled, to act out his own character. Hence not always good to take the advice of one of a different *richtung*—it chills. A plan or schedule or programme hinders the work, *quoad genialitat*. A book should be a *growth* rather than a *building*. The most taking books have been written off-hand. There is too little " abandon " in my writing ; my best have had the most—e. g. the review of Macaulay, and in a less degree the review of Chalmers.* The best things are those which do not come into your head till you begin to write, and which cannot, therefore, be in-cluded in a plan made before-hand. To write in the way I mean, a man must be in earnest, and without a trammel ; hence every degree and kind of *fiction* is adverse. The novel, the poem, the pretended letter, even the anonymous one, are un-favourable to this perfect freedom.

§ 83. *Be careful for Nothing.*—Our pleasures and pains are often trifles, when Providence hangs out greater pleasures and pains just before us. Why am I so much troubled about these little crosses or disappointments ? They will come and be over in much less time than I have spent in carping about them. Time and oblivion have already washed out a thousand such impressions on the sandy beach of my heart. To be abased is to be happy. A large proportion of our cares would go, if pride were to depart. Our distress after failures is often chagrin as to what man will think of us, rather than contrition for having of-fended God.

§ 84. *How shall Mankind be made Happy.*—What a poor pitiful thing do the little niceties and elegancies of science and letters appear, when placed by the side of true religious and philan-trophic wisdom. I can scarcely look with patience on myself or others, spending solid days on petty philosophy, criticism, poetry of the minor sort, belles-lettres, or on botany, archæology, antiquarianism, or any of these things in which the pedantry of learning boasts itself, when the great question is trumpeted in our

* In Princeton Review.

ears, *how shall mankind be made happy?* When a man has attained middle life, he ought to be doing something towards the solution of this problem. He ought to be in earnest. I, therefore, respect Channing for his choice of subjects, though not always for his way of treating them. The grand problem regards *the application of Christianity to the progress of Society.* Nations are tumultuating like oceans. Society seems like to be thrown anew into the crucible. The power that is to order the future mould is the power of *opinion*. Unless it be Truth, all must go wrong. The great thing then is to impregnate the existing mass with truth—moral truth—divine truth. How to do this, should be our question. Many of our old and round-about methods will probably have to be given up. They stand in relation to the measures needed, as the tactics of old Wurmser, to those of Napoleon. We must go to work more directly than heretofore. And methinks it were well if some of us old-fashioned martinets in religion and literature, could cut off our pig-tails and work away in the dishabille of the age. Do so we must, or be left in the rear. Learning we want indeed, but not pedant-learning, names and classifications, but good living truths, such as lie deep, and as yet unquarried in the Book of Books, but which are yet to be brought out for the revolution of the world.

§ 85. *Against Solitude.*—A life of study has always appeared to me an unnatural life. Is it not better to converse with the living than the dead? Some one will yet have to write a book on the excess of literature. The ancient Greek way of studying abroad, in the Porch, or the Academy, on the Ilissus and under the platanus, among the haunts of man, was better for the health both of body and mind. Recluse habits tend to sadness, moroseness, selfishness, timidity, and inaction. The mind has better play *in aprico*. Collision produces scintillation of genius, and proximity of friends opens a gush for the affections. The early Christians seem to have been out-of-door people, rehearsing to one another the wisdom which had been given to them orally. Lessons which go from mouth to mouth, take a portable shape, because dense, pithy, and apothegmatic : such are the proverbs of all ages. We are made for action, and life is too short for us to be always preparing. A breath of pure air seems to oxygenate the intellect, and the best thoughts of the scholar are sometimes during the half-hour of twilight, when he has laid aside his books, and taken his walking-stick. Then he is more of a man, feels his fellowship not only with nature, but with his kind. I sometimes wish I had been less a reader of books ; that I had exercised my prerogative over the beasts of the field, mastered horses, or traversed countries as a reckless pedestrian. Ever turning the thoughts inward produces corrosion. We should have something, it is true, within, but it should tend outwards. He has not fulfilled his vocation, who has spent his score of years in solitary delight over ancient authors, and eaten his morsel alone. Gray, with all Greece in his mind, pacing up and down the green alleys of a college walk, was but half the man he should have been. Horace Walpole, revelling in the virtù of Strawberry Hill, degenerated into a mere toyman, and filled the most elegant letters extant with the matching of old chairs and Sevres china. It is to let the mind run to seed in a corner ; transplantation is necessary. To live for others is the dictate of religion. And what to do for others is best done by actual approaches, face to face, eye looking into eye, and hand pressing hand. It is not enough to say, this or that recondite pursuit may turn to somebody's advantage. So it may, if you live to be a Methuselah or a Lamech. But your ever-increasing stock should not be all hoarded. The sum is, go forth among mankind. Lay aside the cowl, and make one of the great company. Every day renew the electric touch with the common mind. Fall into the circle, to give and take good influences. It is not too late if your heart is not ossified to the core. I hope it is not so bad as that in Tully's phrase, *locus ubi stomachus fuit, concaluit.* It is worth an effort. The air of a saloon or a market-place will do you good, and you will gain something for brushing the crowd in a thoroughfare.

§ 86. *Dying Evidences.*—Between sleep and wake, these thoughts came to me. When I am dying, what will certify to me these truths of Christianity, which are my support? Suppose I doubt them. What will prove them to me in that brief urgent trial? Can I then go over all the evidences? No! the truth will be in me self-evidencing—the same truths which I now have in notion I will then have in faith. That which is now the matter of opinion and probable judgment will be transformed into real truth—faith rather than knowledge.

§ 87. *Pain.*—When a bodily pain occurs, every man who has any sense of religion feels that it is his duty to acquiesce in it, as sent of God, for some end unknown as yet. But the feeling is not so prompt, when a mental pain arises, such as is produced by a fear, an insult, an injury, or the like. Yet the latter, no less than the former, are under the disposal of God, and form a part of his providential arrangement. We should in such cases feel this.

§ 88. *Blessings of Trial.*—The trials which befall us, are the very trials which we need. The little daily excoriations of temper speedily heal themselves, but when the pain lasts, they have an errand to accomplish, and they accomplish it. These, as well as greater sufferings are ordered. They must be submitted to with patience, resignation, and meekness, and if they enable us to see ourselves, and gain a victory over our pride, they are of great value. Instead of vain and impotent wishes to fly from them, or the circumstances which occasion them, it is the part of manly virtue to fear and forbear, and by grace to wax stronger and stronger.

§ 89. *Look forward.*—To look forward is better than to look back, and this is as true of literature as of life. How long has the world been looking back on the remains of the classics, and how slowly did modern Europe disentangle itself from the perplexities of pagan mythology. Dante and Ariosto, Chaucer and Milton are all encumbered with it. Goethe tells us how he came to give up all the pantheon but Amor and Luna. Another school reverts to a later era, and with an antiquarian spirit endeavours to live over the baronial or the conventual life of the middle ages. But literature, to have a true life, must adapt itself to the age in which it exists, and breathe forth the very spirit of the time. And as Christianity, now opening on the world with a new power, is the grand element of the age, our literature is Christian. It should take its post above the common level, and look forward into the great tracts which are opened by the advance of science and civilization, and on which the sun of prophecy throws a cheering light. I often think we should gain, if men of letters, when somewhat possessed of what has been achieved in past ages, would close the ponderous volume, and take wing on their proper pinions, into the inviting regions of futurity.

§ 90. *Influence of our Actions.*—With a mighty but imperceptible influence, divine truth is going on, working in the world the change which has been predicted. Every church that is founded, every soul that is converted, every Bible that is printed, every minister that is ordained, and every sermon that is preached, tend towards this result. Nothing is more certain than the result; but as it is to be accomplished by free beings, under the influence of motives, it is highly important that we watch over all our actions, as tending to this result. Our talent is not for the napkin or the earth, but for trade and increase. The very formation of our individual character tends in a certain degree to the great result. Every example and every word of ours has a bearing on the same ; all we do, in our most careless hours, is so much to help to or hinder. No wrong action is neutral. Could a single individual stand forth all his life embodying some great principle, his influence would be felt on future generations.

§ 91. *Musing.*—Few habits are more injurious than musing, which differs from thinking, as pacing one's chamber does from walking abroad. The mind learns nothing, and is not strengthened, but weakened ; returning perpetually over the same barren track. Where the thoughts are sombre, the evil is doubly great, and not only time and vigour are squandered, but melancholy becomes fixed. It is really a disease, and the question, how should it be treated, is one of the most important in anthropology. The subject of this evil is generally aware of it. He is conscious that the longer he continues in these trains of thought, the less able he is to fly from them; that the troubles on which he ponders grow greater with his thoughts. But the mistake into which the sufferer commonly falls, is that of supposing himself able to throw off the painful burden by a process of counter-thinking. Nothing can be vainer. It is but floundering in the same slough. The only possible escape is by cutting off the whole train—and the more abruptly the better. Whatever does this is good. Sometimes even a new wave of trouble comes in with happy effect, to obliterate the old one. Active employment is still better, indeed the best of all cures for spleen —"fling but a stone, the monster dies." The thing needed is energy to put forth this effort—power to originate a new series of action—motive to abandon the painful objects, which exercise a mysterious fascination, leaving the patient in the belief, that some great evil will ensue, if even for a season he stops thinking about them. To counteract this last hallucination is one of the main points. The sufferer must settle it in his mind, that no possible good can arise from persevering in meditation on the evil : that no possible evil can ensue, if he never thinks of it again. What a blessed thing would it be if the melancholy man could have an infusion of daredevil recklessness for a little while, and if, instead of lashing himself to the helm in the long dark night of storm, he could for once leave the vessel a little to be the sport of the winds. There is no danger of his going too far in this, and, therefore, he may be safely advised to it. Caution and foresight are morbid and unreasonable when they are directed to objects beyond their sphere, and when they are for ever at work, without any results. How true, how wise, how philosophical, how beneficent, is the advice of our compassionate Redeemer, "Take no thought for the morrow." How self-evidencing its wisdom! how certain a cure for the disease ! Yet how difficult of self-application.

§ 92. *True Poetry.*—How can poetry ever reach its acme till its theme is religion ! Not the outward, but the inward. Milton, great as he is, has not touched the greatest themes of religion. Watts, and Wesley, and Rowe have done so, but not with the height of poetic afflatus. I think the world yet waits to behold a Christian poet of the highest order. There never was a falser notion than that of great earthen Johnson, that religion was not a fit theme for the highest poetry. Yet I must acknowledge that, to my mind, it exists only in hypothesis. If we could perfectly understand the Hebrew of the prophets, we should know what it means. A mind loosened from all earthly regards, and singing *unto God*, would produce it. Such a mind must be so rapt as to forget all that belongs to human praise. The heathen sometimes sang thus to their false gods ; why do not Christians sing thus to Christ? What greater inspiration do they wait for ?

§ 93. *Day Thought.*—*The People.*—Every shadow is a shadow of something.

The cry which echoes from so many writers, and even sects, in behalf of the people, and the poor, means something. There are prescriptive evils which have come down for ages—yes, for ages ! Think of it ! What Owen, St Simon, and Fourier *aim at*, is a real desideratum, but their way is wrong.

I pity, I love the poor, and it goes to my heart to hear the scoffing way in which they are often treated. Even the little wretches who plague everybody with their white mice, awaken my affection. This is not the world's philosophy. May I never learn philosophy from the world !

§ 94. *Religion as Excitement.*—Religion is just the excitement which many men need to make them happy. There are apertures in the human soul which nothing else can fill. The soul was made for this. We look back with a sigh to the animation of childhood, and even to the passion of youth. The craving for excitement leads us, in manhood, to pleasure, to business, to gain, to the chase for power. All these are successively, and often too late, discovered to be insufficient. In such a state of disappointment, what a pearl is found by him who believes in Christ! Religion surpasses all other excitements in this, that it is an excitement of love, and love is pleasurable, essentially. It exceeds all other love, in this, that its object is infinite. 'Till men learn to love God, they have powers which are altogether latent. As if certain cells of the lungs should never be filled by a perfect inhalation.

§ 95. *Books and Solitude.*—Much may be learned without books. To read always is not the way to be wise. The knowledge of those who are not bookworms has a certain air of health and robustness. I never deal with books all day without being the worse for it. Living teachers are better than dead. There is magic in the voice of living wisdom. Iron sharpeneth iron. Part of every day should be spent in society. Learning is discipline; but the heart must be disciplined as well as the head; and only by intercourse with our fellows can the affections be disciplined. Bookishness implies solitude; and solitude is apt to produce ill weeds: melancholy, selfishness, moroseness, suspicion, and fear. To go abroad is, therefore, a Christian duty. I never went from my books to spend an hour with a friend, however humble, without receiving benefit. I never left the solitary contemplation of a subject in order to compare notes on it with a friend, without finding my ideas clarified. Ennui is not common where men properly mingle the contemplative with the active life. The natural and proper time for going abroad is the evening. Such intercourse should be encouraged in one's own house as well as out of it. Solitary study breeds inhospitality: we do not like to be interrupted. Every one, however wearisome as a guest, should be made welcome, and entertained cordially. Women surpass men in the performance of these household duties; chiefly because they are all given to habits of solitary study. The life which Christ lived among men is a pattern of what intercourse should be for the good of society. I have a notion that the multiplication of books in our day, which threatens to overleap all bounds, will, in the first instance, produce great evils, and will afterwards lead men back to look on oral communication as a method of diffusing knowledge which the press has unduly superseded; and that this will some day break on the world with the freshness of a new discovery.

§ 96. *Daily Conflict.*—Our resignation and our faith must not be merely general, but particular. It is in special instances we are put upon our trial. We must not say, I could endure another sort of vexation, but not this. I could bear a different annoyance, but not this. This is precisely the one which God assigns to us, and perhaps, for the very reason that we are so intolerant of it.

The duty of humble submission is as imperative under this as under any other trial. The privilege of faith is as great under this as under any other. The promises of the Gospel are not excluded from this case. Could we look into the reasons of state in the mediatorial kingdom, we should see that we are visited with this annoyance rather than any other for a definite purpose, and that one of infinite grace. When this purpose is accomplished, it will assuredly be removed. But to bear it is better than to have it removed. True wisdom counsels us not to shrink from the trial, but to face it, in God's strength. Great fruits are reaped in this field. 'We account a man cowardly who shrinks from an enemy in natural things. We should apply this to our daily mortifications and distresses. It would be a noble habit of soul, if we could bring ourselves to regard every occurrence of this sort as a means of exercising our graces, and gaining new strength.

§ 97. ὁ Μιϰροϰοσμος.—The ancients talked of the *microcosm;* the little world within. We might have done better than disuse the pregnant phrase. We measure things too much by a *material* scale. There is a scale, on which Niagara, or a universe of matter, as such, measures no more than a sigh or an aspiration. The world *within us* is great. Revolutions take place there. It is mind that moves matter. Who can tell the moment of *one thought,* of a Napoleon or a Pascal! So in comparing two men, we compare only the outside: we cannot sound the cavern within. So of depravity: a man says he performs his duty, and is not a sinner; God will not punish him. But God sees a world within him, *which is godless.* There the mind is *everlasting.*

§ 98. *"Thy Word is Truth."*

> Poor twinkling man! thy ray can little pierce
> The scanty circle of thy nearest cloud,
> Far less the spaces of infinity.
> Let modest Reason fold her wing and learn!
> See in the darksome void a guiding beam,
> A glimmering point at first, a star, a sun—
> 'Tis light from higher worlds to guide thee on,
> Ten thousand volumes, laboured by the wise
> Of other ages, cumber still our shelves,
> Vex all our schools, and fill the roll of fame.
> In all how mean a portion that is true,
> Save what is borrowed from the Sacred Word.
> There, in few sentences is writ the lore
> Which king and prophet, master, priest, and sage,
> Toiled for in vain, and died obscure and lost.
> Let me hang breathless on the page divine!
> Here ends my quest, for God has spoken here.
> None can reject, improve, or wrest;
> None need discover, for the end is found.
> Interpret, ponder, practise, and believe,
> This thy sole task—be humble and be wise.
> While others search all nature to explore
> Her treasured secrets, finding thus at best
> Only some laws of this our lower state,
> And feeble inklings of the world divine,—
> My soul contented shall the record view
> Of God's own deeds of old, and gifts of love,
> And ample promise, and foreshadowing sign,
> And gaze upon the bright and lovely form
> Of the Messiah, God incarnate, given
> To image forth the Lord invisible.

§ 99. *Modes of Self.*—How hard, even on questions touching the honour of God and the purity of his church, to keep out self! How hard to be willing to appear to others what we are to ourselves, no more, no less! In regard to ignorance, inde-cision, vacillation, &c., we wear a mask. We often through pride affect the very qualities which we know we want, and over the want of which we secretly mourn. It is hard to say how far a man should go in keeping his own frailties secret. But silence is often safe. A debate arises; we grow warm, we take positions, we stick to them. After thoughts make us doubt whether we have not gone too far; but we act Pilate's part; *Quod scripsi, scripsi.* This pride must be brought low. Truth must triumph. Suppose we lose; very well. Truth gains. Our character is in God's hands. If we do his will, he will take care of our good name.

So many things commonly received seem to me to have no ground in the Scriptures that I often tremble. Then again certain things which I have got out of the mine myself, seem so plain and firm that my soul reposes on them. Hence, the more I go to the word itself, the freer from shaking.

§ 100. *How to view Nature.*—The work of nature, to be viewed aright, should be viewed under the σχεσις under which the inspired saints viewed it. But this is opposite to that of the Pantheist, who looks on nature, and as his soul expands with a philosophic or poetic admiration, lets his reverence terminate on the φαινωρενον, as a divine development. Not so David: "Praise ye HIM, sun and moon; praise him, all ye stars of light. Praise him, ye heaven of heavens, and ye waters, that be above the heavens. Let them praise JEHOVAH; for he commanded, and they were created."

§ 101. *Apothegms for the time:*

(1.) Every evil that befalls is deserved: but every evil is ordered in covenant love.

(2.) With what is past, beyond amendment, we have nothing to do but to repent and submit.

(3.) Pride being one of your greatest ills, must be slain: and what mortifies it is a real, unspeakable good.

(4.) Man's judgment of us is a mere nothing; God's judgment of us is of infinite moment.

(5.) It is idle and wicked to resist the will of God.

(6.) God has never forsaken: He never will.

§ 102. *Thoughts on reading Kant:*

(1.) How little the body and essence of our philosophy of life is affected by such speculations !

(2.) They are ever-varying from age to age, and they determine nothing.

(3.) The best light in which they can be received, is as an intellectual luxury.

(4.) They foster a dreamy disposition, and disqualify for the business of life.

(5.) True wisdom tends to the happiness of the race, It is the science of philanthropy.

(6.) Let me honour those forms of truth which tend constantly and directly to elevate the mass of men, and lessen human misery.

(7.) Consider the teachings of Christ as the incarnate wisdom ; in regard to its beneficence. His action and his precepts are simple, plain, and popular; but behind them lie the profoundest principles.

(8.) The more conversant you are with real distress, the more you will escape that which is imaginary.

§ 103. *The Scriptures.*

> Guideless and darkling; Oh, how poor
> Is man ! forsaken and impure,
> He cannot for a day, an hour,
> Go safe, without superior power.
> Away, ye false lights of an age,
> When pride enveloped every sage.
> The garden where Platonic lore
> Its honeyed current once did pour;
> The Porch of Zeno, and the walk
> Where once the Stagyrite did talk ;
> The haunts of Epicurus—all
> Are desert, and to ruin fall.
> Nor could their lordly patrons show
> The way of life they could not know.
> In vain, bewildered, o'er their page
> I hang, my sorrow to assuage.
> An endless guessing is the best
> They give, to put my doubts at rest.

A truth, half seen, may twinkle far,
As murky evenings show a star,
But in their most meridian light
There glimmers but a Greenland night.
The hour-glass notes the noon of day,
The dial owns the sun away.
From these conjectures, lo ! I turn
To sources which, while sceptics spurn,
I see, I feel, I know, are fraught
With wisdom, by a Saviour taught.
I hail thee, sacred volume, then,
Product of many a burning pen,
By sage, and seer, and martyr driven,
To picture forth the charms of heaven.

§ 104. *Maxims:*

(1.) He is too busy, who is too busy to be kind.

(2.) Nothing is cheaper than kind looks and kind words; but nothing is dearer.

(3.) What we suffer from another's injury, teaches us our own.

(4.) Half humility and half meekness will not answer; be meek and humble, and you conquer.

(5.) Our trials are in a multitude of cases such as produce mortification rather than grief. These are trials of our pride, and they are good for us, though painful to the flesh.

§ 105. *Goethe.*—I have just finished a reperusal of Goethe's Autobiography. It reaches to 1775, *i. e.* to his 26th year. To many persons the book is dull; to many it would be injurious; to me it has been deeply interesting. It is a frank development of his thinking and feeling during the formation period; and in the bad parts I see myself over again. Goethe is not an amiable character. He seems to have looked on himself as on a great development, wonderfully working from day to day, by a kind of fatality, or rather by an irresistible *nisus.* He lets every thing go on, careless whether it be good or evil; himself being the phenomenon, which to inspect, is the business of his life. Therefore there is no compunction about his worst works; and his apology for Werther, is as if one apologized for a viper—a natural curiosity which must be as it is. Goethe had two grand defects—want of conscience, and want of benevolence. Hence his great mind, exquisite taste, and amazing erudition, under the fostering patronage of an Augustian Court, and acting through a literary life, longer than Voltaire's, resulted in nothing which tends to make the world wiser or better. His whim, whatever it was, became embodied in prose or verse. It was not argument settling truth, or goodness arriving at beneficence, but genius and taste, revelling in their own development.

His faithlessness in love, his wassail, his darker excesses dimly set forth, his disregard of friends, his errantry and abandon, are detailed with coolness, and without contrition, even in his old age.

It is interesting to study the manner in which his youthful melancholy, of which both Werther and Faust are symptoms, was sloughed off, and how the almost Chinese sang-froid of his serene manhood supervened.

In religion he was a hopeless infidel. If neither Lavater nor the saintly Mademoiselle von Klettenderg could win his youthful mind, there could be little hope for him in mature life. All that he says about theology and the Bible, is a melancholy proof that the greatest genius, when intellectual pride leads him away from God's revelation, plunges deeper and deeper into self-contradiction. To me Goethe seems as little a believer as Voltaire. Without the persiflage and venom of the Frenchman, he is as godless. Since his death, the extreme Hegelians, and " Young Germany," as represented by Heine, have shown to what his principles lead. Moral evil, as such, seems not to exist for them. Sin, in their vocabulary, is a mere specific form. The *beautiful*, even in morals, they recognize, not, however, morally, but æsthetically.

§ 106. *John Howe.*—A little reading in pages of great thought will sometimes set one thinking, as if by a happy contagion, or as the sight of ten prophets caused Saul to prophecy. Such pages are those of John Howe. Do not go to them when you are gay, and wish to skim the surface. Do not search in them for sentences, brilliant quaintnesses, or the sacred mirth that sparkles in Gurnall or Flavel. Howe moves heavily and strikes out lengthily in a medium of resisting density, but then it is an ocean; and if you accompany him, he will lead you to depths which contain secrets unknown to those who play above. His argumentation is like none other. It throws off the common habiliments of the school-logic, and girds itself for a less regular but more athletic contest. Wait upon him, and he will reward you with abundant spoils.

Sometimes Howe rises to flights more sublime than those even of his great brother Puritans. Less terse than Bates, less polemic than Owen, less pathetic than Baxter, he is more philosophical, original, profound, and impressive than all these. Especially does he command our admiration and love, when he touches his favourite theme, the unity of Christian experience, as above the party differences of all the sects. How mean the squabbles of Christianity appear under the strokes of his overwhelming sarcasm! How we grow ashamed of our Shibboleths, when he takes us up from the fords of Jordan, to the top of Pisgah, and shows us the goodly prospect of a united church.

It was eminently his province to disparage and depreciate worldly things, without one shade of melancholy. The very dimness of this life is produced by the effulgence which he shows in another

§ 107. *On Reading the Epistles.*—Having this day read, without note or comment, a great deal in the epistles, I have endeavoured to open my mind to their genuine impressions, and am much impressed with the result.

(1.) The absence of every thing that savours of the ritualism of the Oxonian school. No stress is laid on priests, altars, ceremonies, or even sacraments. It is wonderful how largely sacraments figure in modern liturgies, and how little in the New Testament, which contains not even the word.

(2.) The intense *supranaturalism* of the New Testament writers. Every good thing is from above. Calling, faith, love, joy, all are of grace, and all of the Spirit. The communication is perpetually alluded to, as a matter of fact and experience. Early Christians lived in a heavenly atmosphere, and felt that by the grace of God they were what they were.

(3.) The heavenly *ethics* of the New Testament. Trust, love, patience, courtesy, meekness, forbearance, gentleness, long-suffering, forgiveness, hospitality, humility; these are what they felt and recommended. The power of Christianity was in these things. Believers lived in a tender love one to another. The world saw it, and were reproved and attracted.

(4.) The attachment of saints to the person of Jesus. He was not an abstraction. He was known of them, as one who had recently been among them, who had left them only for a season, and who was still within reach; a priest abiding continually, and ever living to make intercession for them.

§ 108. *One Truth.*—He who sets one great truth afloat in the world, serves his generation.

§ 109. *Central Truths.*—No truth can be unimportant, or be without advantage if uttered. But the nearer a truth lies to the great centres, the more important is its utterance. To utter one such is more than to gain a field at Granicus or Waterloo. To attain such truths, is one of the great objects of living. Prayerful thought, in moments deemed idle, is often fruitful of such. They come in many a moment of repose, and absence from books and papers; we are less masters of our own trains of thought, than we flatter ourselves.

§ 110. *Truth in Trains.*—Those meditations which are in such a sense our own that they are little mingled with names, authorities, citations, and other men's thoughts and words, are most valuable to us, and most useful to others. They are worth waiting for. We cannot expect many of them; but we should seize them with thankfulness. In no period of my life has this so much struck me as lately; forming a sort of epoch in my mental experience. I think it a little affects my preaching.

The trains of thought I mean are not scholastic ratiocinations. Though unspeakably above all experience or attainment of my own; the reflections of Bacon and Pascal exemplify my notion.

§ 111. *Rules often Constrain.*—Many of the common rules for the conduct of the mind, are too much like rules for the management of the body. Even the body, if alive, must not be dealt with altogether as brute matter.

I never could understand those people who divide their day into portions, with a pair of compasses, and allot so much to one study, and so much to another. I used to make such schedules when I was a lad. Great credit did I take to myself for making them, and great shame for breaking them; which I did day by day. I am now convinced that any attainments which have fallen to my lot, were really not made in these compulsory hours.

When a man is roaming about his library, taking down now this book, and then that, pacing the floor, scribbling on a bit of paper, humming a tune, and seeming to others and to himself to trifle, he is often engaged in his most profitable exercise.

Where there is an active inquiring mind, something is always brewing. There is no such thing as idleness. If he is not eating, he is ruminating. If he is not gathering the raw material, he is elaborating that which has been gathered. Many of these processes go on without our control. Our best trains of thought come and go without our bidding. The man who never knows what it is to throw himself upon these waves, and go whither they carry him, is not likely to have very genial thoughts.

Every kind of knowledge comes into play sometime or other not only that which is systematic and methodized, but that which is fragmentary, even the odds and ends, the merest rag or tag of information. Single facts—anecdotes—expressions— recur to the mind, and by the power of association, just in the right place. Many of these are laid in during what we think our idlest days.

All that fund of matter which is used allusively in similitudes and illustrations, is collected in diversions from the path of hard study. He will do best in this line whose range has been the widest and the freest. A man may study so much by rule as to lose all this: just as one may ride so much on the highway as to know nothing that is off the road.

The mind is capacious in its workings. It loves to assert its independence, and insists upon being consulted as to whether it will do this or that. Therefore in her highest actings she abhors taskwork, and shakes off the yoke.

§ 112. *Diversities of religious Opinion.*—With one and the same Bible before them, how wonderful are the differences of human creeds! The catalogue of sects, schools, and doctrines, might itself fill a volume. This is at times a most painful thought to every considerate mind. I have sometimes thought those happy who cling without scruple to what they have been taught, and have no agitations about other people's opinions. But such cannot be the condition of one who is set for the defence of the truth. It is doubtful, also, whether an independent mind can enjoy firm confidence, except as the result of some shaking from the arguments of opposing reasoners. I have observed that in perusing any able statement of a heterodox creed, I am for the time being affected with their force; and it is not till afterwards that the mind recovers itself, and comes to rest. It may be likened to the needle of a compass, drawn aside by an accidental attraction. At length it finds its true meridian: but not without some anxiety and disquietude.

This state of mind is never produced by reading the simple text of the Scripture. The mind then points towards its proper pole and is at rest.

It is not good to be much conversant with error, even though the object be to refute it; it is disturbing, if not defiling.

Private and unlettered Christians, who value their own peace, will not willingly hear preachers, or read books, which inculcate error.

The same reasons show the importance of dealing as much as possible with the sacred oracles themselves.

§ 113. *Reflection.*—The error is great of supposing that the mind is making no progress and acquiring no knowledge, when it is not conversing with books; and it is one of the errors of bookish men. There are pauses amidst study, and even pauses of seeming idleness, in which a process goes on which may be likened to the digestion of food. In those seasons of repose, the powers are gathering their strength for new efforts; as land which lies fallow, and recovers itself for tillage.

To be worth much the mind must sometimes be left to itself. It must pursue its bent, and sometimes condescend even to trifles. Perpetual readers violate this law of the mental constitution, and never with impunity. Those especially who are so exclusively professional in their pursuits as to do everything by rule and compass, to the neglect of all generous literature, and gentle, graceful entertainment, never fail to become rigid, barren of invention, and cold in expression. The grateful interruption of family hours and company are as good for the mind as for the body. Hence I think a married man is more likely to be a successful scholar than a bachelor.

Reflective minds cannot be wholly idle. Even in play, they work on, in spite of themselves. Seasons of intermission often give birth to the best thoughts.

§ 114. *Regulate the Heart.*—It is more important to regulate the *spirit* than the *steps.* A right heart is better than a right method. A man may have ever so good a plan of duties, but he will do none of them if the feelings be wrong; whereas, if the affections be right, he will be almost sure to do what is proper. Hence praying is better than planning.

This derives force from the consideration that we seldom find the duties of any one day exactly what we laid out on the day before. Our performance, when it is best, is often called forth by emergencies.

There may be fruitless care about even the *duty* of the morrow.

The best preparation for the week's work is the communion of the Sabbath.

The best preparation for the coming day is the devotion of the previous evening.

When the Scripture is let alone, the wheels of duty roll heavily.

§ 115. *The power of the Will.*—The power of the Will to change states of mind and trains of thought, deserves consideration. It is not a direct power, and it has certain limits ; yet we all know that man's activity has a certain scope, even in regard to this class of objects. It is true, a man who hates cannot by volition cause himself to love that which he just now hated. Nor can one who is in deep sorrow cause himself to instantaneously to rejoice, by merely willing it. Yet we are not therefore to lie down in a condition of absolute passivity, and yield ourselves to the cogency of evil tempers by a sort of fatality. There are moments in which we all feel that we are aroused to a sudden exercise of volition, which scatters the preceding feelings as the sun scatters clouds. The melancholy man, brought to a sense of the folly, wretchedness, and danger of his brooding, resolves to break the charm, and is successful. Query : How far this concerns the faculty of Attention ? The mind checks its present current—it directs itself to new objects —it regards motives which have hitherto lain in the shade—it finds a corresponding and often immediate change in its temper and moods.

§ 116. *Aphorisms on Self-denial of Appetite:*

(1.) Pain is to be incurred, or else there would be no self-denial : it is, therefore, to be expected and submitted to.

(2.) The pain of denied gratification may be very great, especially in the beginnings of self-denial : but there is no pain which so surely decreases and disappears. Short pains, for a good end, certainly resulting in pleasure, may be encountered with cheerfulness and borne with resolution. There is even a sort of pleasure in bearing such pains.

(3.) Solicitations of appetite address themselves to our lower nature through animal senses, and must therefore be put down harshly and summarily. It is not enough to plead and reason against them. *Venter non habet aures.* They must be ejected instantly, without parley, as you would cast out a noxious beast.

(4.) For this reason, every animal association should be cut off, which might remain as a fomes of the appetite. Therefore most attempts to break off an evil habit by degrees fail, when the habit is complicated with an appetite. This is frequently observed in the case of ardent spirits. Suppose a reforming drunkard to take a teaspoonful of brandy *per diem.* This would suffice to keep up the taste, and suggest indulgence. The only safety is therefore in absolute abnegation.

§ 117. *God Overrules.*—God overrules even those events in which we have acted erroneously. Wretched should we be, if he did not. None of our choices, purposes, and arrangements, are free from sin. All need to be washed in the blood of Christ. Take an instance : Hastily, and perhaps carelessly, I allow a dear friend to set out on a perilous journey. In this there is certainly a measure of sin, which God might visit. I am in great anxiety for the safety of this friend ; and this anxiety is increased by the fear that I have done wrong, which prevents filial confidence. But how gracious is our Covenant God ! He prevents our errors from coming back upon us in judgment. The Covenant of Grace, being founded on Christ's perfect merits, works its blessed fruits even when we are sinners. Even in such junctures we should confidently roll our burden on the Lord, with penitence for our sin, and trust in his abounding mercy.

§ 118. *More Maxims :*
(1.) He who begins to love his neighbour as himself, will be more cast down for the sake of others than for his own sake.

(2.) Melancholy is so much promoted by musing idleness, that the best preventive of it is to pass rapidly from one employ-ment to another, all day long, without any intervals of solitude or reverie.

(3.) As we go on in life, we ought to be more public-spirited, and to make our anxieties, projects, and prayers devote themselves to some matter of general concern.

(4.) Never give over the endeavour to overcome bad habits of mind or body, or those complicated of both.

(5.) Seize the happy moment of enthusiasm, when the impulse is in a right direction. In the same degree, flee from those sudden exaltations which tend to evil. Cry avaunt! and encourage the feeling of abhorrence.

(6.) Our need of preventive grace is nowhere more felt than when a temptation comes upon us suddenly. At such moments, if left to ourselves, we are weakness itself. Under such access of the enemy, great crimes have been committed.

§ 119. *Think for Yourself.*—A thinking man's thoughts gradually grow into a system. The less he follows other men's lives, the more will his own fabric of method compact itself. It is not always best to counterwork this tendency. The great points of any one's scheme will come out in his preaching. In treating these favourite topics will be his principal strength.

Those on which he dwells most frequently, and with most delight, are such as are central to his system of belief.

§ 120. *Physical Discipline.*—My mind turns upon the subject of physical discipline as subject to religious principle. The New Testament is somewhat remarkable for the entire absence of that ascetic element, which reigns so much in many false religions, and which played so large a part in the Christian Church during all its period of decadence. The body is not treated as necessarily evil. Abstinences are not enjoined. There are no fasts assigned to particular days. Macerations and penances are not so much as alluded to, except in the way of rebuke.

But while this is true, it is not less undeniable, that the New Testament makes it a duty to keep the body in a subordinate place, namely, in subjection to the soul, and in perpetual obedience and fitness to be the holy instrument of all spiritual acts. We perceive at once, that there is a pampering of the flesh which is inconsistent with a holy life. There must be some self-denial and subjugation of the lower part, in order to keep it from that horrid inversion in which appetites and passions acquire the dominancy. All habits of self-indulgence are to be prevented and broken up. We form in our better moments the ideal of a life, in which the character is produced by moderation, temperance, reserve in things lawful, frugality, simplicity, adherence to natural tastes, the cutting off of pleasures which are seducing, or in any degree tend to enslave.

§ 121. *A Simple Rule.*—Do that which you think will please God, and you will keep a good conscience. By so doing you will, in the long run, as much avoid the censure of men as if you made it a special object to please them. Every act of your life will be tending to form the right kind of character. You will be more likely to be useful, and will certainly be happier. If you fail, you will not have the additional pain which arises from blaming yourself.

This is the simplest of all rules of life. It admits of perpetual application, nor is there any conceivable case which it does not reach.

Please not yourself, nor vain human creatures, but God.

§ 122. The man who undertakes to go through life upon a settled plan, which he is not to modify according to circumstances, is much like one who should undertake to traverse a country in a mathematical straight line.

§ 123. *Use of Knowledge.*—There are two very common but very opposite ways of employing erudition and science. The one is that of learned commentators and disquisitioners, who accumulate stores of antiquarian and recondite lore, multiply quotations, and produce great volumes, which may have a zest for a few virtuosos, but which in the common mind can awaken only amazement or alarm. This is the method by which men acquire great fame in the republic of letters.

The other way is the humble mode of those who write for

the instruction of the people. Equal perhaps in real learning to the former, they never acquire the same notoriety. Their ambition is to smooth the way for humbler minds, to make the profundities of science accessible and to furnish the high distillation from varied researches. It is my ambition to belong to the latter class. Even if no higher object should be gained than to simplify science for children or apprentices, or to make religion fully known in a plain way, to the sons of ignorance, I should think it a task worthy to employ a lifetime.

§ 124. When we summon the worldly to abandon the world, it is not so much like asking the mariner to cast his wares into the sea in order to save his life, as it is like the command to the Israelites to leave their farms and their possessions, and go up to the temple-feast, in the assurance that God would provide for them.

§ 125. *Philosophical Studies.*—Lately my mind has been much engaged about the ethical heresies of Paley and the Utilitarians. It has almost seemed my duty to go into the investigation, and I have been reading some of Plato and the Platonists. I am deterred chiefly by the fear of that philosophy, falsely so called, which is denounced in Scripture. My object is truth, and I am sure if it were revealed to me to be right, I would this moment forswear all other reading but the Bible for life. But I am almost sure this would be altogether wrong.

I like good F. Scott's notion, that we are bees, that we seek every sort of flower, but bring our gains back to one Hive, namely, the Bible.

It is one of the glories of the Bible, that it expresses the grandest principles of the highest philosophy in the language of children.

§ 126. *Take no Thought for the Morrow.*—We might accomplish more if we were not foolishly asking ourselves so often, how long such and such a great work would take us. Professor Rob. B. Patton used to engage in most laborious lexicographical works. When asked how he had patience to go on, he said, that he never thought of asking how long it would take him, but went on as if it were to be his work for life.

Dr John Breckinridge made the same remark, when asked about those immense journeys which he takes to collect money —he never looks upon them *as* things which must end.

Addison tells me he finds the same thing good in his commentary on Isaiah. Our Lord's maxim about taking thought for the morrow, seems to have very wide applications.

§ 127. *A Student's Sabbath.*—Preachers and other students seldom have any day of rest. True, they make, if conscientious, some change in labours, but on the Lord's day they read, read, read, as *indeserenter* commonly as on other days. This is a great fault and folly. Just as really as the working man needs rest from the hammer and flail, does the thinking man need rest from thought. I think students ought to make the Sabbath a delight, by closing books, except the lighter and devotional parts of Scripture, by gentle nursing, by cheerful religious talk, by singing God's praise, and by works of mercy.

§ 128. *Variety in the Bible.*—The Scriptures are not the same to all readers, any more than the flowers of the garden are the same to all insects. One man seek this, another seeks that ; none extract all the sweetness. Under the guidance of the Spirit, each believer gains that which is needful for him, discovering and assimilating this by a gracious affinity. When such men systematize their deductions, they are far from being the same. How unlike the Scriptural treasures of Augustine, of Luther, of Howe, of Edwards, of Bunyan, of Hale, and of Chalmers ! Yet each one may get truth and holiness in this garden. These trees yield twelve manner of fruit.

The Scriptures are not the same to the readers of all ages. Primitive believers saw not all that we see. Let me here be guarded. Truth is the same for ever; that which is Scripture truth to-day will be so to eternity. Nothing can be added to the truth of the inspiration. But there may be great additions to our knowledge of it ; and it is not unreasonable to believe, that the Holy Spirit in leading believers into all needed truth, adapts his ministrations of light to the exigencies of particular times.

This should guard us against relying too much on the deductions of other men, however great and good, as if they had seen all, and left nothing to be gleaned in the field of original inquiry. However wonderful the discoveries of an Austin, a Calvin, or an Owen—however true, however extensive—they are not the inspired originals ; I may not confine myself to their teachings. They saw and appropriated all that the Spirit saw to be suitable for their own personal good and the good of the church in their day, and I will thankfully sit at their feet, and be guided by their experience. But my personal good, and the personal good of the church in our peculiar day, may demand other truth in other method, and these I must endeavour to get for myself from the Scriptures, under the guidance of the same Spirit. As we approach the latter glory and the return of the Messiah, there is reason to believe that the scroll of prophecy will be yet more unrolled, and that truths hitherto left in the shade will be brought out in brilliant prominency.

What an inducement have we here to study the Bible day and night—to look with our own eyes for hidden veins in this mine —to seek for it as for *hid treasures !* In expectation of this, and in faithful reliance on that Spirit who gave the revelation, and seeking that anointing which abides with all the elect (1 John), we may well leave for a season the commandments of men, and ponder on the pure original text. Perhaps as we pray and wait over the holy word, we may receive communications better suited to our personal wants and our relations to the world that now is, than if we were to master all the fathers, all the schoolmen, and all the reformers.

§ 129. *Argument the Basis of Devotion.*—The following experience I have often had, but, I believe, never committed to writing. On Sabbath and other occasions, I have wearied myself with attempts to awaken devotional feeling, by reading compositions of a merely hortatory kind—practical and experimental writings.

Our devotion must have a solid basis, and I believe it is in many cases the best thing we can do to go into the very strongest parts of theological argument, and feed upon such strong meat as one finds in Calvin, Rivet, Turretin, Witsius, and Owen.

§ 130. *Thought of the Day.*—We must work more *outwards*. We must bring Christian principles to bear more on the masses of men. We must show them that what they seek by vain philanthropy, is realized wherever true Christianity takes effect. If all men were good Christians, the evils of society would be in a good degree abated. Prescriptive wrongs would cease. Property would be equalized. The rich would communicate of their wealth, and the poor would rise by industry, temperance, frugality, and wisdom. The Bible is made for all ages, and with every new discovery in science, it meets us and shows a coincidence. The worldly philosopher and philanthropist dreams of a perfect state of society—good-will among men and universal peace. Now, the Bible not only predicts this, but shows how it is to be attained. The principles of Christianity tend to produce that very state. All the high civilization and humanity of the best nations is in fact the product of Christianity. In countries where science, literature, and the arts are in a high state, without true religion, we see luxury, excessive pleasure, hardness of heart, false honour, duelling, and suicide. Of this France is a great instance. The true way then to benefit, and even remodel society, is to make it Christian. This method is as simple as it is powerful. It proceeds upon no false or doubtful hypothesis, either of politics or economy. While men endlessly differ and dispute about these, and change one experiment for another in an endless round, loosing their beginnings by the change, and destroying human peace in the fruitless and soon abandoned trials, the humble Christian endeavours are going forward, with a noiseless but mighty efficacy.

Place a thousand men in a Utopian community, such as Owen's, and try to mould them by the visionary principles of the "New Social World," and the result is discord, failure, and misery. But place a thousand men anywhere in the world, and make them true Christians, and you attain really all the good ends sought in the former experiment, and render them as happy as men can be in our world. Hence the man who does most to bring over those around him to the principles and practice of true religion, is the truest philanthropist.

§ 131. *Take Time to Decide.*—When a difficulty, or an objection, or a specious error is presented to the mind, so as greatly to stagger it, we are not forthwith to be disconcerted. All minds are not capacious enough, or quick enough, to resolve such doubts at a moment's warning. Let the matter rest a little. The intellect will collect its strength, and after some rest and meditation, the judgment will come to a sound conclusion. This I have experienced many times. It takes place sometimes without occupying the thoughts in any stated or deliberate manner on the subject, during the interval. The process resembles the oscillations of a pendulum, which at length settles in its proper direction. Hence it is not always right to answer an objection immediately. This slow process is perhaps most commonly that of judicious and experienced persons. Temporary scepticism is distressing; but when we find by experience that it is relieved by wise delay, it need give no serious distress.

With a crafty man, who suspects others, because he knows his own way to be the way of stratagem, the best way of dealing is the freest and most open. It wonderfully confounds his toils, while here as elsewhere it is the most easily maintained.

§ 132. *Thoughts for the Time:*

(1.) Learned labours give little help in hours of alarm.

(2.) Sudden fears and troubles startle us, and drive us to thoughts of plain religion.

(3.) A certain important habit of soul is produced by the custom of daily silence and meditation.

(4.) The more bookish a man is, the more does he need both for his intellect and his heart, these moments of contemplative retreat.

(5.) Pauses of indisposition often force on us that self-communion and thought of God.

(6.) All is well when we apprehend God's ordering. His will is supreme law. Holiness is acquiescence in that will.

(7.) Faith is indispensable in times of panic : great knowledge is not so. Here the humblest mind commonly fares best.

(8.) Peace in trouble comes not from reasoning, but from faith, hope, and love.

(9.) The graces which sustain us in trial, proceed from the immediate and almighty agency of the Holy Ghost.

(10.) In affliction, especially in surprises, the soul falls back on its prevalent habits, whether wavering or fixed.

(11.) In the religious habits of our common days, we are all the while preparing for the hour of affliction and the hour of death.

(12.) It is all-important to be every day living in the belief of the unseen world, and as in the felt presence of Christ.

(13.) A few minutes in the busy day spent in absolute abstraction from the world, with a complete rupture of worldly threads, are among the best means we enjoy. They are to the day what the Sabbath is to the week.

(14.) Well would it be, often in the day, to seek those quiet frames which sometimes come when we compose ourselves for sleep.

(15.) In true retirement of soul there is nothing of perturbation or of gloom, but rather of cheerfulness. It is a healthy state.

(16.) These states of mind are allied to humility and meekness.

(17.) The true position of the soul is like that of constant childlike waiting on God for these influences.

(18.) The medium through which these graces descend, is the Lord Jesus Christ.

(19.) We cannot reason ourselves into holy frames; it is better to say, Lord, increase our faith.

(20.) Keep very low before God, and seek to please him rather than man, and you will find yourself armed against mortifications.

(21.) Cherish those views which agree most with pity for

every kind of human suffering, and active labours for Christ's people.

(22.) Nothing is more remarkable in the religious experience of the Bible, than its childlike simplicity. It is the aroma of the patriarchal life, as of a field which the Lord has blessed. See it in the Apostle John. I know an ancient disciple in whom it is very apparent.

(23.) Much in our religion is borrowed from the accidents of individual religious experience, and not from the Bible.

(24.) We are healthy in our frames when they lead us much to the Bible, and much to the throne of grace.

(25.) External beneficence is a happy antidote to the poisons that grow rank in the shade of scholastic study.

§ 133. *Wait for Uncommon Grace.*—Life is too short to be spent in renewing vain experiments. What I ought to be, I should seek to be without delay. I have been brought to feel to-day that there is a snare in many books as much as in abundance of company. They occupy the thoughts and keep them away from holy objects. This explains what I have long found true, that my best religious thoughts are in two situations, when I am abroad, and when I am in bed ; in both cases away from the literary objects of my study. There is scarcely any moment, in which a student may not take down some volume, to gratify the craving, or suit the present mood. But this brings in thoughts of other men, which is the same as the diversion of company ; and how seldom do we make conscience of the kind of book. It may be innocent or useful, it may be needed, and yet it may have nothing of spiritual nurture. The case is different, when we make our chief book the Bible ; and hence the great advantage of a preacher and pastor. And hence also a certain disadvantage in my professorship, which leads me in no case directly to the Scriptures, in their spiritual meaning. Nothing is more fully made out to me by observation and experience, than that the way of holiness and happiness is that of constant reading of God's word, with prayer.

§ 134. *Great Christians.*—How little adventurous independent piety! Bold thinking, but tame mimic religion. We feel and do as others feel and do; reproduce their diaries, rehearse their prayers, and catch the fashion of their awakenings. To be a great Christian, would be to become very unlike the men around us; hence great Christians have been in solitudes, in missions, or among persecutions. Sometimes I think we are more tied down to a conventional piety than the very Romanists. Their great saints went astray, and are not to be imitated; but they did not adhere to the old, hereditary ways; they broke out in a new direction. Are not yearnings after better things among God's ways of producing them? Are not strange trials, pains, mortifications, and humblings, among God's ways of training the soul? Should not such junctures be faithfully seized upon, for making higher reaches of experience? Have not special seasons of devotion, with long continued prayers and praises, been remarkably owned of God? Can eminent piety be reached without them?

We are presumptuous in figuring to ourselves the type of piety which we ought to attain. Perhaps God is forming us to a different type. Perhaps God intends a type unknown in any other; for the inward countenance of man is as peculiar to the individual as the outward. It is only by waiting in comparative quietude, that we can discern which way this divine tendency guides, and there is danger of running whither we are not sent, and even of grieving the holy Spirit of grace.

It seems to me that in our day we take the pattern and measure of our religion too commonly from what is popular, that is from what is bustling, outward, and full of eclat. But it may appear in another world, that some of the mightiest influences have proceeded from souls of great quiet. No book it is supposed of human composition, has had greater influence than the Imitation of Christ, by Thomas à Kempis. Some of the greatest characters have been formed in secret, as some of the wonders of nature are wrought under the earth. No man knows what God has made him for. Some men, for all we know, may be sent into the world chiefly to form other men. The grand act of a servant of Christ, for which God has been preparing him for many years, may be to give an impulse to some other man, and this may be accomplished in a moment, and when neither of the two suspects it. No man knows when the great act of his life takes place. No man knows when he is doing the greatest good. The old monk who directed young Martin Luther, possibly did nothing so important in his life. Sometimes it is a child, and whom would a Christian more joyfully influence than the son of his bosom? It is for him we labour, pray, suffer, and live. How do we know but the chief purpose for which God has spared our lives is, that we may form an instrument for his work in our own family? Thus the flowering plant dies when it has matured a fruit full of seed. How insignificant was Jesse, or Obed, or Boaz, compared with David; or Zacharias and Zebedee, compared with the two Johns and James. A due sense of what God demands of our sons, and an insight into his method of planning and bestowing for a series of generations, would make us importunate for gifts of the Spirit in our character as educators, and gifts on those who sit as loving learners at our knees.

Philip the Evangelist probably preached no sermon like that in the chariot. We may, therefore, err by forcing matters. The guard must be set here against inaction, under pretence of spiritual waiting. But after a certain point of experience is attained, we readily distinguish humble waiting for God's influences, from indolent, carnal sloth.

The more we believe in a direct influence of the Holy Spirit in sanctification, the more ready shall we be to expect this influence in ways which are uncommon. We have no pledge that we shall be operated on, after the rubrics of other men; nor that the ways in which we may be led shall always be pleasing to other men, even of the household of faith. Our tendencies are not to be necessarily of the Spirit because they seem so: they are to be tried by the word; and they are most apt to be so, in and over the world. Earnest prayer for so vast a blessing is all-important. There is no promise more explicit or more precious, than that of the Spirit. It is sealed by the reference to our beloved children, and the gifts which we, though evil, give to them. It is all things in one. Therefore it is not wonderful that so much is made in the New Testament of the Spirit; the contrast being painful between this and the popular theology.

After all, if God did not work in us, beyond our knowledge and our seeking, we should come to nothing. O, give us thy Holy Spirit.

§ 135. *Song in the Night* :

> Safe in thine arms I lie,
> Dismissing every fear,
> For sure my Lord is here,
> And every ill shall fly ;
> While from his throne above
> The dews of heavenly love
> Shall fall continually.
> Be thine o'erspreading wing
> Above us every one,
> Till the rejoicing sun,
> A bridegroom from the east
> Shall pour his ray of joy,
> And give serene employ
> To every sacred power,
> As when the opening flower
> Turns its fair chalice to the dawn,
> And o'er the greening lawn
> A thousand flowery eyes look out and smile.
> Come, everlasting Light,
> Thou fount of what is bright,
> Source of all life and bliss,
> Let no ill dream of night
> Dare to despoil of this.

§ 136. *Spiritual Changes.*—Few truths have been more sacredly impressed on me than this : We must seek great and needful spiritual changes, not so much from bringing our own minds under rational considerations, however true and useful, as from direct influences of the Holy Spirit. Experience shows that God, in his sovereign pleasure, often leaves us to do wrong, under the very presence of admitted reasons to the contrary. It is a part of the Christian conflict, set forth in the 7th chapter of

Romans. The understanding is convinced; the will itself is somewhat moved; yet there is not such an active volition as secures right action. This motive power must be supplied by the Divine Spirit. There is then nothing we have such need to ask, as the influences of the Holy Spirit.

§ 137. *Real Knowledge and Book Learning.*—Often and often I have thought of the superfetation of books. Look at libraries, trade-sales, catalogues. Hear the bibliographical talk of some men. Recall the innumerable books you have turned over.

Distinguish properly between real knowledge and book learning. Oral wisdom, methinks, will one day resume its ancient honours, for this very cause. Books will crowd one another out. What is said by word of mouth is simplest and most lasting. The early progress both of Christianity and philosophy, was by such means. The best part of education is so conveyed now. Extempore speaking derives some of its advantages from this. We ought all to practise it more.

§ 138. *The Manifestation of God:*

(1.) It is made the duty, as it is the happiness of man, to admire, love, and imitate the character of God.

(2.) God is infinitely removed from human apprehension, and cannot be known any farther than he is pleased to reveal himself.

(3.) The affections the man is bound to feel towards God, are impossible without some knowledge of God.

(4.) If there were no points of likeness between, God and man, we do not see how man could arrive at any knowledge of God. If, as is probable, there are attributes of God which have no analogy in man, we can arrive at no more conception of them, than of objects or qualities for which we have no sense.

(5.) But man was made in the likeness of God, and on this is founded his knowledge of God.

(6.) Though this likeness has been impaired, it is not entirely destroyed. Man still has mind, morals, immortality.

(7.) Still the character of God is at an infinite distance, and must be brought nearer to the analogy of humanity to be contemplated with satisfaction or profit.

(8.) This is accomplished by the Incarnation, whereby God becomes man.

(9.) Morality is the same in God as in man, as to kind, but infinitely different in degree.

(10.) But the holiness of God, in itself considered, is so far removed from our sphere, that we need to have it brought nearer to us, and as it were projected on the plane of humanity. Holy attributes are not appreciated till we behold them in the guise of manhood. Then we sympathize with them, understand them, and feel as if we could imitate them.

(11.) The divine excellencies are there embodied before our eyes in the Lord Jesus Christ.

(12.) These are really divine excellencies, though appearing in the human nature. For holy affections and volitions, in the man Christ Jesus, are perfectly coincident with the holy affections and volitions of the united Godhead; and so they reveal God to us. It is God in Christ, whom we see, admire, love, and imitate.

(13.) The historical representation of Christ in the New Testament is thus to us a manifestation of God.

(14.) This manifestation in the gospel is the great study of man's life. It reveals God. It shows us our law, our model, and our portion.

(15.) There is no other manifestation of God that shows so much of his moral glory.

(16.) Our contemplation of this is the great means of sanctification. " Beholding us in a glass," &c.

(17.) The Holy Spirit makes use of this contemplation to make us like God.

(18.) When the Spirit takes the things of Christ, and shows them unto us, he doubtless takes these very things which are recorded in the gospels.

(19.) We are therefore in the way of duty and of improvement, when we place ourselves before these things in the way of meditation and study.

§ 139. *Death-bed Repentance.*—Perhaps we do great wrong to God's infinite grace, by talking as we sometimes do about Death-bed Repentance. To terrify sinners from their sins is a good object, but it should be sought by no means but truth. Shall we please God by exaggerating in his behalf? Shall we not in the end even frustrate our own end in the awakening of sinners? True, the ungodly will abuse the doctrine that God sometimes gives repentance on a dying bed; but which of the doctrines of religion is it which they do not abuse? The case of the dying thief is the great Scriptural instance. But there are numerous instances of the same, so far as we can judge, on dying beds now. In my own ministry I have seen many. "Train up a child," is often here fulfilled. There is a wonderful tendency on dying beds to take on afresh the experience of childhood. What an encouragement to pious mothers! Infantine emotions I am sure often return in the last days of life, and a mother's voice rings in the ears of the prodigal son. This gives me greater hope in talking with those who, however wicked, have been trained for God in their infancy.

§ 140. *Chrysostom and Augustine.*—Many a person, on being asked which were the sounder and soberer interpreters, the Greeks or the Latins, would answer the Latins. Yet the reverse is true in many cases. Augustine is full of childish allegories; Chrysostom is almost always close to the letter.

§ 141. Christianity operates on mankind in two ways, viz., in the church, and out of the church. In the church it is constantly operating, and legitimately; but each church-organization seems after a time to lose its charm. Churches grow effete, but the church lasts, and we see the vigour breaking out in vital action in some new place. But we must not be surprised to find doctrine, feeling, and life going behind-hand in once favoured churches.

Out of the church Christianity also operates; and this too much escapes notice. Beyond question, the principles of Bible humanity and philanthropy are gaining ground in the world.

Infidelity indeed claims this as its own triumph; but these principles were all borrowed from the Bible. As the world advances, we may hope to see this becoming more and more true.

§ 142. *Dr Green.*—Two things Dr Janeway said about Dr Green, which are too good to be lost. 1. "Dr Green, from the time of his early ministry to the close of his life, used to spend the first Monday of every month as a day of fasting and prayer. 2. In one of my visits to him in Philadelphia, he said, 'Brother, I pray for you every day, and for both branches of our church, and for that church of which you and I were so long collegiate pastors.' "

§ 143. *Likes and Dislikes.*—How far a man should be governed by his penchants and antipathies, his likes and dislikes, in the conduct of his life, is a very difficult question. The *juste milieu* is hard to be found. Suppose we go to the rigorous extreme, and say that one ought to work out his course on principles of severe duty, and follow this implicitly, without paying the slightest regard to the promptings of nature, or to any constitutional tendencies, shutting his ears to every whisper of disgust, and steeling himself against every repugnance. Men have been found who, under strong moral or religious convictions, have so lived: indeed this is the very soul of the ascetic life. When the constitution is firm, and the will imperative, no doubt great actions have proceeded from this source. There is something great in getting the victory of natural cravings, and keeping under the flesh by a perpetual struggle. Men who have so lived have often aimed high, and accomplished wonderful results.

It may be questioned, however, whether in any case these have been the most genial and creative minds. Nature does not move in right lines, nor grow well in moulds and frames, however wisely adjusted. A certain violence is done to the heavings of inward forces tending towards development. These inward forces are often the very indications of Providence, by which man learns whither he ought to go. It is universally allowed, even by the sternest moralists, that, in the choice of a profession, of connections in life, of one's place of abode, and the like, the inward propension is to be taken as an element in the calculation.   Even in so grave and sacred a matter as a call to the Christian ministry, all men give a certain weight to the powerful, and sometimes almost irresistible, tendency towards it in the mind of the proponent.   Great geniuses, in every depart- ment of science, literature, soldiership, the fine arts, and philan- thropy, have broken away from the heartless toil to which seeming duty first tied them down.   How remarkably has this been the case with painters.   All the strait-lacing of Pensly- vania quakerism could not keep Benjamin West from the easel. The same has been true of poets and theologians.   And on looking back upon the lives of such, we cannot but recognize in these interior struggles a providential guidance towards parti- cular ends.   How can we deny then, that, in some of the most important concerns in life, it is allowable to have some regard to the strong promptings of inward desire ?

Excellency in every human calling has some dependence on the zest and enthusiasm with which it is pursued.   Few things which are done in cold blood are well done.   Providence does not mean all men to follow the same things ; and, in nine cases out of ten, that which a man follows is pointed out to him by some dominant taste which is not in other men, and for which frequently no adequate cause can be assigned.   Hence some are lawyers, some generals, and some laborious students in recondite and new branches of learning.   Obedience to such monitions has produced the greatest works known among men.   And it is re- markable that the order of Jesuits, which, above all other com- munities, has adopted for its principle of education, the suppression of individual will, and subjection of all private like and dislike to the dictate of superiors, has produced no great and world- renowned work on any subject.

It seems clear that we may go to an extreme in governing our whole path of life, in contempt of all natural propensities and preferences.

But the question still returns, how far we may be governed by such in the daily steps of our ordinary vocation. Even here it would be an overstrained virtue, which would altogether for-swear a consultation with feelings of like and dislike, which may sometimes be the indications of Providence. Where there is nothing else to decide the question between contending claims, we may very naturally and wisely bring in the consideration of the agreeable and disagreeable. A man's daily work may be to such a degree repugnant to his feelings, that it will be next to impossible for him to persevere in its prosecution.

§ 144.—The days we call idle, sometimes produce as much eventual strength as is derived by vegetable growth from the fields lying fallow, or from the winter repose of the tree. We walk the floor, we open book after book, we read a little, write a little, muse a little, and in the evening condemn ourselves for want of diligence, perhaps justly, so far as the motive is con-cerned. Yet in nothing am I surer, than that this very process results in subsequent energy. Especially when I consider that those who have these lapses, on certain occasions, are, at others, employed for hours, or even days together, at the very stretch of all their powers. In a studious life, if the scholar did not sometimes leave his formal prescribed tract, and expatiate, as it were at random, to pick up the scattered, variegated, unclassed flowers of common, and even little truths, he would fail to have his mind filled with a thousand things which, however hetero-geneous at first, go through the digesting and assimilative process ; become the material of future argument, or furnish embellishment, illustration, or example. Casting ourselves on Providence, in studies as in all things else, we find ourselves led by ways that we knew not.

§ 145. *Consecration of Learning.*—To consecrate all that one has to Christ, is the ruling purpose of every Christian. In the esteem of the Master it is this purpose, or this abiding tendency of soul, which is the thing regarded. Is it a draught from the well, an alabaster box of ointment, or a gift of funeral spices ? it is received. Is it a visit to the prisoner or the invalid, or clothes to the naked? it is accepted as done to Christ. The rich disciple bestows his gold, and the scholar may bestow his learning. These are as frankincense and myrrh. The great point is, that he who has aught must make a free-will offering at the beloved shrine. The accumulations of learning and the refinements of taste may be withheld, even after voluntary designation, and thus the sin of Ananias and Sapphira may be repeated, in a matter more precious than goods and lands. But when all the fruits of study are made over with a full and ready mind, science and literature may be truly said to be laid in the temple. These are the votive treasures, which will be more numerous, as better days dawn on a more enlightened and holier church. Then it is that erudition ceases to be idolatrous and selfish, when their choicest fragrance exhales towards heaven.

The carved work of the Sanctuary, the chasing of Bezaleel, and the graving of Aholiab, the music of Heman, and the song of David, were as welcome offerings as the beasts which smoked in the courts of the Lord's house. There is such a thing as reaping in the fields of classical entertainment, and then suffering the sheaves to perish on the earth, instead of garnering them up for God. When we feel the inspiring influence of books, when we are lifted on the wings of ancient genius, we should jealously avoid the perversion of the gift. The children of this world have their research and accomplishment, and enough is done for pleasure and fame; but the Christian scholar will rebuke himself, unless he finds it in his heart to be more alive in devotion to heavenly things, at the very moment when he has breathed the aroma of poetry and eloquence.

Such a disposition of mind will keep him from being puffed up by his attainments, from resting in the transient satisfaction, from forgetting God amidst his favours, and from sacrificing to gain or ambition what he has gathered from the labours of study. The transition in a Christian disciple from worldly literature to the Scriptures is not violent. He feels the immeasurable disparity, and rises to a new level when he follows the guidance of prophets, of apostles, and of the Holy Spirit himself. Attainments of learning made in such a temple are sacred, however remote the subject may seem to be from biblical research. These gains are for eternity. They are not only not lost in this world, amidst the wreck of fortune and health, but as belonging to the spiritual part in which God's image chiefly resides, they abide and survive the dissolution of death, and emerge in the better state, only to be the germs of new devolopement in that unexplored world of everlasting progress.

Powers strengthened by all the most effective discipline of earthly schools, are dedicated to the greatest and holiest work. High as the intellect may soar, it will never cease to have above it the august cope of heaven; human philosophy will never exhaust or even reach the greatness of divine ideas. These mysterious objects, like the starry heavens, are liberally offered to every eye, and the poor man, the slave, and the very infant gain and enjoy something from the celestial wonders, which Pascals and Newtons lose themselves in vainly attempting to comprehend. Yet the tribute rendered, by different capacities, though equally sincere, is not equally great. When God bestows genius and cultivates talent, and enlarges by providential culture the opening reason, he does this in order to draw from such natures a service far vaster than that of common minds, however pious. Education is, therefore, a fearful gift, bringing tremendous accountability; it should lead to humility, thanksgiving, activity, and devotion. When these are wanting, a godless prostitution of the powers is the result; offensive to God in the proportion in which the subject of these qualities is raised above the vulgar population of the globe. Witness the extreme cases of a Voltaire and a Byron. When such instances are numerous, giving character to a nation or a generation, we have the spectacle of Atheistic France, and apostate Germany. The Christian scholar should pray with every breath, that he be not high-minded, but fear. In proportion as he rises in attainments, he should sink in veneration, and dissolve in love; striving to increase his simple devotions as he increases his mental discoveries. Is there not reason to think, that many learned persons feel somehow absolved from the private daily duties of religion which they would themselves enjoin on humbler minds?

that they pray less, read God's word less, and sing God's praise less, while they are filling up every hour with eager pursuit of knowledge? To live thus is to belie our own professions. We declare our belief that truth concerning God in Christ, is the summit of all truth, and that cold science is insufficient; that these glorious objects are to be tasted by faith, and kept constantly before the mind by devotion. Thus believing, we should not grudge the time bestowed on closet exercises. If these are animated by the Spirit of grace, they are the most sublime engagements of the mind, this side of heaven. And as religion in general is the highest science, so those truths of religion which are cardinal, are the noblest eminences of the mighty range. The plan of Grace, the Incarnation, the Person of Christ, the Atonement, the Paraclete, the Second Coming, are the local points on which the spiritual mind will be fixed, exercising itself according to the degree of its previous culture.

§ 146.—As a man gets older, his pursuits should change, and it is important to consider how. Till a certain point of feebleness, action should have more, and study less. After that point, example, counsel, and prayer, would seem to be the duties of a Christian old age. But plans of suitable change should precede these decays. When one feels himself to have no longer any ascending ground in the journey, he should pause, and readjust his methods. What is good for 40, is not good for 50. In regard, for instance, to study; all studies of preparation, are merely auxiliary studies, and most studies of education should be put away. New languages, unless they can be made to fall under the head of necessary amusement, should be dropt. New sciences and arts fall under the same rule.

To consolidate and methodize, and complete what has been most successfully begun in former years—to turn theory into practice—to attack with vigour the great task of life—to cast out old evils, and by grace to exhibit a holy character, these are the duties of him who is growing old. The whole prospect is deeply serious, though it need not be alarming.

§ 147. Powerful exertion of the will, under influences of the

Holy Spirit, tends to drive away the tempter, and confirm habits of holiness.

§ 148. *Moral Education.*—Reading a passage in the Apology of Socrates, I was more forcibly struck than ever before with the grand defect of our education. What should be the aim of all our education of youth? It should be to make them *good men* and *good citizens.* This should be apparent in every hour of every day. It is not so apparent. The languages and sciences are taught, but what morals and duty?

Leaving out the question of the Bible in schools, closely connected with this subject, how remarkable that we have no textbooks and no classes, having reference to morals. There are no examinations to discover whether pupils are prepared for the duties of life. When we ask a boy concerning his progress, it is " How far have you got in Algebra?" or " Have you read Homer?" and not " What are the temptations of youth?" " What are the evils of gambling or strong drink?" " What are the dangers arising from corruption in voters?"—The moral and practical part of education kept out of view.

Education includes *teaching* and *training.*

§ 149.—Morality may exist in practice without religion. Here we do not mean universal holiness, or the highest virtue, which is itself religion. Morality is equivalent to the maintenance of certain relations between man and his fellows, or between man and society, or between man and his own interests considered objectively. These relations may subsist without any inward right feeling.

§ 150.—The mental acts of devotion to God are thought of unworthily by most. In no acts can the human soul be more nobly employed. Nothing we can do is so safe. In this employment of our souls we might well be willing to be arrested by death. No man can gaze long on the face of God in Jesus Christ, without being elevated. No one will love to do so, unless he has been born from on high. God grant me more of the spirit of true devotion.

§ 151.—There is a wisdom which is not in books. It may be gathered from books, considered as parts of innumerable real sources. Into books it may be transcribed, but only they will comprehend it, who have been taught it from some other quarter.

§ 152.—He who comes down from the mount loving God, or from the cross loving Christ, needs no new frame or impulse for loving his brother also. And how beautifully, in all the texture of St John's epistle is Love interwoven with Light! What a radiant holiness; what a holy illumination! The two seem almost one, in the apostle's mind, as they are in the infinite, primeval source; for God is light, and God is love. And so, in regard to the creature, " he that saith he is in the light, and hateth his brother, is in darkness even until now." The acting of this principle in the new creature will be constantly purging out its opposites; and this by painful struggles. Contrary principles of native selfishness will manifest themselves, but will be shamed and excluded. Every successful struggle of this kind will make the next easier, and will put it further off. Selfishness and love will come to be readily known; and here will be a portable rule, to be applied in the absence of all lesser regulations. The study of Christ's character will first educe love to him, and put it into exercise, and then create a disposition to walk in love as he hath loved us. Thus faith will work by love.

O, for greater measures of this Christian grace! O, for quickness to detect, and strength to cast out, the first poisons of anger, malice, envy, jealousy, and covetousness.

§ 153.—It is unreasonable to hope for a situation where men will not be found to oppose, envy, and blame. To expect this would be childish. Humble perseverance in plain duty, is the way to maintain an easy mind. Apply the Lord's rule about anxiety for the morrow. Work by the day, you may not live till to-morrow. Why cripple to-day's exertions by forecasting a trouble which may never come. Such vexations are trials sent of God. They have been common to all saints. Learn to bear the reproaches of even good men, for many sincere Christians are far from perfection in wisdom, and there are degrees in knowledge and experience, and diversities of opinion, and there are strange and extravagant tempers. Some virtue is put to the test by every one of these troubles. Humility, patience, meekness, courage, fortitude, love of truth, faith, hope, and charity, are exercised thus. If a man's ways please the Lord, he will cause even his enemies to be at peace with him.

§ 154. *Work at the Interior.*—Keep right principles. Guard the heart. Do what is right. Approve yourselves to God. Eye the Judgment. Live as before God, and with Christ. Take good counsel, but confer not with flesh and blood. Let you whole life be a preparation for dying. Give your answers clearly, frankly, simply, and meekly; and learn when, and where, and how to answer the fool according to his folly, and when to answer not. Be harmless as the dove. Study Christ's methods under the contradiction of sinners which he endured. Feel your own incompetency for any part of labour, and own your obligation to grace for every measure of success. Throw self overboard, and walk with singleness of mind, and you will certainly have success. Modern preachers ought to be ashamed to complain of opposition when they read of what befell the apostles and early teachers. God's words in vision to Paul at Corinth should be our encouragement, "Be not afraid, but speak, and hold not thy peace, for I am with thee, and no man shall set on thee to hurt thee; for I have much people in this city." At Ephesus this apostle ministered amidst opposition, "Serving the Lord with all humility of mind, and with many tears and temptations." Acts xx, 19. He journeyed on, knowing that "bonds and afflictions" abode him.

§ 155.—The communications of a pastor with a parishioner are not to be made an affair of ceremony. Pastoral visits are not to be regulated by the laws whereby fine ladies govern their morning calls. A spiritual message is what Christ's minister carries to a house, and has in it something too solemn to be treated like a visiting-card.

§ 156.—Great care is needful to avoid harshness and spiritual pride in dealing with weak professors. We must copy the wise physician, who often has to condescend to the nervous and whimsical. The gentleness of Paul and Paul's divine Lord should be always before us.

§ 157. *A Batch of Maxims :*

(1.) Make not too much of maxims; they are, after all, but measuring-rules.

(2.) Give ten thoughts to the question, What will God think of it, before one to, What will men think of it.

(3.) If you could act like an angel, some would blame; do your best, and in the long run you will please more than by doing anything for the bare purpose of pleasing.

(4.) Never give over striving against a bad habit. Begin again and again a thousand times. Victory will come.

(5.) Return daily and hourly to the study of Scripture.

(6.) For comic and childish jocularity, substitute mild, loving, and if you possess it, witty demeanour and discourse.

(7.) Truth is food; falsehood is poison; error is injurious. Apply this to the reading of erroneous books, even when necessary.

(8.) Some minds are more susceptible of harm from contact with falsehood than others.

(9.) Infinite wisdom in the Scriptures is always accessible.

(10.) The more you are dwelling in truth unalloyed, the more healthful will your thoughts be.

(11.) Some minds, from susceptibilty to the unsettled influence of error, are not fitted to be polemics.

(12.) Do not discredit those convictions which have grown out of former investigations, even though the explicit arguments for them are forgotten. The mind should make progress in conviction as well as in knowledge.

§ 158. *Christian Love.*—In this dreary, windy, winter night, when some of my household are ill, and some in bed, I feel in my loneliness the need of communion with other spirits than my own. And how grateful to the soul at such an hour to know, that this inward craving is met by all the teaching of the gospel, and that no man liveth unto himself!

The communion of saints and the communion of humanity are best connected with communion with Christ. Here is their origin and this is their bond. The man who has no love of the brethren has no love of his kind : the widest philanthropy is found in union with Christian graces. The Spirit, who unites men with God, through Christ, unites them to one another. This holy love, which we speak of even to triteness, and against which we are daily sinning, is more worthy of pursuit than all the objects of philosophy. I am from different lines of inquiry brought perpetually to the point, that the chief way of helping mankind is to work deeply within. True charity begins at home. But from its very beginning it cultivates a reference to those who are without. Christ, who teaches as none other ever taught, and wraps up whole volumes in a word, has taught us the grand secret of forgetting self. We are to lay all at his feet. We are to seek his kingdom. We are to cease from loving our own life, nay, we are to lose it. Loving our neighbour as ourselves, we are to lay down life for the brethren, and to do all possible good to those whom we can reach, as if doing it to him. Never forgetting the inimitable and mediatory parts of his life and death, we see in them also an example of self-forgetfulness and sublime benevolence.

The constant effort of the soul in this direction, under the Holy Spirit, is the chief activity in religion. It connects itself with all doctrines and with all graces. Humility, penitence, submission, patience, faith, hope, meekness, gentleness, self-denial, sympathy, diligence, truth, desire of truth, purity, generosity, courage, justice, veracity, candour, and cheerfulness, all ally themselves, as so many sisters with love.

§ 159.* I am reading John Owen on the Sabbath. The difficulties of this subject increase on me very much. To

* This, and the remaining paragraphs, are extracted from letters to his son, while a student in the Theological Seminary at Princeton.

understand what they are, read a page of Owen (Exercitations preliminary to his Exposition of Epistle to the Hebrews.) Part 5, Exerc. 1, § 5, p. 268, of Goold's Edinburgh edition. He gives sixteen queries, which afford matter for deep rumination. My chief puzzles have always been about the questions, How much of Sabbath observance comes from Creation—how much from Moses—how much is abolished—how much remains. Now and then the great old fellow says a mighty sly thing, *e. g.,* " Most men act as if they were themselves liable to no mistakes, but that it is an inexpiable crime in others to be mistaken." " Some men write as if they were inspired, or dreamed that they had obtained to themselves a Pythagorean reverence." " Only I fear some men *write* books about them, because they *read* none." A sentence of his about preaching is worth being copied as a maxim ; " Nor must we in any case quit *the strengths of truth,* because the minds of some cannot easily possess themselves of them." Dr Mason used to say that all his theology was from Owen on the Hebrews, and my father often remarked, that with all Owen's power, erudition, and originality, he never deviated in his theology into anything eccentric or hazardous.

§ 160. Don't make your sermon fine. Remember " great Julius's" word, and avoid *verbum insolitum voluti scopulum.* Don't mistake the language of imagination for the language of passion ; the sin of our young ministry. I wish I had you for half an hour a day, to give you some voice training ; I have paid much attention to this, with one certain result, that I have learned to speak long and loud without fatigue. Nothing can be done on paper, however. All is only an expansion of old Sheridan's *speak as you talk.*

Read aloud and study in your club, Monod's article, Bib. for 1843, pp. 191-211. He " is himself the great sublime he draws." Nothing in all my history ever did me so much good. See the remarkable notes on pp. 205-6, and 208. This last opened my eyes to the matter. Read it and re-read it. I have the noble original, and have heard the matchless exemplification.

§ 161. I hope you will let no kind of reading keep you from looking daily—if only for five minutes—into a class of writers, who are not attractive in regard to letters, but who unite great talents, great Bible knowledge, and great unction. At the head of these stands Owen. My father used to say one should read "Owen's Spiritual Mindedness" once a year. I add his "Forgiveness of Sin ; " his " Indwelling Sin," and his "Mortification of Sin." Here we have philosophical analysis applied to phenomena of experience. Yet more Platonic and seraphic are Howe's "Delight in God," and " Blessedness of the Righteous." Flavel's "Keeping the Heart," is less deep, but more clear, purling, and delicious. As to Baxter, I think his English equal to any ever written. One such book kept near at hand, and opened for a few moments every morning, seasons the thoughts. So of good biographies—so one does not seek to copy details and idiosyncrasies ; *Simeon's Life*—Martyn's—Brainerd's (with due allowance of his diseased gloom)—Edwards'—above all HALIBURTON'S. I have no doubt of your becoming sufficiently learned ; but I have great fears lest you should look for happiness too much in the æsthetic, then the divine part of the To KAΛON ; lest literature and art should occupy the place of spiritual communion. It requires great striving to keep an academical life from promoting habits of mind out of sympathy with the great activities of good men in the arena and battle of the church.

§ 162. In thinking upon any subject, with a view either to writing or speaking, the mind is apt to flit away, or to fall into sterile reverie. Against this, the common remedy is the *pen;* and it is valuable. But it is not indispensable, or even the best. Let me suggest a device which I never met with in books, but which I have practised in bed and on horseback. *Stake down every attainment in your thinking by a verbal proposition.* The thing of emphasis is the propositional form. We are not now considering whether it is true, or important, or in due sequence ; put your thought into words, as affirming or denying. After a little turning of it, put the result into words. Seek to *deduce* another from

the one you have. N.B. These will often prove heads of discourse. If you have a dozen of these on any subject your work
is blocked out. The aid to memory is surprising. Wretched
as that no-faculty is in me, I always remember such propositions
from one day or week to the next. In early efforts it may be
well to *utter them audibly*. It shows you that you are going on—
and how fast—and when you have come to a logical dead-lock.
This has often been my only preparation for speaking. I
consider this so important, and am so much afraid of being mis-
understood, that I will give you an example, being the last
subject which thus engrossed my attention, in Broadway and in
bed; preferring it for the very reason, that it has not yet thrown
itself into any crystallization : 2 Tim. iii. 4, "*lovers of pleasure
more than lovers of God*." 1. Man loves pleasure. 2. The propensity to such pleasure exists by nature in all men. 3. The
merely animal nature is governed by this as a law. 4. Pleasure
must not be taken to include absence of pain. 5. He who gives
full swing to this propensity, so as to do just what he pleases or
wishes, does not thereby reach perfection. 6. He does not
thereby attain moral excellence. 7. Nay, he does not attain
happiness, the very thing he seeks. 8. Such indulgence is
ruinous. 9. Consequently, this cannot be the highest law of
man. 10. Many go great lengths this way, though nature itself
cuts them short. 11. As absolute self-indulgence is ruinous,
the love of pleasure *must be checked*. 12. The normal life is
therefore one of checks and counterpoises. 13. Strength, happiness, and every great quality are produced by such struggles
and antagonisms. 14. Hence men seek pleasure in *toil, labour,
pain*, navigation, hunting, fighting. 15. Happiness is more in
effort than indulgence. 16. Seeing then that propensity must be
checked, it must be considered what principles can be brought
in, to countervail a tendency so powerful. 17. Selfish interest
is not strong enough. 18. Reasoning is not strong enough.
19. Mere conscience is not strong enough. 20. Love is not
strong enough. 21. Honour is not strong enough. 22. The
text declares what is strong enough : *the love of God :* &c., &c.
This will suggest something as to the genesis of thought. Each

proposition brings forth the next. Sometimes the series is not
so much thus,   A   as thus,   A

      ×

      B   B C D

      ×

      C

      ×

      D

Sometimes the next proposition will be only a neater enumeration of the preceding ; and this process is eminently useful to
the mind. Sometimes No. 2 will be an example of No. 1.
Sometimes you will see that the *order* is capable of improvement;
so above, I perceive that the order (on rhetorical grounds),
should be 20, 21, 19, 22. If a man will only pursue this
process far enough, he will acquire plenty of material, in
such quality as agrees with his other knowledge and native
powers.

The principal thing gained by this method is, I own, the *fixing of attention*. But this is after all the principal thing in all
processes of productive thought. What is it that a man does in
thinking out any subject, beyond keeping his mind's eye looking
in a certain direction? What shall arise in that quarter is as
unknown to him as to any one else. This is one of the greatest
mysteries in the origin of thoughts. The turning of certain
leading thoughts, as they arise, into propositions, marks the rate
of progress, indicates direction, and blazes one's way through
the forest. Each stake tethers the thought, which would wander. There is an additional advantage in this, that we never
have the full use of language, as an *instrument of thought*, unless
when we cause our thoughts to fall into assertory shape. These
have been views, regulating by practice for a great many years ;
but I have only of late come to think that they are overlooked
by many. This is to be considered rather as marking progress
than contributing to the generation of thought ; though it indirectly does the latter.—It is to be observed, that many of the
thoughts which rise, and even take this propositional form, are
to be immediately resisted, as false, irrelative, or superfluous.

Making the proposition is only putting them into a shape in which they can be tested.

As the getting of something to say (the ancient *Inventio*) is the *prora et puppis* of all preparation, I have dwelt a little on this point. Such endeavours are not to be made *invita Minerva*. All times are not equally good for production. This belongs to the passivity of the mind in these processes. We must wait upon it; sometimes leave it, to rest or expatiate, return to the task again, and especially catch at moments of inspiration. Generally speaking, *faithful thinking gives pleasure*. But the beginnings are generally tentative. Change the scene. A subject will look differently, in the study, in the forest, by the sea-side, and in the crowded thoroughfare. External circumstances often stimulate, while they seem to interrupt the productive faculty ; just as shaking a solution will sometimes fix a crystallization. *Rest*, especially in sleep, greatly helps. Clearing up of the general health is useful. For these reasons trains given up as impracticable will be successfully resumed after months.

Thus I have spun out a long yarn upon this simple expedient of fixing one's thoughts in propositions, during the process of excogitation. No one method has been so much employed by me in sermonizing, and mostly when walking up and down the floor, or some path among the trees.

§ 163. I have sometimes thought of writing you a letter on *maxims*, but time has failed me. It is a subject which has occupied much of my thoughts, and, I suppose, has somewhat modified my character such as it is. By a maxim, I mean a general principle of conduct, expressed in a concise, portable, applicable manner. When it hits public taste and runs through society, it becomes a *proverb*. The best thing Lord John Russell ever said, was his definition of a proverb : " the wisdom of many— the wit of one." (Study a little on this.) I have a great penchant for proverbs, in spite of Lord Chesterfield's denunciation. I have several collections, and I wish I had more. But to return to maxims, which are not all proverbs, they are generalizations from the wisdom of experience. Here minds

differ very much. Some men seem to lay up no general conclusions, however long they may observe. Your grandfather
used to say, that old Samuel Venable was the wisest man he
ever knew; that, like Franklin, he was continually treasuring up
the lessons of experience, and framing resultant rules, which
often would be highly valuable to others. You may remember
some good things in French on this point. But at present my
aim is not so much to lead you to enjoy other people's maxims,
as to frame your own. No man can begin too soon to philoso-
phize upon mind, manners, morals, and religion. *Make maxims.*
Make a maxim every day. Do not force it—but if you watch
for it, it will come. When you are not looking for quail, the
shrill "Bob White" reaches your ear without impression; but
when quail are your special quarry, you catch the most distant
whistle. He that is on the look out for maxims will find them.
A young man's maxims must be juvenile and often hasty; but
that particular turn of mind which frames them is all important.
Let me take an humble instance. At a certain period of my
life, I was much afflicted with a sort of bodily inertia. If I was
on the sofa, I did not like to take a chair. If I was in my
fauteuil, it irked me to get up. My flute was in the attic, but
the trouble of mounting so high overbalanced the desire to play.
This grew on me so much, and so killed all alacrity, that I laid
down this rule to myself, *Never avoid doing anything, because of
the short bodily trouble it may occasion.* It has saved me a world
of useless regrets. From little things, we shall by degrees
proceed to great. He that has his mind most stored with such
tried conclusions, will be best armed for the battle of life. There
is no reason why he should blurt them out to others: they are
his own pocket rules. It is not a matter of indifference how
these are expressed. A terse, felicitous maxim is like an instrument brought to its perfect state. The thought may pass
through a thousand minds (the wisdom of many) before it comes
to a shape of memorable and crystalline expression (the wit of
one). It may be compared to one of your happy *formulas* in
mathematical analysis. Many a man had discovered it before
one happy punster said, *Amicus certus in re incertâ cernitur.* One

such conclusion (even without the happy form) is a gain for life; and is like a sum laid up in store for coming days. But chiefly do I refer to rules for one's own conduct, derived from one's own experience. This word "experience," means the sum of such knowledge. That man's experience is most service-able, which is most reduced to palpable formulas; as that philosopher's observations are most valuable when distinctly methodized. Do not think I wish to make you a coiner of proverbs. He might be proud, who could make a single good one. But the proverb, like the epic and the fable, is an extinct genus. The collection of Solomon's is wonderful; you may imagine how much is lost by a version which is literal, modern, and occidental. I find lists of proverbs very good reading. But to return—it is not to provoke you to make proverbs, but to lead you to *maximize;* first, to deduce some law, fact, or general rule; secondly, to give it a memorable shape. We are constantly doing so, on a small scale. Thus, after some painful experiments, a young man arrives at a maxim like this—" always to break off any dispute when I find myself growing warm." What we call wisdom, as distinct from knowledge, consists very much in the habit of observing and amassing such conclusions.

A very great fondness for the sententious has made me a lover of what are called adages, or apothegms. There are many such in Horace and Terence. They abound in Seneca. You know how Sancho Panza's mouth was filled with them; there-fore they must have hit the fancy of Cervantes. The Spaniards derived their taste for them from the Arabians. Some of the Spanish proverbs are very racy; *e.g.,* 1. Touch a sore eye only with your elbow. Take your wife's first advice, not her second. 3. Leave your jest while most pleased with it. 4. Setting down in writing is a lasting memory. Apropos of which last proverb, I have found much pleasure in writing down at night what I call the *thought of the day;* that is, some reflection derived from the day's observation, especially if it can be couched in a single sentence.

§ 164.* Prefer a subject with which you have some acquain-

* From a letter to his son in college.

tance. The more *special* the subject, the more you will find to say on it. Boys think just the reverse ; they write of Virtue, Honour, Liberty, &c. It would be easier to write on the pleasures of Virtue, the Honour of knighthood, or the difference between true and false Liberty; which are more special. Take it as a general rule, the more you narrow the subject, the more thoughts you will have. And for this there is a philosophical reason, which I wish you to observe. In acquiring knowledge, the mind proceeds *from particulars to generals*. Thus Newton proceeded from the falling of an apple to the general principle of gravity. A great many particular observations were to be made on animals before a naturalist could lay down the general law, that all creatures with cleft hoofs and horns are gramnivorous, or that all birds with two toes before and two behind built in holes. This process is called generalization. It is one of the last to be developed. Hence it requires vast knowledge and mature mind to treat a general subject, such as Virtue, or Honour, and it is much better to begin with particular instances. It may be added, that this mental process, of deducing general laws or principles from numerous instances, is also called Induction. It is by a consideration of minute facts, called an "induction of particulars," that we infer (in-ducimus) a general principle. And this, simple as it seems, is the foundation of the whole *Baconian* or Inductive philosophy. If you will carefully attend to what I have written, you will have clearer views than are common among young men, on a fundamental point in Metaphysics.

§ 165. I recommend you to keep an Ephemeris, journal, or every-day book, not for putting down religious frames, but facts, notes of conversations, dates, and hints towards more extended composition. Some most valuable Boswellisms are laid up in these volumes. I regret that I did not begin till 1834, but since then my series is full and unbroken. Thoughts jotted down there have a peculiar freshness. Pascal's "Thoughts" had this origin. In Fangier's edition they are printed just as Pascal left them, with all their errors, blanks, &c. In one place he even says that, on taking the pen, he forgets the thought which he intends to record. In my humbler endeavours, these "thoughts of the day" vary from one sentence in length to fifty pages; and on enumeration I find them more than a thousand. It is wonderful how things will grow, if you do *the least bit every day*. It is so in learning languages. Many of these paragraphs of mine are *scholia* upon Scripture passages. Some of them are prayers, the writing of which, as also the re-perusal long afterwards, I have found of great value. When we spend sometime together, I will read to you some of my occasional notes on preaching from these books.

§ 166. My father used to say to me: Think long and deeply on your subject, and as if nobody had ever investigated it before. I did not then know what he meant. One of the chief uses of *writing* sermons is, that it keeps one a-thinking. The pen seems to recall the thoughts. Some cannot think without it; which is bad—very bad. This is all a matter of habit. The greatest other use of writing is that the matter is preserved. For I will not include correctness, and polish of style, &c., which can be fully obtained by the other method.

LETTERS TO YOUNG MINISTERS.

LETTER I.

ON DEVOTION TO THE WORK OF THE MINISTRY.

WHEN I look back on the years which I have spent in the ministry, I cannot but think that much benefit would have arisen from such honest and plain advices as most of my elder brethren could have given me. It is this which induces me to offer you the hints which follow. These must be somewhat like personal confessions ; since the rules which I have to propose are derived in several cases from my own delinquencies. You know the old similitude. Experience is like the stern-lights of a ship, which cast their rays on the path that has been passed over. It will be some little consolation if others shall be benefited, even by our failures. May God of his infinite mercy, give his blessing to these suggestions !

You have lately entered on the work of the ministry : my solemn advice to you is, that you devote yourself to it wholly. You remember the expression, Εν τούτοις ἴσθι : 1 Tim. iv. 15. The complaint is becoming common, respecting young men entering the ministry, in every part of the Church, that many of them lack that devotion to their work, which was frequently manifested twenty or thirty years ago. It is vain to attribute the alleged change to any particular mode of education. In this there has been no such alteration as will account for the loss of zeal. The cause must be sought in something more widely operative. The effect, if really existing, is visible beyond the circle of candidates and probationers. Nor need we go further for an explanation, than to the almost universal declension of vital piety in our Churches, which will abide under every form of training, until the Spirit be poured out from on high. The fact, however, remains. Here and there are young ministers, visiting among vacancies, and ready to be employed in any promising place, who are often well educated persons, of good manners, and irreproachable character : but what a want of fire ! There can be no remedy for this evil, but a spiritual one; yet it is of high importance that the young man should know what it is he needs. He has perhaps come lately from his studies, in the solitude of a country parish, or from some school in the mountains; or from some sound but frigid preceptor, who, amidst parochial cares, has afforded him few means of stimulation. His thoughts are more about the heads of divinity, the partitions of a discourse, the polish of style, the newest publications, or even the gathering of a library, than about the great, unspeakable, impending work of saving souls. He has no consuming zeal with regard to the conversion of men, as an immediate business. Let us not be too severe in our judgments. It cannot well be otherwise. None but a visionary would expect the enthusiasm of the battle in the soldier who, as yet, has seen nothing but the drill. Yet this enthusiasm there must be, in order to any greatness of ministerial character, and any success; and he is most likely to attain it, who is earliest persuaded that he is nothing without it. It is encouraging to observe, that some of the most useful and energetic preachers are the very men whose youthful zeal was chiefly for learning, but who, under providential guidance, were brought at once into positions where they were called upon to grapple with difficulties, and exert all their strength in the main work. Such were Legh Richmond and Dr Duncan.

In the sequel, you will be fully relieved of any apprehensions that I mean to deter you from study, or even from elegant literature ; but this must be subordinated to the principal aim ; its place must be secondary. Some who have been most successful

in winning souls have been men of learning; Augustine, Calvin,
Baxter, Doddridge, Martyn; but they laid all their attainments
at the foot of the cross. As Leighton said, to a friend who admired his books, " One devout thought outweighs them all!"
This is not peculiar to matters of religion. No man can reach
the highest degrees in any calling or profession, who does not
admire and love it, and give himself to it—have his mind full
of it, day by day. No great painter ever became such, who
had it only as a collateral pursuit, or who did not reckon it the
greatest of arts, or who did not sacrifice everthing else to it.
Great commanders have not risen from among *dilettante* soldiers,
who only amused themselves with the art of war. The young
minister, who is evidently concentrating his chief thoughts on
something other than his ministry, will be a drone, if not a
Demas. Look at the books on his table, examine his last ten
letters, listen to his conversation, survey his companions : thus
you will learn what is uppermost in his heart. And if you
find it to be poetry, æsthetics, classics, literary appointments,
snug settlement, European travel, proximity to the great; be
not surprised if you find him ten years hence philandering at
soirées, distilling verse among the weaker vessels of small literature, operating in stocks, or growing silent and wealthy upon
a plantation. It is a source of deep regret to many in review
of life, that they have scattered themselves over too many fields;
let me entreat of you to spend your strength on one. When we
call up in memory the men whose ministerial image is most
lovely, and whom we would resemble, they are such as have
been true to their profession, and who have lived for nothing
else. Some there are, indeed, who have had a clear vocation
to the work of teaching, which is really a branch of the ministry, and one of its most indispensable branches, and who have
served Christ as faithfully in the school-room or the university,
as in the pulpit; such were Melancthon, Turrettine, Witsius,
Witherspoon, Dwight, Livingston, Rice, and Graham. But our
concern is with ordinary ministers, called to no other public
station ; and of these it is unquestionable, that the most successful are those who have lived in and for their spiritual work.

Call to mind the chief Nonconformists; also of later date, New-ton, Cecil, Brown, Waugh, Simeon; the Tennants, Rodgers, M'Millan, M'Cheyne, and of our own acquaintance the "greatly beloved" William Nevins. In these men, the prominent pur-pose was ministerial work. If at any time they wrote and pub-lished, it was on matters subservient to the gospel. This accounts for the holy glow which, even amidst human imperfec-tions, was manifest in their daily conversation. They might have been eminent in other pursuits, but they had given them-selves to the work of Christ.

In another letter, the subject may be more appropriately dis-cussed, but I cannot forbear calling your attention to the bear-ing of this on the tone of preaching. Suppose a man has been all the week with Goethe and de Beranger, or with Sue and Heine, or even with the Mathematicians or Zoologists, not to speak of prices-current, stock quotations, or tables of interest; how can he be expected, by the mere putting on of a black gown or a white neckcloth, and entering the pulpit, to be all on fire with Divine love! No wonder we preach so coldly on the Sabbath, when we are so little moved on week-days, about what we preach. You have perhaps met two or three clergymen lately; what did their conversation turn upon? The coming glory of the Church? the power of the Word? the best means of arousing sinners? even the most desirable method of prepar-ation? or some high point of doctrine? Or were they upon the last election, the last land speculation, the last poem, or the price of cotton and tobacco? According to your answer, will be the conclusion as to the temperature of their preaching. There is indeed a sort of pulpit fire which is rhetorical—proceeds from no warmth within, and diffuses no warmth without; the less of it the better. But genuine ardour must arise from the habitual thought and temper of the life. He with whom the ministry is a secondary thing, may be a correct, a learned, an elegant, even an oratorical, but will never be a powerful preacher.

You must allow me to give prominence to this devotion of heart to your work, here at the threshold, because it is my de-sire hereafter to enlarge more on your theological studies; and

I earnestly charge you to hold all studies as only means to this
end, the glory of God in the salvation of souls. The day is near
when your whole ministerial life will seem to you very short in
retrospect. Let our prayer be that of the sweet psalmist of
early Methodism :

> " I would the precious time redeem,
> And longer live for this alone,
> To spend, and to be spent for them
> Who have not yet my Saviour known ;
> Fully on these my mission prove,
> And only breathe to breathe thy love.
>
> " My talents, gifts, and graces, Lord,
> Into thy blessed hands receive ;
> And let me live to preach thy word,
> And let me for thy glory live,
> My every sacred moment spend,
> In publishing the sinner's Friend."

That which we all need is to magnify our office, to recognize
the sublimity of our work. There would be more Brainerds,
and more Whitefields, if such views were more common ; and
there would be more instances of great men struggling on for
years in narrow, remote situations, but with mighty effects. The
observation of good Mr Adam is striking and true : "A poor
country parson, fighting against the devil in his parish, has
nobler ideas than Alexander had." My dear young friend, if
there is anything you would rather be than a preacher of the
gospel ; if you regard it as a ladder to something else ; if you
do not consider all your powers as too little for the work ; be
assured you have no right to hope for any usefulness or even
eminence. To declare God's truth so as to save souls, is a business which angels might covet : acquire the habit of regarding
your work in this light. Such views will be a source of legitimate excitement ; they will lighten the severest burdens, and
dignify the humblest labour, in the narrowest valley among the
mountains. They will confer that mysterious strength on your
plainest sermons, which has sometimes made men of small genius
and no eloquence to be the instrument of converting hundreds.
Think more of the treasure you carry, the message you proclaim,

and the heaven to which you invite, than of your locality, your supporters, or your popularity. It is recorded of the excellent John Brown, of Haddington—and I regret that I have forgotten his very words—that to a former pupil who was complaining of the smallness of his congregation, he said : "Young man, when you appear at Christ's bar, it will be the least of your anxieties that you have so few souls to give account of." And the same good man said : "Now, after forty years' preaching of Christ, and his great and sweet salvation, I think I would rather beg my bread all the labouring days of the week, for the opportunity of publishing the gospel on the Sabbath, to an assembly of sinful men, than, without such a privilege, enjoy the richest possessions on earth. By the gospel do men live, and in it is the life of my soul." *

On this subject the opinion of such a man as John Livingston will have weight with you; for you know he was honoured of God to awaken five hundred by one sermon at the Kirk of Shotts. His life and remains, as published by the Wodrow Society, show that the secret of his strength lay in his devotion to the work. "Earnest faith and prayer," says he, "a single aim at the glory of God, and good of people, a sanctified heart and carriage, shall avail much for right preaching. There is sometimes somewhat in preaching that cannot be ascribed either to the matter or expression, and cannot be described what it is, or from whence it cometh, but with a sweet violence, it pierceth into the heart and affections, and comes immediately from the Lord. But if there be any way to attain to any such thing, it is by a heavenly disposition of the speaker." † And again : "I never preached ane sermon which I would be earnest to see again in wryte but two ; the one was on ane Munday after *the communion at Shotts*, and the other on ane Munday after the communion at Holywood ; and both these times I had spent the whole night before in conference and prayer with some Christians, without any more than ordinary preparation; otherwayes,

---

* See Waugh's Life, p. 53.
† Sel. Biogr. Wodr. Coll., p. 287, &c.

my gift was rather suited to simple common people, than to learned and judicious auditors." *

Here you have indicated the true source of pulpit strength. It is closely connected with the subject of this letter; for the more you are swallowed up in the vastness of your work, the more will you be cultivating spiritual-mindedness. You will agree at once, that it is a sign we are taking the right view of our vocation, when the means which we employ for our personal growth in grace are the same which most conduce to the power of our ministry. Such an estimate of our work, as is here recommended, can be maintained only by a constant contemplation of the great end of all our preaching and pastoral labour— namely, the glory of Christ, the building up of his kingdom, and the salvation of souls. This should be always in your mind. When you go to bed, and when you are awake, it should be as a minister of Christ; not, surely, in the way of professional assumption, but with a profound sense of your dedication to a momentous work, for which one lifetime seems too short. There are legitimate occasions, on which a minister may deliberately and thoroughly relax himself, by entertaining books, music, company, travel, or even athletic sports, to an extent far more than is common among sedentary men : and I hope you will despise the canting and sanctimonious proscriptions of those who would debar clergymen from any summer repose, or resorts to the springs or sea-side. Nevertheless, in the ordinary ministerial day, there should be no hour not devoted to something helpful towards the great work. This should give direction to all your reading, writing, and conversation. The volume which you have in your hand should be there for some good reason, connected with your ministry. It will appear hereafter, that the territory from which ministerial auxiliaries are to be levied, is exceedingly wide, and embraces all that can strengthen, clear, beautify, and relax the mind ; but the *animus* of all this must be a single eye towards the finishing your course with joy, and the ministry which you have received of the Lord Jesus. Acts xx.

* Sel. Biogr. Wodr. Coll. p. 194, &c.

24. Holding it to be a disgrace to a young clergyman not to be familiar with the Greek Testament, I add, Τὴν διακονίαν σου πληροφόρησον. Each instant of present labour is to be graciously repaid with a million ages of glory.

LETTER II.

THE CULTIVATION OF PERSONAL PIETY.

It is scarcely possible to treat of some subjects without running into commonplaces: their very importance has made them trite, just as we observe great highways to be most beaten. The question has been much discussed, whether a minister should ever preach beyond his own experience. In one sense, unquestionably, he should. He is commissioned to preach, not himself, or his experience, but Christ Jesus, the Lord, and his salvation; he is a messenger, and his message is laid before him in the Scriptures; it is at his peril, that he suppresses aught, whether he has experienced it or not. He is, for example, not to withhold consolation to God's deeply afflicted ones, till he has experienced deep affliction himself. Yet every preacher of the gospel should earnestly strive to attain the experience of the truths which he communicates, and to have every doctrine which he utters turned into vital exercises of his heart; so that when he stands up to speak in the name of God, there may be that indescribable freshness and penetrativeness, which arise from individual and present interest in what is declared.

In every Church there are some aged and experienced Christians. These are specially regarded by the Master, and require to be fed with the finest of the wheat. The ministry is appointed with much reference to such; and they know when their portion is withheld. They may be poor and unlettered, and incompetent to judge of gesture, diction, or even grammar; but they know the "language of Canaan," and the "speech of Ashdod:" I hold them to be the best judges of the ministry. How little does the starched and elegant, but shallow young divine suspect, that in yonder dark, back pew, or in the outskirts of the gallery, there sits an ancient widow, who was in Christ before he was born, and who reads him through and through. Mr Summerfield once related to me, that Dr Doddridge, when other more learned helps failed, used to consult a poor old woman, living near him, upon hard passages in his 'Commentary, and that he generally acquiesced in her conclusions. There is no teacher like the Paraclete; and the promise is, "*All* thy children shall be taught of the Lord." Isaiah liv. 13. To be able to feed such sheep of Christ, if for no other reason, the young minister should seek to attain high degrees of piety.

The truth is, such are the discouragements of genuine crossbearing ministry, and so repugnant to the flesh are many of its duties, that nothing but true piety will hold a man up under the burden; he will sooner or later throw it off, and begin to seek his ease, or preach for " itching ears," or phonographic reporters. It is an easy thing to go through a routine, to " do duty," as the phrase of the Anglican establishment is; but it is hard to the flesh, to denounce error in high places, to preach unpopular doctrine, to labour week after week in assemblies of a dozen or twenty, to spend weary hours among the diseased and dying, and to watch over the discipline of Christ's house. Nothing but an inward enjoyment of divine truth, and a reference to the final award, will stimulate a man to constancy in such labours.

You will be called, as a minister, to spend much time in laborious study, the tendency of which is to draw the mind off from spiritual concerns; and sometimes in the perusal of erroneous, heretical, and even infidel works, that you may know what it is you have to combat. Your condition in this is like that of the physician, who ventures into infection, and makes trial of poisons. You will need much grace to preserve your spiritual health in such perils. The freedom with which you must mingle in society will expose you to many of the common temptations of a wicked world ; and it will require the extreme of

reserve, caution, and mortification, on your part, to prevent your
falling into the snare. In the present day, out of opposition to
the ascetic life, we all probably act too much as if we were
" children of the bride-chamber," and too much neglect the subjugation of the body. That a man is a minister is no token that
he shall not be cast into hell-fire. The instances of apostasy
within our own knowledge stare at us, like the skeletons of lost
travellers, among the sands of our desert-way. No temptation
hath befallen them but that which is common to man. The ap-
paritions of clerical drunkards, and the like, should forewarn us.
" Let him that thinketh he standeth take heed lest he fall!"
The apostle Paul expresses his view of this, in terms of which
the force cannot be fully brought out by any translation : " But I
keep under my body," ὑπωπιάζω. *I strike under the eye*, so as
to make it black and blue, a boxing phrase, indicative of strenuous efforts at mortification ; as who should say, "I subdue the
flesh by violent and reiterated blows, and bring it into subjection,"
δουλαγωγω; "I lead it along as a slave;" having subjugated
it by assault and beating, I treat it as a bondman, as boxers in the
Palæstra used to drag off their conquered opponents. And the
reason for this mortification of the flesh is, "lest that by any
means, when I have preached to others, I myself should be a
castaway." 1 Cor. ix. 27. Dreadful words! but needed, to
deter us from more dreadful destruction. The tophet of apostate
ministers must be doubly severe. It is the " deceitfulness of sin "
which hardens so many of us into carelessness about so great a
danger. Pride goeth before destruction, till suddenly, like Saul,
the careless minister finds himself inveigled into some great sin.
This may never be known to the world, yet it may lead to his
ruin. " I am persuaded," says Owen, " there are very few that
apostatize from a profession of any continuance, such as our days
abound with, but there door of entrance into the folly of back-
sliding was either some great and notorious sin, that blooded
their consciences, tainted their affections, and intercepted all delight of having anything more to do with God ; or else it was a
course of neglect in private duties, arising from a weariness of
contending against that powerful aversation which they found in

themselves unto them. And this also, through the craft of Satan, hath been improved into many foolish and sensual opinions of living unto God without and above any duties of communion. And we find that after men have, for a while, choked and blinded their consciences with this pretence, cursed wickedness or sensuality hath been the end of their folly."

Of all people on earth, ministers most need the constant impressions derived from closet piety. If once they listen to the flattering voice of their admirers, and think they are actually holy because others treat them as such ; if they dream of going to heaven *ex officio* ; if, weary of public exercises, they neglect those which are private ; or if they acquire the destructive habit of preaching and praying about Christ without any faith or emotion ; then their course is likely to be downward. Far short, however, a minister of Christ may be of so dreadful doom, and yet be almost useless. To prevent such declension, the best advice I know of, is to be much in secret devotion ; including in this term the reflective reading of Scripture, meditation, self-examination, prayer and praise. And here you must not expect from me any *recipe* for the conduct of such exercises, or rules for the times, length, posture, place, and so forth ; for I rejoice in it as the glory of the Church to which we both belong, that it is so little rubrical. How often you shall fast or sing or pray, must be left to be settled between God and your conscience ; only fix in mind and heart the necessity of much devotion.

It is good sometimes to recall the examples of eminent preachers. John Welsh, the famous son-in-law of Knox, was, during his exile, minister of a village in France. A friar once lodged under his roof, and on being asked how he had been entertained by the Huguenot preacher, replied, " Ill enough ; for I always held there were devils haunting these minister's houses, and I am persuaded there was one with me this night ; for I heard a continual whisper all the night over, which I believe was no other than the minister and the devil conversing together." The truth was, it was the Huguenot preacher at prayer. Welsh used to say, " he wondered how a Christian could lie in bed all night, and not rise to pray ; and many times he prayed, and many times he watched." Such cases are not altogether wanting in our own days : Mr Simeon, of Cambridge, in more than one instance is known to have spent the whole night in prayer. Let me seriously commend to your notice a paper contained in his life by Mr Carus, page 303, entitled, *Circumstances of my Inward Experience.* Almost every word of it is golden, and among other passages you will note the following : " I have never thought that the circumstance of God's having forgiven me, was any reason why I should forgive myself ; on the contrary, I have always judged it better to loathe myself the more, in proportion as I was assured that God was pacified towards me. Ezek. xvi. 63 Nor have I been satisfied with viewing my sins, as men view the stars in a cloudy night, one here and another there, with great intervals between ; but have endeavoured to get and to preserve continually before my eyes, such a view of them as we have of the stars in the brightest night ; the greater and the smaller all intermingled, and forming as it were one continual mass ; nor yet, as committed a long time ago, and in many successive years ; but as all forming an aggregate of guilt, and needing the same measure of humiliation daily, as they needed at the very moment they were committed. Nor would I willingly rest with such a view as presents itself to the naked eye ; I have desired and do desire daily, that God would put (so to speak) a telescope to my eye, and enable me to see, not a thousand only, but millions of my sins, which are more numerous than all the stars which God himself beholds, and more than the sands upon the sea-shore. There are but two objects that I have ever desired for these forty years to behold ; the one is my own vileness, and the other is the glory of God in the face of Jesus Christ ; and I have always thought that they should be viewed together ; just as Aaron confessed all the sins of all Israel whilst he put them upon the head of the scapegoat." Such exercises as these, you will admit, may well give occasion for more than usual persistency in prayer.

But lest you think only of sorrowing exercises, let me recall a passage, which Flavel gives concerning one whom he modestly calls " a minister," but who is well understood to have been himself; offering it not so much for imitation, as to show how deep were the experiences of one who was busied in various learning, and in all the scholastic argumentation of his day. He was alone on a journey, and determined to spend the day in self-examination. After some less material circumstances, he proceeds thus: " In all that day's journey, he neither met, overtook, or was overtaken by any. Thus going on his way, his thoughts began to swell and rise higher and higher, like the waters in Ezekiel's vision, till at last they became an overflowing flood. Such was the intention of his mind, such the ravishing tastes of heavenly joys, and such the full assurance of his interest therein, that he utterly lost the sight and sense of this world and all the concerns thereof; and for some hours knew no more where he was, than if he had been in a deep sleep upon his bed." Arriving, in great exhaustion, at a certain spring, " he sat down and washed, earnestly desiring, if it were the pleasure of God, that it might be his parting-place from this world. Death had the most amiable face, in his eye, that ever he beheld, except the face of Jesus Christ, which made it so ; and he does not remember (though he believed himself dying) that he had once thought of his dear wife or children, or any other earthly concernment." On reaching his inn, the same frame of spirit continued all night, so that sleep departed from him. " Still, still, the joy of the Lord overflowed him, and he seemed to be an inhabitant of the other world. But within a few hours, he was sensible of the ebbing of the tide, and before night, though there was a heavenly serenity and sweet peace upon his spirit, which continued long with him, yet the transports of joy were over, and the fine edge of his delight blunted. He many years after called that day one of the days of heaven, and professed he understood more of the life of heaven by it, than by all the books he ever read, or discourses he ever entertained about it."*

Even if you should be disposed to treat this as one of the anomalies of religious experience, you will nevertheless do well

* Flavel's Works, fol. ed., vol. i., p. 501.

to remark that the subject of these exercises is John Flavel, a man remote from enthusiasm, and whose extensive writings are characterised by regular argument and sound theology; and also that this very narrative was thought worthy of republication by the cool-headed Jonathan Edwards.   The mention of which name reminds me of an instance given by him, of high religious joy, which has since his death been ascertained to be that of his own wife.*   The narrative is long, but is worthy of your perusal. Among other traits were these : the greatest, fullest, longest continued, and most constant assurance of the favour of God, and of a title to future glory ; to use her own expression, " the riches of full assurance ; " the sweetness of the liberty of having wholly left the world and renounced all for God, and having nothing but God, in whom is infinite fulness. This was attended with a constant sweet peace, and calm and serenity of soul, without any cloud to interrupt it ; a continual rejoicing in all the works of God's hands, the works of nature, and God's daily works of providence, all appearing with a sweet smile upon them ; a wonderful access to God by prayer, as it were seeing him, and sensibly, immediately conversing with him, as much oftentimes (she said) as if Christ were here on earth sitting on a visible throne, to be approached to and conversed with.   All former troubles were forgotten, and all sorrow and sighing fled away, excepting grief for past sins and for remaining corruption, and that Christ is loved no more, and that God is no more honoured in the world ; and a compassionate grief towards fellow creatures ; a daily sensible doing and suffering everything for God, and bearing trouble for God, and doing all as the service of love, and so doing it with a continual uninterrupted cheerfulness, peace, and joy.   This was exempt from any assuming of sinless perfection, the claim to which was abhorrent to her feelings.   Now, though these are the experiences of a woman, will any one say there is anything in them which would be unreasonable or undesirable in a minister of Christ ?   True, we are by no means to make piety consist in transports, as is irrefragably proved by the great man who recorded these things : yet

* Edward's Works, vol. iii., pp. 304, 399.

there are hours or days in every life of long continued piety, which are remembered for years, and shed their light over all the remaining pilgrimage. And who should covet these Pisgah views, if not ministers of the word ? There is among the posthumous papers of the incomparable Pascal, one, which he long carried about his person, and which contains the record of a particular visitation of divine love. It is one of the most seraphic productions of human language : in some places the joy and rapture and dissolving love seem to defy all ordinary expressions, and he can only write down such broken phrases as, joy—joy—tears—tears ; "*joie—joie—pleurs ! pleurs !*" The greatest scoffers will hardly reckon Pascal and Edwards among unreasoning devotees.

Our age is disposed to sneer at high religious passions : it is perhaps the reason why the pathos of the pulpit has to such a degree departed. It is not, however, as a homiletic instrumentality that I would urge you to grow in grace, but far more momentous reasons, which, as a preacher, you have long since learned.

LETTER III.

THE HAPPINESS OF CHRIST'S MINISTRY.

THERE is a romantic view of the clerical office, which may induce a man to assume it, without any religion ; which regards only its social and literary appendages, and the status in society which it secures, even where there is no establishment. Younger sons in England are frequently educated for the Church, as it is called, and spend their lives in a service for which they have no heart. Even though they may not follow the hounds, or belong to the " dancing clergy," they may look no higher than the literary accomplishments of their place. Coleridge has somewhere given an exquisite picture of a secluded, peaceful rectory, seen in this light. Look at the Memoir of Cary, the translator of Dante, by his son, and you will see what I mean. Both were clergymen : yet there is as little religion in the work, as if it had been the life of an ancient Greek. The contributions of this man to letters were vast, but to religion insignificant. Now let us beware lest some thoughts kindred to these creep into our minds, and make us look rather at the repose, than the work, of the ministry. He grossly errs who considers the life of an evangelist as other than a conflict. Yet it is happy ; indeed I hesitate not to express my conviction, that the life of a faithful minister is the happiest on earth. Some there are, it is true, who are dragged into it, like a reluctant witness into court, *collo obtorto*, and who never possess any of its rewards : but there are many who have found it a heavenly service.

In seeking the constituents of this happiness, you should not look at the accidents of the ministry, but at its substance ; not at the quietude, respectability, emolument, or refining culture, but at the lifelong embassy from the Redeemer to lost men. The truest, safest, most abiding ministerial pleasures are those which come from delight in the genuine object of the ministry, the salvation of men. But there is a collateral blessedness, which we may not despise, since God has deigned to bestow it on his servants. Even this you will be most sure of attaining, if you have much love of Christ, love of the gospel, and love of souls.

The private life of a Christian minister ought to be a happy one. The apostle informs us in what it should be spent, to wit, the word of God and prayer. Acts vi. 4. I should account it lost time to go about persuading you, that there is a happiness in the study of great moral and religious subjects, especially of the word of God. To have this made the business of your days ; to find your chosen solace enjoined as your duty to be shut up for life with prophets and apostles, nay, with Jesus Christ himself, speaking in the " living oracles," to be perpetually drawing water from the wells of salvation ; this is but a part of the minister's joy. While others must snatch time from exacting toils, for communion with God, he may devote whole days uninterruptedly to such contemplations and delights as we find recorded in the lives of Augustine, Edwards, and Brainerd; and may live among those gardens of spices, the odours of which hang about the pages of Binning and Rutherford. Catch but one strain from the experience of the latter, and tell me whether he were happy or not; it is from one of his letters: " O glorious tenants and triumphant householders with the Lamb, put in new psalms and love sonnets of the excellency of our Bridegroom, and help us to set him on high! O indwellers of earth and heaven, sea and air, and O all ye created beings, within the bosom of the utmost circle of this great world, O come, help to set on high the praises of our Lord! O fairness of creatures, blush before his uncreated beauty! O created strength, be amazed to stand before your strong Lord of hosts! O created love, think shame of thyself before this unparalleled love of heaven! O angel of wisdom, hide thyself before our Lord, whose understanding passeth finding out! O sun, in thy shining beauty, for shame put on a web of darkness, and cover thyself before thy brightest Master and Maker!" Though these are not professional flights of soul, yet who should enjoy them, if not those who are called to dwell in the house of the Lord all the days of their life, to " behold the beauty of the Lord, and to inquire into his temple?" Psalm xxvii. 4. None of the private studies of the minister are absolutely peculiar; yet the opportunity for them is more remarkably his.

There is happiness in preaching. It may be so performed as to be as dull to the speaker, as it is to the hearers; but in favoured instances it furnishes the purest and noblest excitements, and in these is happiness. Nowhere are experienced, more than in the pulpit, the clear, heavenward soaring of the intellect, the daring flight of imagination, or the sweet agitations of holy passion. The declaration of what one believes, and the praise of what one loves, always give delight: and what but this is the minister's work? He is called to converse with the highest truths of which humanity can be cognizant, and, if God so favour him, to experience the noblest emotions; and this most, while he is standing " in Christ's stead."

I am persuaded, that previously to trial, no young man can duly estimate the glow of public discourse as a source of pleasure. When the soul is carried by the greatness of the subject, and the solemnity of the occasion, above its ordinary tracts, so as to be at once heated and enlarged by passion, while the kindled countenances of the hearers, and the reflected ardour of their glance, carry a repercussive influence to the speaker; or when the tear twinkles in the eye of penitence, and weeping throngs attest the power of truth and affection; then it is that preaching becomes its own reward. This is more than rhetorical excitement and stage-heat; it is caused by Christian emotion. Call it sympathy, if you please; I am yet to learn what harm there is in this: it is legitimate sympathy. If a Christian minister ever has deep impressions of truth, we may expect it to be in the pulpit; there, if anywhere, we may hope for special gifts from above; and these gifts are dispensed for the sake of the hearer, and are reckoned on, as graces, or tokens of individual piety. Yet they constitute a great part of the preacher's happiness. They are not dependent on eloquence, in its common meaning; for they fall equally to the share of the humblest, rudest preacher, provided he be all on fire with his subject, and bursting with love to his people. No scholarship, filing, or varnish, can compass this; it comes from the heart: and many a minister has chipped at the edges of his sermon, and veneered it with nice bits of extract, only to find that its strength had been whittled away. There may be more awakening or melting, in a backwoodman's improvisation, than in all the climacteric periods of Melville, or all the balanced splendour of Macaulay. Certainly the delight of soul is on the side of him who is most in earnest. It is especially love that moves the souls of hearers, and love, in its very nature, gives happiness. It cannot be, that a man can be frequently the subject of those feelings which belong to evangelical preaching, without being for that very reason a happier man.

The better moments of Andrew Gray, Hall, and Chalmers, must have been snatches of heaven. But be not discouraged when I mention these great names: the more you refer the joy of preaching to its legitimate and gracious causes, the more you will see that it may exist independently of what the world calls eloquence. It is not only in the vast assemblies of a Chrysostom, a Bridaine, or a Whitefield, that the service of Christ brings its sacred pleasures, but in Philip Henry's little parish of Worthenbury, which never numbered eighty communicants; or in the early morning-lectures of Romaine, when two candles lighted all the house. Nor is this happiness restricted to great and decorated edifices; it belongs to the itinerant missionary, who dismounts from his tired horse, and gains refreshment by dispensing the word to the gathering under the ancient oaks; or who meets his circuit of appointments in regions where the truth has scarcely ever been heard. I exhort you to seek your highest professional delight in preaching the gospel, so as to be looking forward to the blessed hour during all the week.

Little space is left for me to say that the minister of the gospel has a source of happiness in his parochial work and social communion. It is this, indeed, which distinguishes his calling, and is its grand prerogative. This brings him near to the hearts of his people, and, unless he betrays his trust, embraces him in their affections. The ministry may indeed be so discharged, as that the pastor shall have none of this; he sits with his hat and stick in his hand, makes a morning call, or leaves a card: he is only a ceremonious visitor, from whom the children do not run and hide, only because they see him every day in the high-place. But the genuine bond is as strong and tender as any on earth, and as productive of happiness. Think of this, when you are tempted to discontent. What is it that really constitutes the happiness of a residence? Is it a fine house, furniture, equipage, farm, large salary, wealthy pew-holders? Nay, it is LOVE. It is the affectionate and mutual attachment. It is the daily flow of emotion, and commingling of interest in common sorrows and common joys; in the sick-room, and the house of bereavement, at the death-bed and the grave, at baptisms and communions. These things may be in the poorest, humblest charge: then the " dinner of herbs" is better than " the stalled ox." Growing old among such associations, the pastor becomes like "Paul the aged." Let us strive after a happier, that we may have a more fruitful, ministry.

There is one occasion of joy, which is by no means rare in pastoral experience, and which ought in another of its aspects to be laid before you more at large; it is the season when souls are awakened and converted in great numbers. The revival brings with it the joy of harvest. Too commonly we are content to be like those who "glean and gather after the reapers among the sheaves." How different is the case, when the wide fields are covered with golden ears! Then it is, that "he that reapeth receiveth wages, and gathereth fruit unto life eternal." John iv. 36. Where there have been several such ingatherings, the pastor looks around upon the larger part of his church, as seals of his ministry, and in their turn they regard him with an inexpressible tenderness of filial attachment. Growing old, in such circumstances, he is the patriarch of all the younger generations; and, even when the fire of his prime has departed, can fix the attention and reach the heart, by means of this very relation. See what strength this tie may acquire, even where the pastor is young, in the account of M'Cheyne's return to Dundee, after his mission to Palestine. It was a time of revival, and though he had not been himself the proximate instrument, he rejoiced in the fulfilment of the saying, "that both he that soweth and he that reapeth may rejoice together." This was only the repetition of scenes which occurred among our Presbyterian ancestors in the seventeenth century. Ministers and people must have rejoiced together in uncommon degrees, to have endured the fatigue and protracted services of such occasions as are recorded. Under the preaching, for example, of Mr William Guthrie, author of the "Great Interest," hundreds of his hearers had walked miles to be present. It was their usual practice to come to Fenwick upon Saturday, spend the greatest part of that night in prayer, and in conversation on the state of their souls, attend on the Sabbath-worship, and on Monday return cheerfully to their distant homes. Those long sacramental services of our forefathers, comprising several days, and attended by thousands, sometimes excite a smile; but they remain on record as monuments of the elevated affections of those who joined in them, and enjoyed them. Not only the people, but the ministers—may I not say especially the ministers—were happy in the fellowship thus enjoyed. We know from experience the blessed fraternity and mutual affection, cemented by holy joy, which prevail in those parts of our church, where the meetings of ecclesiastical courts are still made seasons of religious service. Such community of interest in the highest good tends, beyond everything else, to heal dissensions, and to exhibit ministers of Christ to his people in that union which, unfortunately, is not seldom interrupted. The expectation of such gratifications may be lawfully indulged.

After all, what is the scriptural statement of ministerial happiness? "What is our hope, or joy, or crown of rejoicing?" asks Paul; and answers, "Ye are our glory and joy!" 1 Thess. ii. 19, 20. Seek happiness, my dear young friend, in contemplation of this reward. That moment will indemnify the minister for the losses of a whole life. "And is this the end," he will exclaim, "of all my labours, my toils, and watchings; my expostulations with sinners, and my efforts to console the faithful! And is this the issue of that ministry under which I was often ready to sink! And this the glory of which I heard so much, understood so little, and announced to my hearers with lisping accents and a stammering tongue! Well might it be styled *the glory to be revealed.* Auspicious day! on which I embarked in this undertaking, on which the love of Christ, with a sweet and sacred violence, impelled me to feed his sheep and to feed his lambs. With what emotion shall we, who, being intrusted with so holy a ministry, shall find mercy to be faithful, hear that voice from heaven, 'Rejoice and be glad, and give honour to him; for the marriage of the Lamb is come, and his wife hath made herself ready!' With what rapture shall we recognize, amid an innumerable multitude, the seals of our ministry, the persons whom we have been the means of conducting to that glory!"*

When you asked me for some advice respecting a course of

* Hall's Works, p. 151.

ministerial study, you probably did not expect a series of letters so much like sermons as these have been. In due time, if your patience should hold out, I hope to fulfil my original intention; but I desire that we may both feel more and more deeply that none of our studies will be directed aright, unless we begin with just views of the great object of our calling. For this reason, I have ventured to spend sometime in setting forth considerations, which may serve to awaken the true ministerial zeal, and to turn your wishes and hopes towards the right quarter.

LETTER IV.

CLERICAL STUDIES.

WHEN learning in the ministry is mentioned, some are ready to think of a purely secular erudition, such as withdraws a man from his duty, or unfits him for it. Of this there have been too many instances, especially in countries where rich benefices have been afforded by an established religion. Even in a very different state of things, the clergyman may become a mere savant or *litterateur*, and rob his spiritual charge of the time which he spends in his researches. Such scholars may be very useful to society, yet most unfaithful to their vows, and it is under their auspices that evangelical warmth has commonly died out in Protestant Churches. Without going to the extreme of Sterne, who was a licentious trifler; of Swift, who was a Cynic, in both the senses of misanthropy and filth; and of Robertson who was scarcely a believer, one may sacrifice Christ to the muses. The Church of England continues to furnish some brilliant examples of this from the prizes held out to men of learning, and the rich livings and fellowships which support clergymen without the necessity of parochial labour. Where the vocation of such a man is to the instruction of youth, we surely will not complain, if Providence allot to him a high distinction in science or letters, along with faithful discharge of ministerial duty, even though the latter should not absorb all his care: you will remember such men as Isaac Milner, Jowett, and Farish. Yet I beg you to observe, that the ministerial learning which I am recommending is none of these, but is solely the discipline and accomplishment whereby you shall be better fitted for your appropriate work, and is therefore subordinated to your professional activity. This circle indeed is much vaster than some people think, and may in its sweep, comprise, in certain circumstances, and by turns, every part of the field of knowledge; yet the particular aspect under which it is viewed is that of an auxiliary to the preacher and the pastor. The study is not a place for lettered luxury, nor for ambitious lucubration, with views fixed on secular authorship or academical promotion; but the sacred palæstra in which Christ's soldier is supposed to be forging his armour, and hardening his muscle, and training his agility, for the actual combat of the ministry. And you must allow me to tell you plainly, that the danger is not that you will have too much of this preparation, that you will be overeducated, or extravagantly learned, but all the reverse. You may get great learning, with a bad motive; you may get little, with the same: but all·you will ever get, multiplied ten times, will not be too much for your work, or more than the Church and the times demand. Neither devotion, nor active labour, will furnish you an excuse for the neglect of knowledge. This is a question where examples are worth more than reasons. Look at Luther. Who was more devout? who was more active? Yet who was more devoted to learning, or more profoundly anxious, to the very close of life, that literature and religion should never be divorced, in the ministry of the Protestant Churches? This it was which occasioned his famous sermon on the education of children: he perceived, as early as 1530, that in the fervours of reformation-piety there was a disposition to neglect refined cultivation; he therefore penned this address, during a sojourn at Coburg. There is in it a passage so truly Lutheran, that I must give it you, even at risk of not sticking to my text. You will see in it the very presence of the Brother Martin of Goethe's

Goetz von Berlichingen, as knitting his brow against the hard-fisted barons of his day. It shows, moreover, that he thought of labour, and not amusement. "There be some who think that the writer's office is a light, trifling office, but that to ride in armour, and bear heat, cold, dust, drought, and the like, is labour indeed. Aye, this is the old, trite, every-day proverb, *No man knows where his neighbour's shoe pinches*. Every one feels his own disquiet, and gapes after the quiet of his fellow. True it is, it were toil to me, to ride in armour; but then, on the other hand, I would fain see the knight who could join me in sitting still all day, looking on a book. Ask of any chancery scribe, preacher, or orator, what sort of labour there is in writing and speaking; ask the schoolmaster, what toil there is in teaching and training boys. A pen is a light thing, that is true; and there is no tool more easily obtained, among all handicraft, for it asks only the wings of geese, of which there is abundance; but there must be added to this the best part of man, the *head*, and the noblest member, the *tongue*, and his highest work, *discourse*. All these must work together, in the writer; whereas in the other it is only the fist, foot, and loins, for he can sing and joke all the while, which the writer must write alone. 'It is three fingers' work' (so they say of writing); but it takes the whole body and soul to boot. I have heard say of the noble dear Emperor Maximilian, when the great Jacks (*Hansen*) about him used to grumble, because he employed writers so much in embassies and otherwise, that he spoke thus:—'Well, what must I do? You would not let yourselves be useful, so I had to take writers.' And again: 'Knights I can make, but not doctors.' So I have heard of a clever nobleman that he said: 'My boy shall go to studies; it is no great art to hang two legs over a horse, and be a rider; that he has already learnt with me.' It was well and cleverly spoken. I say not this out of contempt for the knighly order, or any other order, but against the losel troopers (*losen Scharrhansen*) who condemn all letters and art, and boast of nought but wearing harness, and bestriding horse; though this they do but seldom, and have for it lodging, ease, mirth, honour, and well-being all the year round. It is true, as the saying goes, ' Harness is heavy, and learning is light;' yet, on the other hand, to learn to bear harness is easy, but to learn, practise, and exercise art and science is hard." Perhaps no one, not even Melancthon, ever uttered a higher panegyric on clerical learning than Luther in one of his letters to Eobanus Hess. " Ego persuasus sum," says he, sine literarum peritia prorsus stare none posse sinceram theologiam, sicut hactenus ruentibus et jacentibus literis miserrime et cecidit et jacuit. Quin video, nunquam fuisse insignem factam verbi Dei revelationem, nisi primo, velut præcursoribus baptistis, viam pararit surgentibus et florentibus linguis et literis."*

But do not imagine from these remarks, that what I recommend to you at present is only, or chiefly, literature, in the popular acceptation of the word, and as distinguished from professional study. It is this last which should awaken your chief interest, and the rest may be more safely left to take care of itself. There is no need of solicitation or stimulation, to bring a man in our day to acquaint himself with the lighter material; it floats on the surface, and is carried by the tide to his very doors. Make sure of the solids, and I have small fear of your suffering for lack of novels, fugitive poems, magazines, and young-lady literature. Familiarize yourself with master-pieces ; you will find in them relaxation enough, and may afford to look on the perishing nothings of the hour, as you do on the drift that plays along the edges of your river. I do not, of course, exclude the master-pieces of our own day; but truly great works are so numerous, that you need no more debauch your taste by reading them, than you need drink Oberlin bread-coffee instead of Mocha.

These things are true, even of simple literature ; but how the subject rises, when you look on yourself as called of God to live for his glory, to labour for souls, to expound his word ! One lifetime is very little for the attainment of the objects which seem indispensable, and some of which I hope shortly to table before you. Who, for example, even of the Chalmerses, Dwights, and Masons, could say that he had travelled round the entire

* Vol. x. ed. Berl. 1841, p. 159. Ep. cccclxxviii.

curriculum of theology ?   Who is the perfect historian ?   I am
sure it will be claimed by any rather than the Schroeckhs,
Gieselers, and Neanders.   Who is *omnibus numeris* complete in
Hebrew, or even in Greek ?   Thus might I go through the ency-
clopædia, and each would say, " It is not in me."   So that the
difficulty will not be to find out what a minister shall fill his
time with in the study, but how, amidst his sacred and importunate engagements, he can obtain any time for private labours.
Looking at the greatness of the harvest, and the shortness of life,
one is tempted at the first blush to say, " Let the study alone ;
go forth and save souls."   And this has been so much the
tendency in every era of church revival, that it would have been
the settled policy to multiply unlettered preachers, if God, in his
wonderful providence, had not, at the forming periods, raised up
men to hold fast by the immovable maxims of sound learning.
Such was Melancthon in Germany ; such was Melville in Scotland.   To the second of these, who can tell how much Presbytery
is beholden ?   When, in 1574, he returned to his native land,
from a five years' attendance on the prelections of such men as
Turnebus, Ramus, and Beza, deeply read in Hebrew and Syriac,
able to declaim fluently in Greek, and a fit comrade for Buchanan, the great Latinist of his day, Melville set up a standard at
Glasgow, which may well surprise us.   " He taught usuallie
twise in the day.   Beside his ordinar professioun of divinitie
and the oriental tongues, he taught the Greek Grammar, Ramus's
Dialectick, Talæus's Rhetorick, Ramus's Arithmetick and Ge-
ometrie, the Elements of Euclide, Aristotle's Ethicks, Politicks,
and Physicks, some of Plato's Dialogues, Dionysius's Geogra-
phie; Hunterus's Tables, and a part of Fernell.   The schollers
frequented, to the Colledge in suche numbers that the rowmes
were skarse able to receave them." *   Thorough learning in the
ministry was builded into the very foundation, and has continued to characterize the structure.   In the earliest struggles of
our Church in this new country, Presbyterian ministers were
constantly seen uniting the self-denying ardours of the mission
with the toils of the school and college.   And when, under

* Calderwood, pp. 111, 339.

temptations almost irresistible, it was sought to change the demand of qualification, the General Assembly chose rather to suffer the loss of a valuable limb, than to swerve from principles which were necessary to the healthful integrity of the body. If our brethren are unanimous in anything, it is, in Luther's judgment, that sound and varied learning must be sustained, if we would preserve the Church.

You will mistake my meaning, if you fancy that the learning which I am holding up as suitable for the minister of the gospel, is such as might be demanded in a professor of the sciences, or a writer on classical and philological literature. It may be as great as these, but it differs in kind, and excludes a multitude of details, on which the other must expend labour. It is ministerial, or in its widest sense theological learning, which is pleaded for: but this is enough for all the powers. No' man need ever expatiate beyond the metes of divine science, from any want of room in the latter, or any excess of faculty above what may be consumed on the Scriptures. Lightfoot and Marckius, and other voluminous original commentators, doubtless were ready to acknowledge that they had touched these waters only *primoribus labiis*. It is therefore with no extenuation of the work, that I say the clerical student is to pursue clerical studies: yet it may prevent misapprehension, and remove objection, by showing the perfect harmony of the discipline proposed, with the daily incumbent duties of the sacred calling.

There is such a thing as maintaining a transient popularity, and having a little usefulness, without any deep study; but this fire of straw soon burns out, this cistern soon fails. The preacher who is constantly pouring out, and seldom pouring in, can pour but a little while. I need hardly caution you against the sententious maxim, prevalent among freshmen, concerning those great geniuses, who *read little, but think much*. They even cite, as of their party, one of the greatest readers who ever wrote, as every work of his goes to prove; to wit, Shakspeare! The greatest thinkers have been the greatest readers, though the converse is by no means true. In reading the writings of those most remarkable for originality and invention—and mark, it is in reference to these qualities only the reference is now made— we know not whether most to admire the adventurous flights of their own daring, or their extensive acquaintance with all that has been written before, on their chosen topics. You will see this remark strikingly verified in the productions of Descartes, Leibnitz, and Hegel. While, however, I say thus much for reading, I own that reading is but a part of study; and that he cannot be admitted to the title of learned, who has not the habit of concocting, methodizing, and expressing his own thoughts. The great point is this: there must be perpetual acquisition. This is the secret of preaching. What theologians say of pre- paration for death, may be said of preparation for preaching; there is *habitual*, and their is *actual* preparation : the current of daily study, and the gathering of material for a given task. It may be compared with what is familiar, in another faculty, that of Law : the lawyer has his course of perpetual research, in the great principles of general jurisprudence, or the history of statutory enactment, or the systematic arrangement of practical methods, and he has his laborious and sometimes sudden read- ing-up for an emergent case. Should he confine himself entirely to the latter, he must become a narrow, though perhaps an acute, practitioner. So likewise the clerical scholar, however diligent, punctual, and persistent, who throws his whole strength into the preparation of sermons, and who never rises to higher views, or takes a larger career through the wide expanse of scientific and methodized truth, must infallibly grow up stiff, cramped, lopsided, and defective. His scheme of preaching may never take him through the entire curve of theology and Scrip- ture ; or the providential leadings of his ministry may bring him again and again over the same portions. These are evils which can be prevented only by the resolute pursuit of general studies, irrespectively of special pulpit performance. Such habits will tend to keep a man always prepared ; and instead of getting to the bottom of his barrel as he grows older, he will be more and more prepared, as long as his faculties last. But the grand evil to be warred against by the younger preacher, is not that of confining himself to pulpit preparation, but that of not preparing at all : and by preparation I mean study. To seize a pen, and dash off a discourse, on a subject heretofore not familiar, and with such thoughts as occur while one is writing, may insure ease and fluency of manner, but is little better than the delivery of the same thoughts without writing ; indeed, the latter possesses some great advantages, from the elevation of the powers by sympathy, passion, and attendant devotion. Engrave it upon your souls, that the whole business of your life is to pre-pare yourself for the work, and that no concentration of powers can be too great. The crying evil of our sermons is *want of matter ;* we try to remedy this evil, and that evil, when the thing we should do is to get something to say : and the labor-ious devotion of some young clergymen to rhetoric and style, instead of theology, is as if one should study a cookery-book when he should be going to market. I yesterday listened to a sermon (and I am glad I do not know the preacher's name), which was twenty-five minutes long, but of which all the matter might have been uttered in five. It was like what the ladies call trifle, all sweetness and froth, except a modicum of cake at the bottom. It was doubtless written extempore. When a young clergyman once inquired of Dr Bellamy, what he should do to have matterf or his discourses, the shrewd old gentleman replied, " Fill up the cask, *fill up the cask*, FILL UP THE CASK ! Then, if you tap it anywhere, you will get a good stream; but if you put in but little, it will dribble, dribble. dribble, and you must tap, tap, tap ; and then get but little after all."

If, in this daily pursuit of knowledge, you keep constantly be-fore your mind the end for which you seek it, there need be no fear of excess : it is studies which divert us from the evangelic work, that are to be deprecated. To the last day of life, regard your mental powers as given you to be kept in continual work-ing order, and continual improvement, and this with reference to the work of preaching and teaching. You will find all great preachers to have lived thus ; and though neither you nor I should ever become great, we shall sink the less by reason of

such struggles. The whole of what we have to learn is, sub-
stantially, in one volume ; for by this, it is declared, the man of
God may become ἄρτιος πρὸς παν ἔργον ἀγαθὸν ἐξηρτισμένος.

LETTER V.

HOW TO FIND TIME FOR LEARNING.

ALL ministers are not called to be equally learned : it would
be idle to expect such a result, amidst the marked differences of
talent and circumstances. There is a gradation in this repect
from the young pastor, who has almost all his time at his command, to the itinerant who thinks he can do no more than read
his pocket Bible. The objection to regular studies which meet
us most frequently is, that there is no time for labour in the
closet, from the pressure of parochial cares. You need no
prompter as to this : indeed, I fancy I hear you exclaiming,
How is it possible for one situated as I· am, to find hours for
learning ? I desire, in the present letter, to answer this very
question, and to suggest a few considerations which will, per-·
haps, clear the path, and open some light through the seeming
forest. After having had the same perplexities, I think I perceive certain principles by which a life of faithful pastoral and
pulpit labour may be made compatible with sedulous application.

First of all, if you would make the most of your scanty hours,
keep the one sacred object in view in every study you undertake. This is the way to secure unity of plan. You bear
in mind the twentieth proposition of Euclid's first book : the
straighter your line, the shorter. I trust it is no wresting of the
apostle's words to say, *One thing I do ;* or more laconically still,
in the four letters of the original, ἐν δέ. Let your intentions
branch out in every direction, undetermined whether you mean
to be a great linguist, or an elegant classic, or a mathematician,

or peradventure, a botanist, or a master of English literature, and it is plain enough that you will find all your time too little. There is such a thing as being very idly and unprofitably engaged in one's study. Far from loving restriction, or from wishing to coerce the mind in pursuing its bent, I would, nevertheless, beseech you, when you go among your books, to know what you are after. Your end in life is sufficiently obvious; and the studies by which it is to be attained are enough to occupy your time, if you are but faithful. It is of deliberate and stated application that I now speak : you certainly will not expect me to plan ways and means of gaining time for the annuals, monthlies, or weeklies. In your regular professional studies, you will find the whole field brought more clearly under survey, and the whole process simplified, by looking on every part of it with reference to your main work of expounding the Scriptures and preaching the gospel.

This leads to a second suggestion of a particular under this general head. Form the habit of contemplating all your study as the study of the word of God. In a large, but just sense, it is undoubtedly so. All your discipline and all your acquisition, all your reasoning power and all your taste, all your library and all your eloquence, are only so many means for learning God's word, and for teaching it. Exegesis, theology, controversy, church history, are only portions of the apparatus for learning and teaching. With this in your mind, you may go much further than many think, and yet return safe. As Scott, the commentator, used to say, " The bee may range widely, so that it brings all to the hive." Say to yourself daily, *En codicem sacrum !* " Here is my hive ; hither all my gatherings must be brought." The range of some men has been wonderful, and their powers of assimilation have been so great, that they have laid every department under contribution, and filled their discourses with the digested results of multifarious and almost incongruous reading : take, as instances, Baxter, Saurin, and Chalmers. But common minds need a strong centripetal force, and this is to be found in reverential love for Holy Scripture. No method known to me is so likely to keep you in the right state of mind, in this respect, as the practice of devoting the first and best part of every day to the perusal of the Bible in the original tongues. Few will the days be, in which you will not discern the directive influence of this on the researches of the subsequent hours; and the influence will be there, even when not discerned.

From what has just been said, you will deduce the all-important rule, to lop off all irrelevant studies. Observe, we are not talking now of amusements, but of dogged labour. And if you mean to succeed, and to save precious time, see to it, that you rid yourself of all impertinent matters. In this age of books, tempting studies will grow rank around you, and creep into your windows, as a great vine has been doing into the chamber where I write; but you must be unrelenting, and make short work with their pretensions. The blue and yellow flowers among the corn must be plucked out, and you must be doing it every day. It is not a bad remark of Helvetius, though a bad man, that in our day the secret of being learned, is heroically to determine to be ignorant of many things in which men take pride. Keep, as Fenelon says, the pruning-knife in hand, to cut away all that is needless : " On a besoin d'être sans, cesse la faucille en main, pour retrancher le superflu des paroles et des occupations." *
Especially must this resolution be exercised towards such branches of study as require a great expense of time, in order to any proficiency. There are some arts which are so jealous as to usurp the whole life. Ælian tells of a young Greek who took up a famous philosopher into his chariot, and, driving round the stadium at full speed, showed him that his wheel had never deviated from a given line : the philosopher replied, " Now you have demonstrated to me that you are fit for nothing else." There are, indeed, cases in which a strong tendency of taste and genius, toward some foreign branch of knowledge, as, for example, mathematics or geology or language, may break through all rule, and force the clergyman to eminence in his chosen or destined pursuit. But these are exempt cases, and we are treating of those persons who avow their determination to live and

* Ep. 338.

die in the work of the ministry. If you, my dear friend, have other intentions, express them frankly, and save me the pains of any further disquisitions. But he who chooses the service of God in his sanctuary is called to great subjects, which are sufficient to fill up all his thoughts. Whatever a man may do as subsidiary to these, or as a healthful diversion from them, it is still true that scriptural or theological learning is the peculiar domain of the clergyman.

Lest this should be thought too exclusive, I must add, that some degree of acquaintance with collateral sciences is absolutely necessary to a full understanding of our own; for, as Lord Bacon says, large prospects are to be made not from our own ground, but from contiguous towers and high places.* But another sagacious observer says : " It is in my opinion, not any honour to a minister, to be very famous in any branch that is wholly unconnected with theology ; not that knowledge of any thing, properly speaking, is either a disadvantage or ground of reproach; but for a man to show a deep knowledge of some particular subject plainly discovers that he hath bestowed more time and pains upon it than he had to spare from necessary duty." † There is more self-denial in acting on this maxim than is commonly thought, and you will often be called upon to lay aside darling entertainments that you may more fully make proof of your ministry. Whatever will enable you to preach better, though it were a fable or a ballad, you may legitimately include in your plan ; but when you lay out your chief strength on matters purely secular, you so far abuse the golden vessel of the sanctuary. Observe this rule, and your will find it more easy to accomplish study, even in your limited time.

It is not unworthy of statement, that there is such a thing as making the line of your studies coincide with the tenor of your preaching, even without the wearisome formality of a declared series. The subject of the sermon ought somehow to be in-

* "Prospectationes fiunt a turribus aut locis praealtis ; et impossibile est ut quis exploret remotiores interioris scientiae alicujus partes, si stet super plano ejusdem scientiae, neque altioris scientiae veluti speculum conscendat." —*Nov. Org.*

† Witherspoon's Works, vol. iv. p. 20.

cluded in some recent course of study, though much of the latter
may never be brought into the sermon. If, for example, you
should be going into those heads of divinity which relate to the
Person of Christ, you might easily draw material for all your
morning discourses from subjects allied to this: in this you will
find great economy of time.

You cannot well overrate the benefit to be derived, in these
respects, from carrying always with you a high estimate of your
study-labours, in comparison with other men's labours, and other
labours of your own. The clergyman's study, which some
people regard as they would a pantry, or a genteel appendage to
housekeeping, is the main room in the house, and (if consistent
with Heb. xiii. 2) ought to be the best. It is the place where
you speak to God, and where God speaks to you; where the
oil is beaten for the sanctuary; where you sit between the two
olive-trees, Zech. iv. 3 ; where you wear the linen ephod, and
consult Urim and Thummim. As you are there, so will you be
in the house of the Lord. A prevalent sense of this will do
more than anything to procure and redeem time for research,
and will cause you to learn more in an hour, than otherwise in
a day. That upper-chamber is also the spot where you will enjoy one of the most valuable means of learning and preparation,
which we too much neglect—I mean conference with brethren
about your work, and especially your preaching. And it will
be your duty to impress on your people the truth, that you are
as really serving them, when you are in your study, as when
you are in their houses. But to render these views efficacious,
you must, from the beginning, look on all your meditation, reading and writing, as a tribute to God, and a free-will offering in his
holy temple. This will lead you to pray over your researches,
and to handle every topic as in the presence of Christ. It will
tend to prevent your lucubrations from lapsing into a selfish,
solitary, anchoretic abstraction from your charge. The more
you are occupied upon the simple text of Scripture, the more remarkably will this temper prevail in you.

In this, as in everything else, there is economy of time in
punctuality and order : as Hannah More says, " It is just as in

packing a trunk ; a good packer will get twice as much in as a bungler." The example of Dr Doddridge on this point, as re-corded in his life, is worth looking at. Lay before yourself some scheme, and have a distinct notion of what you are going to attempt. This is like the builder's working-model ; how sadly would he waste his timber and his time, if he should fall to hewing, squaring, and sawing, without any conception of what he was going to erect ! Allow me to bring this matter a little more closely to you, by proposing the following questions, to be frankly answered by you on the spot, *in foro conscientiæ.* 1. What part of the week do I devote to study ; and, of this, how much to the original Scriptures ? 2. What part of Scrip-ture am I engaged in studying critically ? 3. What head of theology has lately been under investigation ? 4. What work of research have I lately mastered ? 5. What is my plan of study for the coming day ? I think it likely that there are some young pastors (and in none of these letters do I address myself to any others) who may find in these queries a key to their meagre attainments. One of the highest objects proposed in this correspondence, is to afford you some assistance in chalk-ing out your work, and rendering manageable the great business of clerical study.

But after all, it cannot be concealed that there will be need of vigorous and unceasing efforts, to secure time for application, and to cut off all occasions of sloth and waste. You will be under a perpetual attraction to leave your study. The obviously pressing claims of your parish will pull you by the sleeve. You will find it indispensable to have some certain times consecrated to the word of God and prayer. The best proof that time can thus be rescued, is the fact that so many clergymen engaged in laborious charges, do actually spend much of their life in study. If propriety would sanction the disclosure, I would easily go into particulars, and give the names of eminent living pastors, with the laudable devices by which they compass the end proposed. One would be found to trench largely on the hours of sleep ; a method scarcely to be recommended. Another would be seen rising, year after year, a long time before day. Some are known to me, who accomplish all their heavy study before noon. A distinguished preacher in one of the largest churches, allows no interruptions during the last three days of the week. Two others have chambers attached to their churches, where they do not encourage visits, until certain hours. It is not for me to choose among these methods, nor to hold up my own as equal or superior. In nothing it is more important for a man to open his own path, than in habits of study. As a general thing, it would seem to be well (using Scott's words) " to break the neck of the day's work," as early as possible. There have been clergymen of great eminence, who observed no certain hours. Dr Payson never denied himself to visitors; his motto was, " The man who wants to see me, is the man I want to see." Such was also the practice of the late Dr John H. Rice. There are situations where the young minister is constrained to act in this way. Where we cannot get the whole we must make vigilant use of a part. Even itinerants may gain knowledge; and I have heard eminent scholars say, that nothing they ever read made so deep impression on them, as volumes which they found in their chamber window, and which they devoured with the greatest avidity, because they doubted whether they should ever see them again. Great concentration of mind is produced by such traits. John Wesley, as his journals show, perused hundreds of volumes on horseback; you will find his notices of books in French, Latin, and Greek. Reading on horseback, though from no such necessity, was a favourite practice of the late Dr Speece, who was a *helluo librorum;* and also of Dr Campbell, of Rockbridge, whom I may name, though not a clergyman. More than twenty years ago, when I was much in the saddle, I was on a tour of preaching with the Rev. Abner W. Clopton, of the Baptist church. He was a man of much learning, and of such ministerial earnestness, that it was commonly said that he preached at least three hundred and sixty-five sermons in the year. It was summer time, and I observed, that after an early breakfast, he would take his saddle-bags and retire into the shade of the woods for about three hours. For this purpose he always carried a volume or two of solid reading;

and at that time was making a second forest-perusal of Dwight's Theology. By such decision and self-denial, some men counteract all the dissipating tendencies of itinerancy, while they are enjoying its unspeakable advantages. But it is to be observed that such self-control is seldom found, except in those who have been previously subjected to most vigorous scholastic training. Where there is a will, there will be a way; and the resolved purpose to be well furnished for the work is scarcely ever frustrated. But to carry out such a purpose, you must avoid a thousand things, to which, at your age, you will be tempted, and which consume time and preclude habits of application.

Providence so orders it, that generally speaking, the young pastor has a small charge. This is something mortifying; but it affords invaluable opportunities for study, and so fits him for subsequent labours, where he can scarcely call an hour his own. There are many other respects, in which it is of vast moment to let the character grow up and take its settled form, in the shade of retirement. The danger is (and it ought to be fully before your mind) that you will use no more study than is necessary to meet the moderate demands of your little rural congregation; if you yield to this, it may be safely predicted, that you will never rise above the stature you have already attained.

On these subjects, much is to be learned from men of other professions; and I have frequently been struck with the analogy between the busy lawyer's life and ours. In this respect, the maxims of the late Charles Butler, Esq., of Lincoln's Inn, are worthy of being transcribed; especially as, in addition to large practice, and copious legal authorship, he published a number of works on general literature and religion. You will make the necessary modifications to adapt it to clerical life. Butler ascribes his saving of time to these rules : " Very early rising— a systematic division of his time—absence from all company and from all diversions not likely to amuse him highly—from reading, writing, or even thinking, on modern party-politics—and, above all, never permitting a bit or scrap of time to be unemployed—have supplied him with an abundance of literary hours. His literary acquisitions are principally owing to the rigid observance of four rules : 1. To direct his attention to one literary topic only at a time ; 2. To read the best book upon it, consulting others as little as possible ; 3. Where the subject was contentious, to read the best book on each side ; 4. To find out men of information, and, when in their society, to listen, not to talk." " It is pleasant to him to reflect, that though few have exceeded him in the love of literature, or pursued it with greater delight, it never seduced, or was suspected by his professional friends of seducing him, for one moment, from professional duty."* Here let me leave you for the present, convinced that nothing impracticable is required of you, which I hope will be still more fully sustained by my next letter, which will be one of facts.

LETTER VI.

LEARNED PASTORS.

THE early Reformers and later Nonconformists were fond of dwelling on the distinction between the *Pastor* and the *Doctor ;* and the early New England churches had both : as early indeed as the Second Book of Discipline, the proper place was assigned to the schoolmaster and the professor.† It ought to be a matter of devout thankfulness that God has in every age dispensed to his Church both kinds of gifts ; and that while some have been eminent for the cure of souls, others have been as signally fitted for the didactic part. Yet the error would be egregious, if you should think that the ordinary duties of the laborious pastor are incompatible with the pursuit of learning. It is my present purpose to name some men who have remarkably

---

* Butler's Reminiscences, p. 8.

† " Under the name and office of a doctor, we comprehend also the order in schooles, colledges, and universities, quhilk hes bene from tyme to tyme carefullie maintainit, als weill amang the Jewes and Christians, as amangs the prophane nations."—*See Book of D. ch. v.* § 4.

united the two : out of a great number, I am forced by economy of space to select a few.

Passing by Augustine and the early Reformers, as instances familiar to you, let me come to later times. I have before me the works of ROBERT BOLTON, in five quartos. They are purely theological, practical, and experimental, and full of masculine eloquence. The margin is studded with citations from classics, fathers, and scholastics, in the ancient tongues. Bolton is often quoted by Baxter and Flavel. He was probably the most powerful and awakening preacher of his day, and greatly blessed to the conversion of sinners. He wore himself out with almost daily preaching, and the same patience which led him to transcribe the whole of Homer and comment on the whole of Aquinas was manifest in the perpetual labours of his parish. BATES needs no commendation of his piety, his eloquence, or his learning : the point to be observed is, that he spent his life in ministerial duty; in his later years at Hackney, where he was a predecessor of Matthew Henry. His works evince as well his erudition as his pastoral zeal. JOHN OWEN and RICHARD BAXTER, whose works by themselves make a library, were working pastors, through as much of their life as was allowed to them from persecution. Owen was about five years Vice-Chancellor of the University of Oxford, but was even then by no means without charge. But his great ministerial attainments were made while he was con- stantly exercising his ministry. The name of Baxter is insepar- ably associated with his parish of Kidderminster. To look at his controversial works, overladen with enormous quotations from Chrysostom, Jerome, Hales, Scotus, the Reformers, and the very Jesuits, you would say he was never out of his study : to look at his preachings, catechizings, visits, and imprisonments, you would say he was never in it. " His Reformed Pastor" shows his standard in regard to pastoral fidelity ; he probably came as near to it as men ever do to their standards. JOHN HOWE, the least scholastic and most philosophic, if not angelic, of the Puritans, carried on his amazing researches *pari passu* with his pulpit and parish routine. He was very early settled at Great Torrington, in Devonshire, where he remained until his ejectment. You perhaps remember his Latin correspondence, his manner of keeping fast-days with his people, the favour which he had with Cromwell, and his trials. Late in life he preached in the metropolis. He was extraordinary as an extemporaneous speaker, even in the day when that mode was prevalent. Notwithstanding his persecutions and frequent removals, he managed to accumulate vast learning, without being anything but a preacher of the gospel. CHARNOCK deserves to be named here. Less popular as a preacher, he was equal as a scholar to those just mentioned ; being versed in every part of learning, especially in the originals of the Scripture. He was indefatigable with his pen, and was one of those who confined himself almost entirely to his study. But he still preaches by his works. EDMUND CALAMY is famous, as one of the authors of *Smectymnuus*, written in answer to Bishop Hall's Divine Right of Episcopacy : the title indicates the writers' names, by their initials, viz., S. Marshal, E. Calamy, T. Young, M. Newcomen, W. Spurstow. No London preacher was favoured by great crowds, and that for twenty years : as many as sixty coaches were sometimes drawn up at his church. But he had not attained his fulness of preparation without some pains. While chaplain to Bishop Felton, he studied sixteen hours a day ; read over all Bellarmine and his answers ; read the school-men, particular Thomas Aquinas ; and perused the works of Augustine five times. Need I assert the diligence or erudition of MATTHEW POOL ? Look at his tall folios, especially his *Synopsis Criticorum*, the fruit of ten years' toil, during which he used to rise at three and four o'clock. Yet in the evenings he could be " exceedingly, but innocently merry, very much diverting both himself and the company." He was pastor of St Michael's, London, fourteen years, till the Bartholomew's Day, and was a laborious preacher. TUCKNEY is memorable as the principal writer of the Shorter Catechism. He was for a time in Boston, as Mr Cotton's assistant, and afterwards in St Michael's, just named. When ejected, he had become master of St John's, Cambridge. Calamy relates, in regards to the college elections, that Tuckney used to say, " No one shall have greater regard to the truly godly than I ; but I am determined to choose none but *scholars :* they may deceive me in their godliness, but in their scholarship they cannot."

How could I have postponed to this place dear JOHN FLAVEL ? No one needs to be told how pious, how faithful, how tender, how rich, how full of unction, are his works. In no writer have the highest truths of religion been more remarkably brought down to the lowest capacity ; yet with no sinking of the doctrine, and with a perpetual sparkle and zest, belonging to the most generous liquor. It has always been a wonder to me, how Flavel could maintain such simplicity and naïveté, and such childlike and almost frolicksome grace, amidst the multiform studies which he pursued. I can account for it only by his having been constantly among the people, in actual duty as a pastor. Opening one of his volumes, at random, I find quotations, often in Greek and Latin, and in the order here annexed, from Cicero, Pope Adrian, Plato, Chrysostom, Horace, Ovid, Luther, Bernard, Claudian, Menander, and Petronious. His residence at Dartmouth would afford a multitude of pastoral instances, if this were our present object.

JOSEPH CARYL, the voluminous commentator on Job, was a preacher in London, as far as the intolerance of the times permitted. The same church was served by Dr John Owen, David Clarkson, Dr Chauncy, Dr Watts, and Dr Savage. THOMAS GOODWIN was one of the greater Puritan divines recorded in the University-register at Oxford, as " in scriptis in re theologica quamplurimis orbi notus." Living in days of tribulation, he was more migratory than he could have wished ; but the preaching of the gospel was his great work. At first he sought the praise of learned elegance, but " in the end," says he, " this project of wit and vain-glory was wholly sunk in my heart, and I left all, and have continued in that purpose and practice these threescore years ; and I never was so much as tempted to put into a sermon my own withered flowers that I had gathered, and valued more than diamonds, but have preached what I thought was truly edifying, either for conversion of souls, or bringing them up to eternal life."

Other less noted ministers there were among the Nonconformists, known on earth for their learning, and in heaven for their converting of sinners from the error of their ways. Such a man was PETER VINKE, of London, memorialized in a funeral sermon by John Howe. He was a universal scholar. His Latinity was celebrated, and he kept constant journals in the Latin tongue. But yet more remarkable was he for humble, painful affectionate, gospel labour. "From his memorials, it appears that he was much in admiring God for what he had done for him and his, especially for assisting him in his ministerial work, and particularly at the Lord's Supper." Some place ought to be given to JOHN QUICKE, author of the *Synodicon*, which is even now one of the best repositories of facts, respecting the Reformed Church in France. He was a good scholar and an animated and successful preacher. In his days of health, he used to be in his study at 2 o'clock in the morning. He was greatly concerned for the persecuted Huguenots, and zealous for the upholding of a learned ministry. He loved preaching so well that he was seized in the pulpit, in 1663, and made long trial of prison fare. Yet when a cavalier-justice threatened them with a distant gaol, Quicke replied, "I know not where you are sending me, but this I am sure of, my heart is as full of comfort as it can hold." GEORGE HUGHES, of Plymouth, was one who united successful study with constant evangelical activity. He was indefatigable in his ministerial work, and much devoted to the private exercises of piety. He preached twice the Sabbath before he died, being sixty-four years of age. In a period, when learned men were not scarce, Mr Hughes had the reputation of being an admirable critic and expositor, and well acquainted with every part of theology. Baxter considered his Aaron's Rod Blossoming, as one of the best books on affliction. Here might be mentioned Gouge, Truman, Williams, the Henrys, and the Mathers; but I will close my list of Puritans, properly so called, with the name of good Mr JESSEY, the Baptist, whose quaint visage, with beard, bands, and Geneva-cap, adorns the Nonconformist's Memorial. Besides constant labours in the ministry, he was much concerned about bringing out a new translation of the Bible ; for he was a proficient in Hebrew, Syriac, and the Rabbins. For the age in which he lived, it is a singular fact that Mr Jessey had such regard for the poor Jews at Jerusalem, that he collected for them, and transmitted to Palestine £300, and with this sent letters to win them over to Christianity. The inscription which he put over his study door has often been copied :

> AMICE, QUISQUE HUC ADES ;
> AUT AGITO PAUCIS; AUT ABI :
> AUT ME LABORANTEM ADJUVA.

The grace of God did not leave our Scottish forefathers without some striking examples of parochial studies and successes. The value which they set upon ministerial learning is inscribed on the constitution of our Church. It could not be otherwise, where the foundations were laid by such hands as those of Knox, Buchanan, and the Melvills. There is no modern satiric verse in Latin, more resembling the most biting of Catullus, than the *Franciscanus* of Buchanan, and sundry memorable epigrams of Andrew Melvill. JOHN ROW, of Perth, lived in times of disquietude, and is chiefly remembered for his uncommon experiences; yet we must not forget, that the youth who boarded with him, spoke nothing but Latin, and that the lesson of Scripture read before and after meals, was always either Hebrew or Greek. JOHN M'BIRNIE " used always to have, when he rode, two Bibles hanging at a leathern girdle about his middle, the one original, the other English." When JAMES MELVILL was dying, he repeated a number of the Psalms in Hebrew. ROBERT BRUCE, that saintly preacher, favoured beyond most with near approaches to God in prayer, and marvellous power in awakening sinners; and whose life you ought to examine in detail, thus speaks of himself in old age :—" I have been a continued student, and I hope I may say it without offence, that he is not within the isle of Britain, of my age, that takes greater pains upon his Bible." But he understood Luther's *bene orâsse.* John Livingstone was one morning at Mr Bruce's house, when he came out of his closet with his face swollen with weeping; he had been praying for Dr Alexander Leighton, who was pilloried in London, and for himself that he had not been counted worthy to suffer. In his public prayers, "every sentence was a strong bolt shot up to heaven." Of his success, Didoclavius says, " Plura animarum millia Christo lucrifecit." DAVID DICKSON'S name is a precious ointment in Scotland. He was exceedingly blessed in an age of wonderful revivals. Multitudes were convinced and converted by his means while he was at Irvine, to which place they flocked from a great distance around. He was an active and fearless member of the General Assemblies of that stormy time. The *Sum of Saving Knowledge* was dictated by him and his friend Mr Durham. He was the author of the hymn, " O Mother dear, Jerusalem," which has since suffered so many garblings and transformations. When dying, he was asked by Mr Livingstone, how he found himself. He replied, " I have taken out all my good deeds, and all my bad deeds, and cast them through each other in a heap before the Lord, and fled from both, and betaken myself to the Lord Jesus Christ, and in him I have sweet peace." Dickson was the author of several learned works ; one of these, *Therapeutica Sacra*, is a quarto volume in the Latin language. In his latter years, he was professor of theology in Glasgow.*

WILLIAM GUTHRIE, author of the *Christian's Great Interest*, was one of the most graceful, elegant, accomplished, and commanding preachers that Scotland ever possessed. He belonged to a small class of men who have blended eminent devotion with charms of manner. Far from being a recluse, he excelled in manly exercises, indulged in angling, fowling and hurling on the ice, by which he maintained vigorous health. To say that he was admired and loved by Rutherford, is almost enough. His prayers were such that whole assemblies were melted into tears. Of his authorship, Dr Owen once said, pulling out a little gilded copy of the *Great Interest*, " That author I take to be one of the greatest divines that ever wrote ; it is my *vade-mecum*, and I carry it and the Sedan New Testament, still about with me. I have written several folios, but there is more divinity in it than in them all." Guthrie laboured most of his life in one

* Select Biog. Wodrow Soc. vol. ii. p. 114.

place, and with such success, that there were hardly any in his charge who were not brought to a profession of faith and the worship of God in their families. His favourite employment was the study of the Scriptures, which he read much in the original. Next to Guthrie I must mention SAMUEL RUTHER-FORD ; but how shall I mention him ? Christians of the present day, knowing him chiefly by his letters, which glow with hea-venly love, scarcely remember that he was one of the most learned men of his age. Indeed, it is hard to say whether he was greater as a pastor or an author. He was professor as well as preacher. He commonly rose about three in the morning. He spent all his time either in prayer, or reading and writing, or visiting families. His works are numerous, learned and argumentative, both in Latin and English. Read his Letters ; they will prove to you that great study need not quench the flame of devotion. " Rutherford's Letters," says Mr Cecil, " is one of my classics. Were truth the beam, I have no doubt, that if Homer, and Virgil, and Horace, and all that the world has agreed to idolize, were weighed against that book, they would be lighter than vanity. He is a real original."*

The whole space allotted to this letter would be little enough for speaking of GEORGE GILLESPIE. It is the common opinion of Presbyterians, that, taking his learning and eloquence in connection with his youth, Gillespie must be regarded as a pro-digy. He accompanied Henderson and Baillie to the West-minster Assembly, in which body, notwithstanding his youth, he shone as a distinguished light. His learning was extraor-dinary, for exactness as well as compass, and in debate he joined the highest inspiration to the most complete scholastic training. Still he was the humble, pious preacher, relying on his God, as well in the disputation as the sermon. The members of the Assembly usually kept little books, in which to note the arguments to be answered, and the heads of their speeches; but when Gillespie's book was looked into it was found to contain only such entries as these : " Lord, send light !

---

* Rutherford was called to a professorship in Utrecht, as Ames had long before been to one in Franeker.

Lord, give assistance ! Lord defend thine own cause !" If you would be convinced of his learning, read his masterly and famous work against the Erastians, entitled Aaron's Rod Blossoming. It is no vain boast, when he says of this book in his preface : "As I have not dealt with their *nauci*, but with their *nucleus*, I have not scratched at their shell, but taken out their kernel (such as it is), I have not declined them, but encountered, yea, sought them out where their strength was greatest, where their arguments were hardest, and their exceptions most probable ; so no man may decline or dissemble the strength of my arguments, inferences, authorities, answers, and replies, nor think it enough to lift up an axe against the outermost branches, when he ought to strike at the root." He speaks of the time bestowed on this most weighty and seasonable work, as gained with difficulty from his parochial cares. This list might be easily increased. There was HALYBURTON, noted as a deeply experienced believer and a devoted preacher, as well as a student, theologian, and author. There was THOMAS BOSTON, thought of generally, in connexion with his sermons and his Fourfold State, but who also wrote the *Tractatus Stigmologicüs*, a quarto on the Hebrew accents, and was a consummate biblical scholar. In later days we have had the ERSKINES, MACLAURIN, and WITHERSPOON, whose reputation as a man of learning was formed before he left his pastoral charge.

If my knowledge extended a little more into the Reformed Churches of France and Holland, I might doubtless add to these examples. One thing is certain, the great scholars and great authors of these countries, whether professors or pastors, were men laden with the burden of preaching. If my memory fails me not, the celebrated BOCHART, a polyglot of erudition, was the minister of a small church. At and after the time of the Synod of Dort (the most brilliant era of reformed theology), learning was diligently cultivated by private pastors. The late Dr LIVINGSTON, a pupil of DE MOOR, may be taken as a specimen, in this respect, of what was considered ministerial training in Holland, a century ago.

Our own country abounds in examples of ministerial learning.

We speak of *President* Edwards; but how short a time was he president! His Stores of knowledge were treasured while he was at Northampton and Stockbridge; where, as a descendant related to me, he did not know his own cows, and was so stingy of his time, as to wait in his study till the very instant when dinner was served in the adjoining room, and always retired to his books the moment he had finished his sparing meal; a practice to be condemned without hesitation. I need not recall to you the men whose names are familiar, as having lived nearer to our times, such as DICKINSON, WADDELL, MASON, WILSON, GREEN, RICE, SPEECE, HODGE, and MATTHEWS. If it were proper, I could still more easily record the names of clergymen still living, who add to the constant labours of the ministry, regular and persistent efforts to discipline the understanding and enrich the heart by private study. It is with the humble hope of stimulating you to attempt the like that I have collected the materials of this somewhat fragmentary letter.

LETTER VII.

ON EXTEMPORANEOUS PREACHING.

You desire some information from me about extemporaneous preaching. Before I throw on paper my desultory thoughts, I beg leave to premise that you must expect nothing from me in the spirit of those censors who, in the language of King James's translators, "give liking unto nothing but what is framed by themselves, and hammered on their own anvil." After about thirty years of talking for my Master, often in a method *ex tempore* enough to satisfy the most rigorous, I cannot forget that there have been other anvils before mine, and that their work has been turned off by such workmen as Edwards, Davies, and Chalmers. I am not ready to say that their "reading" was no "preaching." This prefatory disclaimer will embolden me to use some freedom in recommending the method of free utterance.

You have expressed fears as to your ever becoming an extemporaneous preacher, and I shall confine myself to practical advices. Many who have excelled in this may have had fears like yours. My counsel is that you boldly face these obstacles, and begin *ex abrupto*. The longer you allow yourself to become fixed in another and exclusive habit, the greater will be your difficulty in throwing it aside. Some of the authors whom I respect and shall quote below, recommend a beginning by gradual approaches ; such as committing to memory a part, and then going on from that impulse. This is what Cicero illustrates by the fine comparison of a boat which is propelled by its original impulse, and comes up to the shore even when the oars are taken in. Others tell you to throw in passages extemporaneously amidst your written materials ; as one who swims with corks, but occasionally leaves them. Doubtless many have profited by such devices ; yet if called on to prescribe the very best method, I should not prescribe these. Again, therefore, I say, *begin at once.* When a friend of mine, who was a pupil of Benjamin West, once inquired of the celebrated Gilbert Steuart, then at work in London, how young persons should be taught to paint, he replied : " Just as puppies are taught to swim— CHUCK THEM IN !" No one learns to swim in the sea of preaching without going into the water.

Such observation as I have been able to employ suggests the following reason for the advice which I am giving you. The whole train of operations is different in reading or reciting a discourse and in pronouncing it extempore. If I may borrow a figure from engines, the mind is *geared differently.* No man goes from one track to the other without a painful jog at the " switch." And this is, I suppose, the reason why Dr Chalmers, in a passage which I reserve for you, cautions his students against every attempt to mingle reading with free speaking. It is not unlike trying to speak in two languages, which reminds me of what a learned friend once observed to me in Paris, concerning the Cardinal Mezzofanti ; that this wonderful linguist, when he left one of his innumerable tongues to speak in another, always made a little pause and wet his lips, as if to make ready for going over all at once. It requires the practice of years to dovetail an extemporaneous paragraph gracefully into a written sermon.

As I am perfectly convinced that any man can learn to preach extempore who can talk extempore, always provided he has somewhat to say, my earnest advice to you is that you never make the attempt without being sure of your matter. Of all the defects of utterance I have ever known the most serious is having nothing to utter. You will say that is not extemporaneous which is prepared, and, etymologically, you are doubtless right. But the purely *impromptu* method, or the taking of a text *ad aperturam libri*, is that towards which I shall give you no help, as believing it to be the worst method possible ; for however suddenly you may ever be called upon to preach, you will choose to fall back to a certain extent upon some train of thought which you have previously matured. In all your experiments, therefore, secure by premeditation a good amount of material, and let it be digested and arranged in your head, according to an exact partition and a logical concatenation. The more completely this latter provision is attended to, the less will be the danger of losing your self-possession or your chain of ideas. I lay the more stress on this because it must commend itself to you as having a just and rational basis. Common sense must admit that the great thing is to have the matter. All speaking which does not presuppose this is a sham. And of method, the same may be observed with regard to the speaker which is enjoined by all judicious teachers with regard to the hearer, namely, that even if divisions and subdivisions are not formally announced, they should be clearly before the mind, as affording a most important clue in the remembrance of what has been prepared.

Early extemporaneous efforts are frequently made futile or injurious by the unwise *selection of a topic*. The opprobrium of this mode of preaching is the empty rant of some who use it. Preachers there are who have mighty vociferation, extreme volubility, highly coloured diction, and glorious pageantry of metaphor, but who prove nothing, teach nothing, and effect nothing. Inexperienced speakers fancy that they shall have most to say upon a sentimental, an imaginative, or a hortatory topic. There is a snare in this. The more special the subject, the richer will be the flow of thought: let me recommend to you two classes of subjects above all others, for your early attempts—first, exposition of the Scripture text, and secondly, the proof of some theological point. Argumentative discourse is best fitted to open the fountains of speech in one whose words flow scantily. There is no one fit to speak at all who does not grow warm in debate. And still more specially confutation of error is adapted to promote self-possession, which, as we shall see, is a prime quality in extempore speaking.

It is hardly possible for any man to produce valuable matter in a purely academical exercise. Hence it is all-important to practise *bona fide* preaching before a real audience. All pretences there vanish; there is an object to be gained; and the true springs of preaching are unsealed. This is the discipline by which all great extemporaneous speakers have reached facility and eminence. You cannot do better, therefore, than to seek some humble by-place where souls are desiring salvation, there to pour into their uncritical ears the truths which, I trust, burn in your heart. I can warrant you that a few weeks of exhortation to awakened sinners will show you the use of your weapons in this kind. Revivals of religion always train up off-hand speakers. It was my privilege to be early acquainted with the late Dr Nettleton. I heard him in most favourable circumstances in Pittsfield, four-and-thirty years ago, and again at two later periods. Though one of the most solid, textual, and methodical speakers, he usually laid no paper before him. His speaking in the pulpit was exactly like his speaking by the fireside. I introduce his name for the purpose of reciting his observation that, in the great awakenings of Connecticut, in which he laboured with much amazing results, he scarcely ever remained in any parish of which the minister did not acquire the same extemporaneous gift.

If you press me to say which is absolutely the best practice in regard to " notes," properly so called, that is in distinction from a complete manuscript, I unhesitatingly say, USE NONE. Carry no scrap of writing into the pulpit. Let your scheme, with all its branches, be written on your mental tablet. The practice will be invaluable. I know a public speaker about my age, who has never employed a note of any kind. But while this is a counsel for which, if you follow it you will thank me as long as you live, I am pretty sure you have not courage and self-denial to make the venture. And I admit that some great preachers have been less vigorous. The late Mr Wirt, himself one of the most classical and brilliant extempore orators of America, used to speak in admiration of his pastor, the beloved Nevins of Balti- more. Now, having often counselled with this eloquent clergy- man, I happen to know that while his morning discourses were committed to memory, his afternoon discourses were from a " brief." A greater orator than either, who was at the same time a friend of both, thus advised a young preacher : " In your case," said Summerfield, " I would recommend the choice of a companion or two, with whom you could accustom yourself to open and amplify your thoughts on a portion of the word of God in the way of lecture. Choose a copious subject, and be not anxious to say all that might be said. Let your efforts be aimed at giving a strong outline ; the filling up will be much more easily attained. Prepare a skeleton of your leading ideas, branching them off into their secondary relations. This you may have before you. Digest well the subject, but be not careful to choose your *words* previous to your delivery. Follow out the idea with such language as may offer at the moment. Don't be discouraged if you fall down a hundred times ; for though you fall you shall rise again ; and cheer yourself with the prophet's challenge, ' Who hath despised the day of small things ? ' " If any words of mine could be needed to reinforce the opinion of the most enchanting speaker I ever heard, I should employ them in fixing in your mind the counsel *not to prepare your words.* Certain preachers, by a powerful and constraining discipline, have acquired the faculty of mentally rehearsing the entire discourse which they were to deliver, with almost the precise language. This is manifestly no more extemporaneous preaching than if they had written down every word in a book. It is almost identical with what is called *memoriter* preaching. But if you would avail yourself of the plastic power of excitement in a great assembly to create for the gushing thought a mould of fitting diction, you will not spend a moment on the words, following Horace :

> " Verbaque *provisam* rem non invita sequentur."

Nothing more effectually ruffles that composure of mind which the preacher needs, than to have a disjointed train of half-remembered words floating in the mind. For which reason few persons have ever been successful in a certain method which I have seen proposed, to wit : that the young speaker should prepare his manuscript, give it a thorough reading beforehand, and then preach with a general recollection of its contents. The result is that the mind is in a libration and pother, betwixt the word in the paper and the probably better word which comes to the tip of the tongue. Generally speaking, the best possible word is the one which is born of the thought in the presence of the assembly. And the less you think about words as a separate affair, the better they will be. My sedulous endeavour is then to carry your attention back to the great earnest business of conveying God's message to the soul; being convinced that here as elsewhere the seeking of God's kingdom and righteousness will best secure subordinate matters.

No candid observer can deny to the Wesleyans extraordinary success in extemporaneous preaching. While the lowest class of their itinerants are all rant and bellow, their mode of gradual training, in class-meetings, in societies, and finally in immense out-door gatherings, is one of the best for bringing out whatsoever natural gifts there may be among their young men; and hence they have from the very days of the Wesleys, had an unbroken succession of eloquent men in their first rank. You will call to mind Newton, Summerfield, and other familiar names. A traditionary manner of elevated discourse, at once colloquial and passionate, has no doubt been handed down from the origin of the society. There is an account of Charles Wesley's *début*, which cannot fail to interest you. It was in the year 1738, and in the little church of St Antholin, Wattling street, originally founded in the fourteenth century, that he first attempted to fly from the nest. " Seeing so few present," says he, " I thought of preaching extempore ; afraid, yet I ventured on the promise, ' Lo, I am with you alway,' and spoke on justification, from Romans iii. for three-quarters of an hour without hesitation. Glory be to God, who keepeth his promise forever ! " * Which reminds me to quote Mr Monod in another place, and to assure you that the true way of being raised above the fear of man in your early services is to be much filled with the fear of God ; and that the only just confidence of the preacher is confidence in the promised assistance of God. Until you cease to regard the preaching of the word as in any sense a rhetorical exercise, it matters little whether you read or speak, or what method of preparation is adopted ; you will be " as sounding brass or a tinkling cymbal."

Contrary to my supposition when I began, the sequel will demand at least one letter more.

LETTER VIII.

ON EXTEMPORANEOUS PREACHING.

You will have observed that in my remarks on this topic, I have not directly approached the question touching the comparative excellence of this method. One must have lived in a very narrow glen and drawn few lessons from observation, not to have discovered long ago that there are different ways of accomplishing the same great ends in Providence, and that a beautiful variety of methods is used in the dispensation of the Spirit.

* Life of Charles Wesley, p. 147.

Much that is written on these matters is a covert self-laudation or, as was harshly said of Reynolds's Lectures on Painting and Sculpture, " a good apology for bad practice." But while you allow your brethren to write and even to read their discourses, you nevertheless desire some hints as to your own discipline in the freer method. If long experiment, innumerable blunders, and unfeigned regrets, can qualify any one to counsel you, I am the man ; for all my life I have felt the struggle between a high ideal and a most faulty practice. But what I offer with an affectionate desire for your profiting is derived rather from the successes of others than from my own failures.

Argumentative discourse, the most methodical, connected, orderly, close, and finished, may be conveyed without previous writing. The forum and the deliberative assembly afford the demonstration. It is not true that writing insures ratiocinative treatment ; it is not true that what is loosely called extemporaneous speech necessitates incoherent declamation. A few of us remember with pleasure that great but singular man, James P. Wilson, of the First Church, Philadelphia. His spare figure, his sitting posture, his serene, bloodless countenance, his gentle cough, his fan, all rise to make up the picture. There was no elevation of voice, there was no appeal to sensibility. All was analytic exposition, erudite citation, linked argument. Yet, from the beginning to the end of his long ministry, he never brought any manuscript into the pulpit. As this has been questioned, his own words may be cited as testimony valid up to the year 1810 ; they are otherwise valuable in regard to their exemplary candour. Speaking of himself as a preacher, he says :— " He never committed to memory, nor read a sermon or lecture in public since he began the ministry. This statement is designed as an apology both for the shortness and other defects of these preparations, which were composed chiefly for private use."* The late President Dwight—certainly not from any incapacity to handle the pen—during the latter years of his life, when his eyes were failing, preached *ex tempore* those great sermons which afterwards, at his dictation, were written down,

* Lectures on some of the Parables. Phil. 1810. Preface.

and so constitute his System of Theology. The excellent commentary of M'Ghee on the Ephesians was taken down in shorthand from his extemporaneous lectures. The same is true of Gaussen's Lectures on the Apocalypse. But why cite recent instances, when we know that all the sermons of Augustine, and a great part of Calvin's expositions were thus prepared? Let this fully rid your mind of the conceit of Freshmen, that to preach *ex tempore*, is to preach what is empty, loose, or turgescent. Let it further conduct you to what is the *puppis et prora* of the whole matter, namely, that everything in a sermon is secondary to its *contents*.

Among continental divines the reading of sermons may in general terms be said to be unknown. The normal method is that of pronouncing from memory what has been carefully written. This is so admitted a point, that special rules are laid down, in all homiletical instructions, concerning the time and manner of getting the *concept* (a most convenient term) by heart. Yet many Italian, French, and German preachers, and among them some of the greatest, easily slide into the way of premeditative discourse. Where a particular method has had some prevalence for centuries, it is natural to expect useful maxims. Let me, therefore, quote the recommendations of a few judicious writers. Consider then what is proposed by Ebrard, Consistorial Councillor in Spire; but take it on his great authority, not on mine:—" Committing to memory should be a *renewed meditation of the expression*. When the sermon has been concocted, let the preacher, on a quarto sheet (no more is needed) draw off a *mnemonical sketch* ; that is, indicate the thoughts or those clusters of thought, according as his memory is strong or weak, by a single phrase, or mnemonic catchword. Let him set down these in a tabular way, strikingly, so that the lines may fall into shapes to seize the eye. Now let him throw aside his manuscript and try, by the aid of this paper, to reproduce the sermon ; that is, to invent afresh equivalent expressions." I have already advanced reasons against all such cumbering of the mind; but my zeal for unbounded liberty and development of subjective peculiarities, leaves me to offer it to you for what it is worth. The remarks of an equally celebrated man, Professor Hagenback, of Bàle, are less exceptionable : " Whether a sermon shall be written and committed to memory, or shall be elaborated only in the mind, must be determined by individual peculiarity, and is a question on which theory has not much to say. In every case, this process of memory must be regarded as a transient one, from which nothing goes over to the actual delivery. Even where the sermon has been written, it must be conceived by the mind as something spoken, and not as something composed." Schleirmacher, who always extemporized, is reported to have said that this was the proper method for tranquil natures, while those less equable should fix the thought and expression by careful writing. On the other hand, Rosenkranz observes :—" Our early familiarity with books and writing, and our small acquaintance with thinking, especially among the learned class, may account for our making so little of extemporaneous discourse." And the enthusiastic and eloquent Gossner characteristically says :—" The Holy Ghost at Pentecost distributed fiery tongues, and not pens." The motto of the great and pious Bengel was, " Much thinking, little writing ;" yet he wrote down his divisions. These gleanings will suffice to disclose to you the German mind on this subject. What you may gather from all these eminent preachers is, that whatever be your particular method, nothing can be accomplished without laborious thought.

There is a caution, derived from personal misadventure, which I would seek to impress upon you, with reference to your early trials. *Beware of undue length.* Do not undertake to say everything, which is the secret of tiresomeness. Oh, the grievousness even of calling to memory the exhaustive and exhausting teachers of patience! Avoid the notion of those who think they must occupy up a certain time, as by hour-glass. Fifteen minutes, well and wisely filled, can insure a better sermon than two hours of platitude and repetition. Touch and go in these early attempts. Only be on the watch for moments when the thought unexpectedly thaws out and flows, and give the current free course. Beginners, who apprehend a paucity of matter, and have small power of amplification, will be much relieved by carrying out the scheme or plan of their sermon into more numerous subdivision. On each of these, something can certainly be said, especially if, after the Scotch method, each particular is fortified with a Scripture passage. Neither in these exercises, nor in any other, act upon the mean policy of reserving your good things till afterwards. Believe, with Sir Walter Scott, that the mind is not like poor milk, which can bear but one creaming. Therefore, always do you best. It is unfair in some who lament the decay of extemporaneous preaching to assume that it has gone altogether into desuetude in the Northern States. This is so far from being the case that there is scarcely a settled pastor of my acquaintance who does not frequently, if not every week, address his smaller audiences without what, in Scotland, are called "the papers." Some of the happiest efforts I have heard, were made by preachers who elaborate their more important discourses by thorough writing. It is in such meetings, then, as these that the young preacher will find his most favourable school of practice. Here he will be sustained by the sympathy of pious and loving fellow-Christians, who, with minds remote from everything like critical inquisition, will seek from the pastor's lips the word of life. I strongly advise you to seek out and delight in such assemblages. If they interest you, they will interest those who hear you; and the more you forget the scholar and the orator, the more will you attain the qualities of the successful preacher. It was in such free gatherings, where formalism was excluded, and discourse was colloquial, that Venn, Houseman, Cecil, Simeon. Scott, Martyn, Richmond, Scholefield, Carus, and other blessed servants of God in the English Church, learned to break through the trammels of the age. It was my great privilege to hear Professor Scholefield preach a warm extempore discourse to a crowded assembly in St Andrew's Church, Cambridge. The theme was the repentance of Ahab; and as I listened to the plain, evangelical, ardent utterance of this simple-hearted Christian, I could hardly persuade myself that I had before me the celebrated Greek editor and accomplished successor of

Porson. Who can calculate the blessings conferred on Great Britain and the world through the labours of Charles Simeon and his school?

In order to give a turn still more practical to my advices, I will throw them into hortatory form. Single out some service among the most serious of your neighbours, and where you can be undisturbed in your sincere endeavour to do them good. Aim honestly at having the devotional sentiment uppermost. Block out your matter with much care and exactness, and assure yourself of perfect acquaintance with the entire order. Set about the work with an expectation of being very short. Do not allow yourself to dally long with any single point. Be simple, be natural, be moderate, and use no means to pump up fictitious emotion; above all, use no tricks of voice or gesture to express emotion which you do not experience. On this point I will copy for you Ebrard's comic advice, which may suggest something even by its exaggeration and caricature:—"The preacher should not seek to make the thing finer than it really is. He should not prank common-place thoughts with rhetorical ornaments. He should not attempt by verbal artifice a pathos which is foreign to his heart. Let him say what he has to say clearly and naturally. This is what is meant by the rule—Not a word more than the thing itself carries along with it. If the preacher's heart is warm and excited, this movement and animation will find natural expression in words. *Pectus facit disertam.* In like manner, individual colouring will take care of itself; so that if two preachers treat the same text, and in the same view of it, the proverb shall still hold true of them, 'If two do the same, it is not the same they do;' *Duo si faciunt idem, non est idem.* One will unintentionally speak more warmly and nobly than the other. These two constituents, to wit, warmth and individual colouring, enter of their own accord; the latter *we need* not seek, the former we *ought* not. The desire to preach a fine sermon is a sin." And in regard to the vicious amplification of slender minds he thus writes:—"Instead of saying in plain terms, 'Everything on earth is transitory,' and clenching it out by a verse from the Psalms [such a preacher], says:—

'Let us cast our eyes upon the flowers of the field, the slender lilies in their silver lustre, the glow of the rose, the blossoming decoration of the trees, which gladden us with their fruits—Oh, how refreshing to our eyes are these sights in the vernal season! But, alas! that which was blooming yesterday, droops withering to the earth to-day! A mortal breath sweeps over the scene, and the frail flower sinks weak and sickly to the ground!' How beautiful!—Nay, more, it is wonderful, among these flowrets of amplification, that not only a simple thought, but sometimes the veriest negation of thought, a mere logical category without contents, may be dressed up in pompous words. 'Every man has proof already of God's goodness and providence.' Here proceed to inflate the 'every man' thus:—'Go and ask the aged; ask the young; go to the man of hoary hairs, whose silver locks tend towards the earth; go to the children gambolling amid the grass; the sprightly boy; the aspiring youth; abide in the circle of friends, in the faithful home, or speed away in the distance; traverse the foaming flood of the perturbed ocean; fly to the north, the south, the east, or the west; go, I say and ask where thou wilt and whom thou wilt; the sage and the fool; inquire of his experience, and thou shalt find in the history of each and every one traces of divine providence and proofs of divine benevolence, &c." * The American variety may differ from the German; but you recognise in this a familiar mode of beating the matter out thin, which disgraces such extempore haranguers as attempt " to split the ears of the groundlings; who, for the most part, are capable of nothing but inexplicable dumb shows and noise." The consideration of this will, I am very sure, guard you against striving after protraction of talk and grandiloquent blowing up of common thoughts. Therefore content yourself for some time with being true, intelligible and earnest, without any remarkable flights of eloquence; for I wish to see you fairly established on your skates before you essay pirouettes and double-eights upon the ice. But *manum de tabula.*

* Ebrard Prakt. Theologie, p. 341.

LETTER IX.

ON EXTEMPORANEOUS PREACHING.

If the least thought had crossed my mind that familiar advices on a point which interests you would have grown from one letter to three, I should certainly have attempted a more formal disposition of these desultory remarks. Take them, however, as they rise and flow. I have written in earnest, because I know your solicitude and augur success. Do me the justice to believe that I am not exalting my own little method as the only one in which excellence may be attained. I should painfully doubt my enlargement of view and maturity of judgment, if I felt myself sliding into such a pedantry. From our own poor pedestrian level let us look up at the mighty preachers of the past—the Bossuets, Whitefields, Wesleys, Chalmerses, and Masons, and own that God accomplishes his gracious ends not only by a variety of instruments, but in a variety of ways. If there is any maxim which you might inscribe on your seal-ring and your pen, it is this, *Be yourself.* As Kant says, every man has his own way of preserving health, so we may assert that every true servant of the gospel has his own way of being a preacher; and I pray that you may never fall among a people so untutored or so straitened as to be willing to receive the truth only by one sort of conduit. Every genuine preacher becomes such, under God, in a way of his own, and by a secret discipline. But after having reached a certain measure of success, it will require much humility, much knowledge of the world, and much liberality of judgment, to preserve him from erecting his own methods into a standard for even all the world.

When you resolve to attempt preaching *ex tempore*, in the qualified sense of that phrase, you by no means renounce order, correctness, or elegance. Of all these we have repeatedly known as great examples in those who did not write as in those who did. All these qualities will be found to depend less on writing or not writing, than on the entire prèvious discipline. As well might you say that no one can speak good grammar unless he has previously written. Whether he speaks good grammar or not depends on his breeding in the nursery, in school, and in society. He who has been trained cannot but speak good English; and so of the rest. You have read what Cicero says concerning the latinity of the old model orators—they could not help it: "*Ne cupientes quidem, potuerunt loqui, nisi Latine.*" * Madison, Ames, Wirt, Webster, or Everett, could not be cornered into bad English. Cicero goes aside even in his great ethical treatise to relate with gusto how delicious was the Latin speech of the whole family of Catulli.† And in regard as well to this as to flow of words, he lays down the grand principle when he says: "Abundance of matter begets abundance of words; and if the things spoken of possess nobleness, there will be derived from that nobleness, a certain splendour of diction. Only let the man who is to speak or write be liberally trained by the education and instruction of his boyish days; let him burn with desire of proficiency; let him have natural advantages, and be exercised in innumerable discussions of every kind, and let him be familiar with the finest writers and speakers, so as to comprehend and imitate them; and *(Næ ille haud sane)* you need give yourself no trouble about such a one's needing masters to tell him how he shall arrange or beautify his words!" ‡

Your own observation will predispose you to accept the testimony of all competent persons, that method, closeness of thought, and the utmost polish may exist where there has been no use of the pen in immediate preparation. Fenelon, Burke, Fox, Robert Hall, and Randolph, are cases in point. Let me dwell a few moments on the first-named, for these two reasons: first, that he is unsurpassed in correctness and elegance; and, secondly, that he is the most celebrated advocate of *ex tempore* preaching. His remarks are too long to be fully cited, but they furnish a qualification which is needed just in this place, to show you what degree of rhetorical elegance should be craved. The extemporaneous preacher (says Fenelon) on the supposition that, "as

* De Oratore III. 10.   † De Officiis I. 37.   ‡ De Oratore II. 31.

Cicero enjoins, he had read all good models, that he has much
facility, natural and acquired, that his fund of principles and
erudition is abundant, and that he *has thoroughly premeditated his
subject*, so as to have it well arranged in his head, will, we must
conclude, speak with force, with order, and with fulness.   His
periods will not amuse the ear so much : all the better; he will
be all the better orator.   His transitions will not be so subtile :
no matter ; for—not to say that these may be prepared even
when they are not learned by heart—such negligences will be
common to him and the most eloquent orators of antiquity, who
believed that here we must often imitate nature, and not show
too much preparation.   What then will be wanting ?   He may
repeat a little ; but even this has its use : not only will the hearer,
who has good taste, take pleasure in thus recognizing nature,
who loves to return upon what strikes her most ; but this repetition will impress truth more deeply.   It is the true mode of
giving instruction." *   But read and ponder the whole of these
matchless " Dialogues on Eloquence."

You will have observed my disposition to cite authorities on
this difficult subject, rather than to vent opinions peculiarly my
own ; authorities, let me add, who have themselves exemplified
what they taught.   Among all contemporary preachers whom I
have had the good fortune to hear, I cannot hesitate to give the
palm of oratory to Adolphe Monod.   And with what solemnity
and tenderness do I write this beloved name, as fearing lest, even
before these lines reach you, he should have departed to that
world of which he has spoken so much, and for which he is so
graciously prepared.   The point to which I ask your attention
is, that the most elegant pulpit writer in France is equally elegant in extemporaneous discourse.   But then it is the elegance
of a Grecian marble ; it is beautiful simplicity.   It is nature—
nay, it is grace !   What a lesson is contained for you in his remarks on *self-possession in the pulpit!*   I will quote them from a
lecture which Mr Monod delivered to his theological class at
Montauban, sixteen years ago.   Observe that he has been speaking on the incompatibility of perfect eloquence with "self-observ-

* D'œuvres de Fenelon. Paris, 1838. Ed. Didat. Tom. II. p. 674.

ation," or thinking how one is doing it ; and he has been showing that such constraint is not confined to those who get their sermons by heart, but may exist in extempore preaching.

" Suppose," says he, " you have the finest parts ; of what use will they be to you unless you have presence of mind ? On the other hand, he who is at his ease says only what he means to say ; says it as he means to say it ; reflects : stops a moment, if need be, to cast about for a word or a thought ; borrows even from this pause some expressive tone or gesture ; takes advantage of what he sees and hears ; and, in a word, brings all his resources into play ; which is saying a great deal ; for ' the spirit of man is the candle of the Lord, searching all the inward parts.' " " You will perhaps tell me," adds this delightful writer, " that this self-possession which I recommend is rather a boon to be wished for than a disposition to be enjoined ; that it is the happy result of temperament, of previous successes, of talent itself, and that it is not in a man's power to be at ease whenever he choses. I admit that it depends partly on temperament, and this is a reason for strengthening it when timid ; partly on previous successes, and this is a reason why a young man should apply all his powers to take a fair start in his course ; and partly, also, on talent itself, and this is a reason for diligently cultivating that measure which has been received. But there is yet another element which enters into the confidence which I at the same time desire for you and recommend to you ; IT IS FAITH. Take your stand as the ambassador of Jesus Christ, sent of God to sinful men. Believe that he who sends you will not have you to speak in vain. Seek the salvation of those who hear you, as you do your own. Forget yourselves so as to behold nothing but the glory of God, and the salvation of your hearers. You will then tremble more before God, but you will tremble less before men. You will then speak with liberty, according to the measure of facility and correctness which you possess in other circumstances of life. If our faith were perfect, we should scarcely be in any more danger of falling into false or declamatory tones in preaching, than we should in crying out to a drowning man to lay hold on the rope thrown to him to save his life."*

It is in perusing such passages as this that I begin to comprehend the source of power in this writer and other great masters of pulpit eloquence, and discover at the same time why such treatises on extempore preaching as those of Ware are cold and inoperative. The study of unapproachable exemplars must not stimulate us to experiments like that of Æsop's frog. According to our measure, we may succeed here as elsewhere. I would most earnestly counsel you to throw aside, by every possible effort, all that resembles self-critical observation, while you are speaking in the name of the Lord. If your tendency should be towards scantiness of vocabulary, broken sentences, or involuntary gaps, halts and pauses, by all means *encourage a flow*. The advice which might be fatal to a voluble loquacity is all important for you. Keep up the continuity. Let trifles go. What Dr Johnson says to a young writer, to wit, "It is so much easier to acquire correctness than flow, that I would say to every young preacher, Write as fast as you can," is even more necessary for a young speaker:—Speak as uninterruptedly as you can. Let little things go. Return for no corrections. The wise will understand your slips and forgive them. Whitefield's rule was, "Never to take back anything unless it were wicked." This is very different from rapid utterance or precipitancy. Deliberate speech is, on the whole, most favourable. Good pastor Harm's three L's are worthy of being applied to delivery, but are poorly represented in English by the aliteration, Lengthened—Loud—Lovely.† Luther's maxim for a young preacher is still more untranslatable; but the sense is—"Stand up cheerily—speak up manfully—leave off speedily." *Tritt frisch auf, thu's maul auf, hoör bald auf.*

It is high time I obeyed the last direction by leaving off. As I do so, let me again remind you that great eloquence is not necessary to great success; that there may be great power of

---

* Discours prononcé à l'ouverture d'un cours de débit oratoire, à la faculté de Montauban, le 26 Novembre, 1840.

† "Langsam, Laut, Lieblich."

discourse where there is little elegance: that the mighty works of Divine grace have not been always or chiefly wrought by the popular preachers who draw vast assemblies; that no man can be always great, and no wise man will seek to be always so; and that, after all, a man can receive nothing except it be given him from heaven.

LETTER X.

ON DILIGENCE IN STUDY.

In what was said to you about Extemporaneous Preaching, I sought to draw away your attention from the manner to the matter. He can never preach well who has nothing to say. The all important thing for a messenger is the message. Of all the ways of preaching God's word, the worst, as has been admitted, is the purely extemporaneous—where a man arises to speak in God's name without any solid material, and without any studious preparation. A thousand-fold better were it to read every word of an instructive discourse, in the most slavish and uncouth manner, than to vapour in airy nothings, with suavity of mien, fluency of utterance, and outward grace of elocution. It is this which has become the opprobrium of extempore preachers; and it must be admitted that the danger is imminent. As all men dislike labour in itself considered, the majority will perform any task in the easiest way which is acceptable. And as most hearers unfortunately judge more by external than internal qualities, they will be, for a certain time, satisfied with this ready but superficial preaching. The resulting fact is, that in numberless instances, the extemporaneous preacher neglects his preparation. If he has begun in this slovenly way while still young, and before he has laid up stores of knowledge, he will, in nine cases out of ten, be a shallow, rambling sermonizer as long as he lives. Immense gymnastic action and fearful voci-

feration will probably be brought in to eke out the want of
theology ; as a garrison destitute of ball, will be likely to make
an unusual pother with blank cartridge.

Omitting, for the moment, the unfaithfulness of such a ministry,
the man who thus errs will find the evil consequences rebound
upon himself.   It is only for a time that the most injudicious or
partial congregation can be held by indigested and unsubstantial
matter, however gracefully delivered.   They may not trace it to
the right cause, but they know that they are wearied, if not
disgusted.   The minister, having rung all the changes on his
very small peal of bells, has nothing for it but to repeat the old
chimes.   " Somehow or other, Dr Windy seems to hitch into
the old rut.   He gives us the same sermon.   Especially he
wears us out with the same heads of application."   While this
is going on among the hearers, it is wonderful how long the
offender may remain ignorant of the reason ; just as we old men
do not know how often we repeat the same story.

Another inevitable result of unstudied preaching, is the habit
of wandering or scattering.   Nothing but laborious discipline,
unintermitted through life, can enable a man to stick logically
to his line of argument.   Discerning hearers know better than
the careless preacher, why, after stating his point, he constantly
plays about it and about, like a boat in an eddy, which moves
but makes no progress.   " Skeletons," as they are ludicrously
called, however good, do not prevent this evil, unless they be
afterwards thought out to their remotest articulations.   The idle
but voluble speaker will flutter about his first head, and flutter
about his second, but will mark no close ratiocinative connexion,
and effect no fruitful deduction.   Evidently he who is continually pouring out, and but scantily pouring in, must soon be at
the empty bottom.

Indolent preachers fall upon different devices for concealing
the smallness of their staple, and for preaching against time.   I
have alluded to the bringing in of irrelative matter ; kindred to
this, and generally accompanying it, is undue amplification.   The
minute bit of gold must be beaten out very thin ; hence wordi-
ness, swoln periodicity, and Cicero's *complementa numerorum.*

Such ministers seldom remain long in a place. The Presbytery is not, indeed, informed that Mr Slender has preached himself out; some reading elder, or surly Scotch pewholder is made the scapegoat; but the fact is, that the preacher goes away to fascinate some new people with his soft voice and animated manner.

Ministerial study is a *sine qua non* of success. It is absurdly useless to talk of methods of preaching, where there is no method of preparation. Ministerial study is twofold—special and general. By *special study*, I mean that preparation for a given sermon, which is analogous to the lawyer's preparation of his case. If faithful and thorough, this may lead to high accomplishment; but, as in the instance of *case-lawyers*, it may be carried too far, and if exclusively followed must become narrowing. The man who grows old with no studies but those which terminate upon the several demands of the pulpit, becomes a mannerist, falls into monotony of thought, and ends stiffly, drily, and wearisomely. At the same time, he wants that enlargement and enriching of mind derived from wide excursion, into collateral studies, of which all the world recognises the fruits in such preachers as Owen, Mason, Chalmers, and Hall. Yet even this inferior way of study into which busy and over-tasked men are prone to slide, is infinitely better than the way of idleness, oscitancy, and indecent haste. For thus the student who begins betimes, manages to pick up a great deal more than is necessary for his special task. In premeditating one sermon, he often finds hints for three more. By tunnelling into the rock of a single prophetic passage, he comes upon gems of illustration, nuggets of doctrine, and cool spring of experience, all which go into the general stock. Yet no wise student will restrict himself to the lucubration asked by next Sunday's sermon.

By *general study* I mean that preparation which a liberal mind is perpetually making, by reading, writing, and thinking over and above the sermonizing, and without any direct reference to preaching. Such studies do indeed pour in their contributions to every future discourse with a continually increasing tide; but this is not seen at once, nor is this the proximate aim. No man can make full use of his talent, who does not all his life pursue a high track of generous reading and inquiry.

Your general studies will again subdivide themselves into those which are *professional* and those which are *non-professional*. Both are important and mutually advantageous. But the first claim is that of biblical and theological literature and science, upon which, at present, my remarks shall be brief, and respecting on the point in hand. Let *Theology* afford us an instance; though every word I write may be just as well applied to History and Interpretation. Besides all your sermon making, *Theology, as a system, must be your regular study.* Neglect this, and your pulpit theology will be one-sided; many topics will never have due consideration. I shall augur badly for your career, if you are found uninterested in great theological questions. Some established works should be daily in your hands; and of such works a few should be often re-perused. Find a clergyman who knows nothing of such pursuits, and you will observe his preaching to be unmethodical, and little fitted to awaken inquiry among deep thinkers in his flock. He will soon attain his acme, and will continue to dispense milk where he should give strong meat. The analogy of other professions will occur to you; the lawyer or physician who reads law or physics only for this or that case, can never take high rank.

Non-professional studies open a wide field, and every minister must be governed by the indications of Providence. Extremes are perilous, and I know too well how, under the pretext of cultivating general literature, and even art, a servant of Christ may almost alienate himself from what should be the darling studies of his life. Witherspoon has observed, that it is not to the credit of any gospel minister to be famous in any pursuit entirely unconnected with theology. Yet he who is a mere theologian, is a poor one. Bacon said, long ago, that no man can comprehend the canton of his own science, unless he surveys it from the heights of some contiguous science. Take *Law*, for instance, though this is only one example out of a hundred. An acquaintance with jurisprudence is of the greatest value to the minister. No man can understand the practice of our Church Courts who does not discern their connection with the Civil, rather than the Common Law. Our very terms, especially in the older forms of process, savour of Justinian and the Code ; and ignorance of this has frequently led to the substitution of English for Roman modes, altogether subversive of the unity of our system. This will be more clear if you compare the progress of a Scottish ecclesiastical action with that of one in America, and observe how utterly we have lost all reference to the *libellus*, and other civil forms of trial. Matthew Henry was sent by his father to Holborn Court, Gray's Inn, that he might study law, as a preparation for theology ; and every part of his commentary shows familiar acquaintance with the terms of this science. This was not a rare opinion among the old Presbyterians. " I must be so grateful as to confess," says Baxter, " that my understanding hath made a better improvement of Grotius' *De Satisfactione Christi*, and of Mr Lawson's manuscripts, than of anything else that I ever read. They convinced me how unfit we are to write about God's government, law, and judgment, while we understand not the true nature of government and law in general; and he that is ignorant of politics, and of the law of nature, will be ignorant and erroneous in divinity and the Sacred Scriptures." Half the disputes about Imputation could have been precluded, if the combatants, instead of acquiescing in definitions of Webster, had familiarized themselves with the usage of genuine English writers in regard to the word *guilt*.* But this is only a single specimen. The times demand that a well-furnished preacher should draw both argument and illustration from every science. Tell me how you spend your forenoon in your early ministry, and I shall be better able to predict how you will preach. If you idle, stroll, or even habitually visit, before noon, your mental progress may be divined.

* Take one example out of many. "But concerning the nature or proper effects of this spot or stain, they have not been agreed : some call it an obligation, or a *guilt of punishment;* so Scotes."—*Jeremy Taylor, Apples of Sodom, Part II.*

REMARKS ON THE STUDIES AND DISCIPLINE
OF THE PREACHER.

The habits of a young minister, in respect to mental culture, are very early formed, and hence no one can begin too soon to regulate his closet-practice by maxims derived from the true philosophy of mind, and the experience of successful scholars. Early introduction to active labour, in an extended field, partaking of a missionary and itinerant character, may, amidst much usefulness, spoil a man for life, in all that regards progress of erudition, and productiveness of the reasoning powers. Such a person may accomplish much in the way of direct and proximate good ; but his fruit often dies with him, and he does little in stimulating, forming, and enriching the minds of others. On the other hand, a zealous young scholar, captivated with the intellectual or literary side of ministerial work, may addict himself to books in such a manner as to sink the preacher in the man of learning, and spend his days without any real sympathy with the affectionate duties of the working clergy. The due admixture of the contemplative with the active, of learning with labour, of private cultivation with public spirit, is a *juste milieu* which few attain, but which cannot be too earnestly recommended.

We assume it, without the trouble of proof, that every young minister, whose manner of life is in any degree submitted to his own choice, will strive after the highest Christian learning. But here there are diversities in the conduct of studies and the regulation of thought, which demand the most serious discrimination. We are persuaded that grave errors prevail in respect to what should be the aim of the pastor, in his parochial studies and discipline. For this cause, we would venture a few suggestions, not altogether without previous experiment and careful observation.

Let us suppose a settled minister, after the usual career of academic and theological training, to be seated in his quiet parsonage, with a sufficient and increasing apparatus of books around him. His tastes and predilections dispose him to account the hours blessed which he can devote to reading; and many a man under this early impulse, makes his greatest attainments during the first ten years. Yet hundreds go astray from the outset. It is not enough to turn an inquisitive mind loose among an array of great authors. The error against which we would guard such a one, is that of mistaking a large and various erudition for wise and thorough culture of the faculties.

The knowledge of authors, however great and good, is an instrument, not an end; and an instrument which may be misdirected and abused. There is much to be attained from other sources than books; and all that is gained from these, must, in order to the highest advantage, be made to pass through a process of inward digestion, which may be disturbed or even precluded by indiscriminate reading. The attainment of truth demands more than what is termed erudition. One may have vast knowledge of the repositories of human opinion, of what other men, many men, have thought upon all subjects, what in modern phrase is known as the *literature* of science; one may have a bibliographical accuracy about the authors who have treated this or that topic in every age, about systems, and schools, and controversies; and yet be vacillating and undecided as to the positive truth in question. We meet with men—and they are not the least agreeable of literary companions—who never fail, whatever topic may be started, to display familiarity with all the great minds who have treated it, to cite author after author, and to pour out reminiscences the most curious concerning the history of opinion in the Church, but who seldom strike us by the utterance of a single original conclusion, and never evince a rooted firmness of private judgment. Such are they who amass libraries of their own, and flutter among great public collections; who dazzle by quotation after quotation in sermons and treatises; who deck the margin of their publications with a catena of references to volume, page, and edition of works often inaccessible to ordinary scholars; but who discover or settle no great principle. They are felicitous conversers, walking indices to treasured lore, and sprightly essayists, but not investigators, in the true sense, not producers, not solid thinkers. Indeed it would seem as if in the very proportion of such encyclopædic knowledge, there was an incapacity for the mental forces to work up the enormous mass of superincumbent information. All this we believe to be true, while we scorn the paltry self-conceit of those who would denounce learning as injurious to originality, or would contrast readers and thinkers as incompatible classes. Our position is only that care must be taken that the great reader be also a great thinker.

The clerical student will of course add to his knowledge of books every day; but these accumulations of knowledge must be governed by some law ; must be directed, nay, must be limited. There is surely some point beyond which the acquisition of other men's thoughts must not be carried. This we say for the sake of those *helluones librorum*, who read forever and without stint ; browsing as diligently as oxen in the green herbage of rich meads, but, unlike these, never lying down to ruminate. Life is too short, Art is too long, for a human mind to make perpetual accretion of book-learning, without halt. *Sufflaminandum est.* There must be more circumscription of the range ; for if a hundred volumes, in a given science, may be read, why not a thousand; and why not, supposing so many extant, ten thousand ? At this rate, no scholar could ever find his goal. And as uninterrupted research shuts out continuous reflection, it is observed that those who go astray in this road become the prey of never-ending doubts, even if they do not fall into latitudinarian comprehension and indifference to truth. The faults of some truly great men appear to have had this origin ; we might adduce as instances, Grotius, Priestley, and Parr.

The mind must be allowed some periods of calm, uninterrupted reflection, in order to librate freely, and find the resting-point between conflicting views. That time is sometimes expended in learning, examining, and collating arguments of all kinds, on different sides of a given question, which might, by a much more compendious method, have served to discern and embrace positive truth, or to make deduction from acknowledged truth. No wise counsellor would proscribe the perusal of controversies. Yet he who reads on different sides, must necessarily read much that is erroneous; and all tampering with falsehood, however necessary, is, like dealing with poisons, full of danger. If we might have our choice, it is better to converse with truth than with error; with the rudest, homeliest truth, than with the most ingenious, decorated error; with the humblest truth, than with the most soaring, original, and striking error. The sedulous perusal of great controversies is often a duty, and it may tend to acuminate the dialectical faculty; but none can deny that it keeps the thoughts long in contact with divers falsities, and their specious reasons. Now these same hours would be employed far more healthfully in contemplating truths which in their own nature are nourishing and fruitful. To confirm this, let it be remembered, that truth is one, while error is manifold, if not infinite; hence the true economy of the faculties is, wherever it is possible, to commune with truth. Again, while error leads to error, truth leads to truth. Each truth is germinal and pregnant, containing other truths. Only upon this principle can we vindicate the productiveness of solitary meditation. Link follows link in the chain, which we draw from unknown mysterious recesses. A few elementary truths are the bases of the universal system.

If it should be urged, that defenders of sound doctrine must be acquainted with all diversities of opposition, we admit it, with certain limitations. But we must be allowed to add, that he who thoroughly knows a truth, knows also, and knows thereby, the opposite errors. Let any one be deeply imbued with the Newtonian system of the material universe, and he will be little staggered by denials of particular points, however novel and however shrewdly maintained. But the converse is not true. There may be the widest acquaintance with forms of false opinion, while after all the true doctrine may elude the most laborious search. And therefore we believe that the reading of error, known to be such, for whatever cause, just or unjust, never fails, at least for a time, to have bad effects ; producing pain and dubiety, collecting rubbish in order that it may be removed, and inflicting wounds which it is necessary to heal. Without rushing, then, to any extremes, we may employ these incontestable principles in the regulation of our studies.

There is a sort of independence and adventure which leads inquiring and sanguine minds to contemn the thought of using any special precautions in the handling of error. They feel strong in their own convictions, and fully exempt from all danger of being seduced. But they neglect the important principle that the very contact of what is false tends to impair the mental health. Hence we are not ashamed to avow it, as a canon of our intellectual hygeine, that we will not, except from necessity, read books which contain known error. We would advise youthful students especially not to be inquisitive about such. As in regard to morals, prurient curiosity leads to concupiscence and corruption, so in regard to the pursuit of truth, eager desire of knowing bad systems undermines the faith. This is the weak place in some truly excellent minds. They spend a whole literary life in acquiring the knowledge of strange, conflicting, heterogenous systems. There is no infidelity or heresy, from Epicurus and Pelagius, down to Spinoza and Comte, into which they have not groped. The perpetual oscillations of Coleridge's great understanding are due, in some degree, to this morbid penchant; hence his delight in Plotinus, Böhm, and Schelling; and hence his long gestation, resulting in no definite faith, and no completed work. Continual wandering in the mazes of theories which after all are not adopted, ends only in dissatisfaction and pain. It is a trial to converse with mistaken minds, even for the purpose of refutation ; but to make such commerce the habit of life, is to court disappointment and weakness, if not to be betrayed and supplanted. With no common earnestness of entreaty we would therefore exhort the enterprising student to devote his days and nights to the search of verity, rather than the discovery, or as a first object, even the confutation of error. Offences must needs come, and must needs be removed ; the

Church must still have its controvertists; but in regard to the actor in these scenes, unnecessary polemics do harm.

We have thus prepared the way for a view which we have kept before us from the beginning, and which we trust will elucidate both the object and method of ministerial study. Granting that positive and unadulterated truth is the sole result to be sought, the question is natural and just, how such truth shall be discovered, amidst the multitude of varying opinions. To the Christian enquirer the problem need cause little hesitancy. If there is a revelation from God, this is to be the capital object of meditation. The truth of the Scripture stands forth at once as the grand topic for life; and this one book is at once the professional guide and the chosen delight of the sacred student. He need no longer ask what shall be the principal aim of his inquiries, or what his line of direction in the research of knowledge. Reason and truth are correlative; and only what is true can afford nutriment and growth.   In our mingled state, we receive truth with additions of error; but all the benefit is from the truth, and all falsehood is poison, which overclouds, pains, and weakens the mind.   It is not too much to affirm, that even the momentary inhalation of such miasma works some lesion of the inward powers. Who can say how many of our prejudices, distresses, and sins, arise from this single cause?

In the conduct of mental discipline, it will not be difficult to see the applications of this principle, though it may call for constraint and self-denial. There is occasion for circumspect walking in the study of opinion. We desire the knowledge of good and evil; but let us be cautious; let us employ a wise reserve; let us distrust our own strength of judgment; let us be sparing in our familiarity with seducers. It were well, in all cases, to take our stand on the firm ground of divine verity, and thence to make our survey of all that is opposed.   Instances may be given of men long trained in the best schools, who, from a sickly taste for strange opinions, have fallen from soundness of faith, and landed in the bigotry and superstition of popery, or the delirious ravings of Swedenborg.   Amidst conflicting judgments respecting the doctrinal contents of revelation, there is a just presumption in favour of those which are catholic, those which are prevalent among good men, those which are obvious in the record, those which tend to sobriety and holy living, those which are least allied to enthusiastic or fanatic innovation, those which grow out of first truths, and those which are consistent with themselves.

In the investigation of truth, it is important to bear steadily in mind the great foundation of valid belief. All argumentation runs back into certain propositions which sustain the entire structure of argument, and which commend themselves to the unsophisticated mind, as light to the healthy organ of vision. This is especially important in our study of the Bible. It is less observed than it deserves to be, that while the sacred writers sometimes argue, they oftener assert the truth. This is, above all, true of Him who spake as never man spake; and it became Him, as the authoritative Teacher, the Source of truth, yea, the Truth itself. The same declarations, even now repeated by mortal lips, have, we believe, a penetrative force, greater than is commonly acknowledged. We may accredit reason, without going over to rationalism. The first truth and the first reason are coincident in God. Here subject and object are identical. Even in fallen man, as a reasonable being, truth is fitted to reason. Like Light, it makes its own way, is its own revealer, and, to a certain extent, carries its own evidence. However fully we may consent to receive whatever is divinely revealed, there is a previous point to be settled before opening the volume, which is, that God is to be believed ; and this is a discovery of natural light. There are truths, the bare statement of which is mighty. The repeated statement of truths propagates them among mankind ; most of our knowledge is thus derived. These propositions may be made the conclusion of ratiocinative processes, of processes differing among themselves, and indefinitely multiplied; for men have various ways of proving the same thing. But many a man believes that which he cannot prove to another. It is shallow to deny or doubt a proposition, simply because he who holds it is unable to bring it within logical mood and figure. Thought is very rapid.

Middle terms are often faint in the mind's vision, so as to vanish, while yet the conclusions remain. Nay we are sometimes sure of that, on the mere statement of it, which, so far as conscious-ness reports, has not come to us as the result of linked reasoning. This seeming intuition may extend to a greater sphere of objects than those which are usually denominated First Truths.

From these considerations we may be encouraged, both in private inquiry, and in the teaching of others. We are not to be deterred from stating the truth, because we have not time to argue, nor even because it is denied. Assertion propagates falsehood; how much the rather should we use it to propagate truth? The statement of a great truth conveys to the hearer a form of thought, which, although he deny, he may come to believe. Therefore let it be stated. The medium of proof may come afterwards. Truths confirm one another, and become mutual proofs. In this way our study of Scripture perpetually build up our knowledge and faith. THERE IS A GOD : here is the sublimest asservation which human lips can utter. It is declared to the babe, and he receives it. Shall no man enjoy the great conception, but one who has mastered the arguments? The arguments are multiform, unlike, perhaps sometimes insuf-ficient; yet the truth abides. There are a thousand arguments, and a thousand are yet to be discovered, just as there are a thousand radii, all tending to one point in which to centre. There is no truth which the mind so readily receives; and we adopt it as a palmary instance of the use of declaring a truth, as the Scriptures often do, independently of ratiocination.

But that which settles the mind as to the real warrant for believing Scripture, is that all inspired teaching is authoritative and triumphant. In the baffling search of truth, the weary mind needs such a resting-place and acquiesces in it. The Word of God, considered as a body of religious truth and morals, is the chief fund of those who receive it, and the treasure-house of the instructed scribe. It has made the wisest philosophers and the happiest men; and the true business of the Christian philosopher is to subject the sacred text to a just interpretation. This suddenly defines and lightens the territory of the clerical student. His work in a certain sense is wholly exegetical. His

function, in regard to the divers declarations of the Bible, is like
that of the natural philosopher in regard to the complete phenomena of the universe. And here is task enough; for life is too
short for even the united powers of Christian interpreters to
exhaust all the meaning of the Scriptures. The prophetic word
alone seems to lie before us as a great continent, concerning
which as great mistakes have been made as by the early Spanish
discoverers about the new world they had touched, and of which
only one here and there has taken any safe bearings. The same
may be said concerning the border-land between revelation and
physical science; many lucubrations must ensue, before the
obscure equivocal voices of science, antiquities, and seeming
discovery shall be duly corrected by the everlasting sentences of
God's word.

So truly are perverse methods founded in an evil nature, and
so prone are we to abuse the best principles, that, with the Bible
in our hands, as a chosen study, we may slide into the old
blunder of undigested and impertinent erudition. The text may
be swallowed up of commentary. Indeed, we know not a field
in which pedantic erudition careers with more flaunting display,
than this of interpretation. Young clergymen there are, whose
proudest toils consist in the constant consultation of a shelf of
interpreters, chiefly German. We protest against this pretended
auxiliary when it becomes a rival. The commentary, like fire,
is a good servant, but a bad master. The state of mind produced
by sitting in judgment to hear twenty or fifty different expounders
give their opinions on a verse, is morbid in a high degree; and
cases are occurring every year, of laboriously educated weak-
lings, rich in books, who are utterly destroyed for all usefulness
by what may be called their polymathic repletion. No—more
knowledge of Scripture is generally derived from direct study of
the text, in the original, with grammar and lexicon, than from
examining and comparing all the opposite opinions in Pool's
Synopsis, De Wette, or Bloomfield. Again we say, commentaries must be used, and thankfully, but just as we use ladders,
crutches, and spectacles; the exception, not the rule; the aid in
emergency, not the habit of every moment. There are times
when what we most of all need, is to open the eye to the direct

rays of self-evidencing truth; and at such times every intervening human medium keeps out just so many rays from falling on
the retina. Holy Scripture cannot make its true impression
unless it be read in continuity; a whole epistle, a whole gospel,
a whole prophecy at once; and with repetition of the process
again and again; but this is altogether incompatible with the
piecemeal mode of leaving the text every moment to converse
with the annotator. The best posture for receiving light is not
that of an umpire among contending interpreters. So far as the
text is understood by us, our study of it is converse with positive
truth. Suppose some errors are picked up, as they will be, in
individual cases: these will be gradually corrected by the
confluent light of many passages. The sum of truths will be
incalculably greater than the sum of errors. The healthful body
of truth will gradually extrude the portion of error, and cause it
to slough off. The analogy of faith will more and more throw
its light into dark places. All these effects will be just in
proportion to the daily, diligent, continuous study of the pure
text. Generally it will be found, that the more perusal of the
text, the more acquisition of truth. And in application to the
case of preachers, if we have learnt anything by the painful and
mortifying experience of many years, it is, that of all prepara-
tives for preaching, the best is the study of the original Scripture
text. None is so suggestive of matter; none is so fruitful of
illustration; and none is so certain to furnish natural and attractive methods of partition. If we did not know how many live
in a practice diametrically opposed to it, we should almost blush
to reiterate, what indeed comprehends all we are urging, that
God's truth is infinitely more important than good methods of
finding it.

We have sometimes thought that over-explaining is one of
the world's plagues. There are those things which, even if left
a little in enigma or in twilight, are better without being too
much hammered out. Who ever failed to be sick of the prating
of the *cicerone* in a foreign gallery? Why should we deluge an
author's inkhorn with water? Wherefore should Æsop and
John Bunyan be diluted with endless commentary? And all

this applies itself to the young minister's private study of Scripture.   Experience shows that for pulpit and pastoral purposes, one is more benefited by scholia, or sententious seedlike observations, such as those of Bengel's *Gnomon*, than by the Critici Sacri, Doctor Gill, or Kuinœl.   Baxter says of himself: "Till at last, being by my sickness cast far from home, where I had no book but my Bible, I set to study the truth from thence, and so, by the blessing of God, discovered more in one week than I had done before in seventeen years' reading, hearing, and wrangling."   To which add Bengel's maxims: *Te totum applica ad textum; rem totam applica ad te.*   And again: "More extraordinary proof there is not, of the truth and validity of Holy Scripture, and all its contents of narratives, doctrines, promises, and threatenings, than Holy Scripture itself.   Truth constrains our acquiescence; I recognise the handwriting of a friend, even though the carrier does not tell me from whom he brings a letter.   The sun is made visible, not by any other heavenly bodies, still less by a torch, but by itself; albeit the blind man apprehends it not.

The hive of books on interpretation and religious philosophy, in our day, is the German press.   Great readers among the younger clergy seem ashamed not to have an acquaintance with these.   The question is frequently asked, whether a knowledge of the German language is a necessary or highly important part of ministerial accomplishment.   If the ministry at large be regarded, we hesitate not a moment to reply that it is not.   There are other attainments far more valuable.   Some men indeed, called to lead in theological instruction, to publish expository works, and to wage controversies, may well apply themselves to this medium of knowledge; and as no one can predict what shall be his future vocation in these respects, violence is not to be done to the impulses of Providence, which draw and urge the young student to this field; as Carey was attracted to Eastern philology, while yet a shoemaker.   Such exempt cases, however, cannot be made the basis of a general rule.   So far as exegesis is concerned, with its preparations and cognate branches, all that is indispensable in German literature is regularly transferred into English. Much even of this is impure, seductive, and utterly false; and he may regard his lot as happy, who finds no duty summoning him to meddle with such a farrago. In respect to theology, properly so called, and the philosophy of religion, we know of no single German work which the young minister may not do without. Even those which are orthodox are only approximations to a system of truth from which the theologians of that country have been sliding away; gleams of convalescence in a sick-room, which was almost the chamber of death; laboured vindications of what none among us doubt; or refutations of heresies which happily have not invaded our part of Christendom. Why should the parish minister in New Jersey or Wisconsin toil through the thirty volumes which have been educed by Strauss's portentous theory? Why should he mystify himself by labouring among the profound treatises which show that God is personal, or that there is such a thing as sin? And why should he wear himself out in mastering a theosophic, metaphysic hypothesis, which has exploded by the expansion of its own gases, before the volume has been brought to his hands. All that we have written about the infelicity of living in a tainted atmosphere has its application here. Upon many a brilliant book from abroad, we may write, as did the great Arnauld upon the fly-leaf of his Malebranche, *Pulchra, nova, falsa.* After some observation, we cannot recall a single instance of one who has become a more effective preacher, by addicting himself to the modern authors of Germany.

Keeping in view the great importance of being something more than a warehouse for other men's thoughts, the earnest minister will early seek the art of original meditation. To himself he will sometimes appear to be making little progress; perhaps even to be walking over his own circular track. But thinking over the same trains is not useless, if one so thinks them over as to secure truth. Novelty is the last object which a wise inquirer will seek. We may be sneered at for the suggestion, but we hold it a wise purpose *quieta non movere,* and till cause be shown, to rest on settled positions. As we did not discover the tenets which we profess, but were taught them, so we may hold them, till maintenance be denial of Scripture reasons. In meditation on these truths, we may so conduct the process as to revise and correct definitions and notions ; to secure just connection of arguments ; to change the order of the same ; to reject useless steps ; to supply chasms ; to reassure the memory, and thus to have materials for daily thinking, even by the way, in the crowded street, or in the saddle. We may thus be carrying on the entire column of truths into the regions of further discovery.

When in pursuing theological lucubrations, the student finds himself advancing by cautious deduction from known truths, he has this special safeguard, that such deductions correct previous errors and confirm previous truths ; the former by startling us with manifest falsehood—the *reductio ad absurdum*—the latter by arriving anew at familiar truths, or truths consistent with former truths, or inconsistent with the denial of former truths. Or the same may be thus expressed : Every advance in true reasoning adds confirmation to the general system. These are good reasons for studying sometimes without books ; a great attainment which some eminent scholars never make in a whole lifetime.

It is, we trust, impossible for any so far to mistake our drift, as to suppose that we utter a caveat against reading or even against extensive reading. Books are and must continue to be the great channels of knowledge, and fertilizing stimulants of the mind. But we would have the young preacher not to look on them as the sheaves of harvest. Great importance attaches itself to sound views of the place which human compositions occupy in mental training. Crude, immature learners regard their courses of reading, especially when rare and diversified, as so much ultimate gain ; as furnishing propositions to be remembered, and as the material of future systems ; and according to their quickness and tenacity of memory, they exercise themselves to reproduce the contents of favourite authors, in their very sequence, if not in their very words. But the same persons, if destined for anything greater than slavish repeaters, soon arrive at a discovery, that a day of multifarious reading needs to be followed by an evening of reflection, in order to conduce to any progress. And let it be observed, as a curious phenomenon of thought, that these subsequent reflections are not the reproduction or re-arrangement of notions gathered during previous study. This is useful and encouraging in the premeditation of sermons. It is even possible that none of the foregoing propositions reappear in their modified shape; the mind may work on a track entirely new. This part of the process ought to be well marked. What has been gained is not so much information as discipline; the training of the athlete before contention. Yet the previous reading, indeed all previous reading, is felt to have tended somehow towards the favourable result. This is to be accounted for by several reasons. The powers have been stimulated; thus we manure the ground, in order to crops. In addition to this, the generalizing faculty arises to wider statements, and laws, for which the particulars of the discursive reading have furnished the instances. And further, the analogy of things read suggests new resemblances and opens new trains. But for all this there is no room, where the reading is perpetual, so as to become the only mode of study. Even where the mind, after converse with books, is put upon original activity, care must be taken that these later trains of thought are in the direction of what is useful, and above all what is divine. The best flights of the preacher's meditation are those with which he is indulged after copious perusal of the simple word of God.

While many will assent to the general correctness of these statements, few, we apprehend, will consent to put them into practice, in the earlier years of mental training; and with some, the faulty methods of these years become the habit of life. But where a man belongs to the class of productive minds, he will spontaneously seek retirement and self-recollection, after the laborious reading of some years. Whether he write or speak, he will do so from his own stores. It is true that much of what he so writes and speaks will be the result of long intimacy with other minds, but not in the way of rehearsal or quotation. Wise and happy quotation adds beauty and strength; but the general truth holds, that the highest order of minds is not given to abundant citation, except where the very question is one which craves authorities. Masculine thinkers utter the results of erudition, rather than erudition itself. For why should a man be so careful to remember what other men have said? Of all that he has read for years, much if not most, as to its original form, has irrevocably slipped away; and it is well that it is so, as the mind would else become a garret of unmanageable lumber. The mind is not a store or magazine, but partly a a sieve, which lets go the refuse, and partly an alembic, which distils the "fifth essence." The book-learning of any moderate reader, even if not increased, would afford material for this process. The lust of novelty betrays some young preachers into a feverish thirst for new reading, in the course of which they scour the fields for every antithetic pungency, and every brilliant expression. For fear of commonplaces, they forbear to give utterance to those great, plain, simple, everlasting propositions, which after all are the main stones in the wall of truth. The preacher errs grievously, who shuns to announce obvious and familiar things, if only they be true and seasonable, and logically knit into the contexture. The most momentous sayings are simple; or rather, as Daniel Webster once said, "All great things are simple."

In hours of discipline, it would not be unprofitable for the student to make it his rule, every day, to bring freshly before his mind some solid truth, and if possible some new one; but rather the solid than the new. Let him fix the truth in his mind as something founded and immovable. Let him proceed to deduce other truths, but with caution. Let him abjure haste and dread paradox. Let him humbly strive to ascend to the highest principles. And let him be more concerned about the laws of thought, than the matter of knowledge. In a word, let him think for himself.

This last advice sometimes works noxious results on a certain class of minds. As given from the desks, without explanation, it is just indeed, but often nugatory. Original and independent thinking is one of the last attainments of discipline. The novice does not know how to go about it. He cannot say, "I will now proceed to generate a thought, which neither I nor others ever had before." The ludicrous attempt is most likely to be made by the Icarus or the Phæthon, of least strength and skill. Whole classes of youth, under famous teachers, have sometimes been stimulated into rash speculation and innovating boldness by the abuse of this very counsel. It is necessary, therefore, to qualify and guard it. All the beginnings of knowledge proceed upon a principle of imitation. Not more truly do we learn to speak and to write, by following a copy, than we learn to investigate and to reason by imitating the processes of others. Something of this must pertain to the whole preliminary stage of development. But by degrees, the native powers fledge themselves for a more adventurous flight. And when such beginnings are made, and the young thinker is animated with the desire of expatiating for himself, it is prudent that he should consider the nature of the procedure, or how the mind orders itself in original thinking. Briefly, then, most of our effort concerns the faculty of attention. We must look steadily in the direction of the dawning thought, as we look eastward for the sun rising. We can often do no more than hold the mind fixed. When Sir Isaac Newton was asked how he effected his vast discoveries, he replied, " By thinking continually unto them." Hence the preacher, who earnestly searches for truths to be uttered in God's house, will often feel himself reduced to a posture of soul which seems passive. Thought is not engendered by violent paroxysms of conscious invention ; any more than a lost coin or a lost sheep is found by running hither and thither in a fury of pragmatical anxiety. Let the wise thinker seat himself, and eschew vexing, plaguing cogitations. Those are not the best thoughts which are wrung out with knitted brows. Something must be conceded to the spontaneity of thinking. We do not so much create the stream, as watch it, and to a certain degree direct it. This is perhaps the reason why great thinkers do not wear themselves out; but often attain longevity. It is not meditation which weakens and distempers clerical students, so much as long sitting at the desk, and unrestrained indulgence at the table. Placid, easy philoso-phizing is one of the delights of life, and is fruitful. It may be

carried on in gardens, on horseback, at the seaside, amidst
pedestrian excursions. It is the testimony of Malthus, who says :
" I think that the better half, and much the most agreeable one,
of the pleasures of the mind, is best enjoyed while one is upon
one's legs." In thinking, we may discreetly let the thread drop
at times ; it will beyond doubt be found again at the right moment. Interruptions thus do good, and secure repose which
might not otherwise be taken. Especially converse with other
minds, on subjects of present interests, is among the most useful
means of suggestion and correction, as it regards our own researches. And what is true of living friends is no less true of
good books ; in their proper place, they afford invaluable helps
to our original inquiries.

As a single example, but that the most important, of what we
mean by the use of good books, as auxiliary to private thinking,
we select works on systematic theology, either such as give a
conspectus of the whole, or such as more largely discuss particular topics. These profess to give the classified results of
biblical investigation. To the production of these systems, either
in the head, in the sermon, or in the printed book, all exegetical
research is subsidiary. Fondness for these will be very much
in proportion to the strength, clearness, and harmonious action
of the intellect. No man can be said to know anything truly,
which he does not know systematically. Every mind, even the
loosest, tends naturally to methodize its acquisitions; much of
every man's study consists in referring new truths to the proper
class in his mental arrangement; every man has his system,
good or bad, and every sermon is, so far as it goes, a body of
divinity. But the great minds of theology have made this their
favourite department; and none can commune with them constantly without catching a portion of their energy, and learning
somewhat of their art. Melancthon, Calvin, Chamier, Turrettine, Owen, and Edwards, are companions who will teach a man
to think, and strengthen him to preach. When studies are miscellaneous and desultory, there is the more reason for employing
frequent perusal of scientific arrangements, in order to give unity
to the varied acquisitions. As a good parrallel, we may

mention that the late Judge Washington was accustomed to read over Blackstone's Commentaries once a year. This, however, was not enough for a genuine blackletter lawyer. " Find time," said Lord Chancellor Eldon, " to read Coke on Littleton, again and again. If it be toil and labour to you, and it will be so, think as I do, when I am climbing up to Swyer or Westhill, that the world will be before you when the toil is over ; for so the Law will be if you make yourself complete master of that book. At present lawyers are made good cheap, by learning law from Blackstone and less elegant compilers ; depend upon it, men so bred will never be lawyers (though they may be barristers), whatever they may call themselves. I read Coke on Littleton through, the other day, when I was out of office ; and when I was a student, I abridged it." Our candid judgment is, that writers such as we intend belong chiefly to a former period of Reformed theology. And we have had a pleasurable surprise, in finding the same judgment expressed by the late Dr Pye Smith, who has been so often quoted as favourable to German divines, with whose works he had a thorough acquaintance. " Perhaps," says he, " the very best theological writings that ever the world beheld,—next to the sacred fountains themselves —are the Latin works of foreign divines who have flourished since the period of the Reformation. It is no extravagance to affirm, that all the toil and labour of acquiring a masterly acquaintance with the Latin tongue, would be richly recompensed by the attainment of this single object, an ability to read and profit by those admirable authors."*

But the great incitement, as well as the true pabulum of thought is to be derived from the Scriptures. It is happy for a student when he finds that his most animated inquiries are over the word of God. This is a study which secures the right posture of mind, not only for calm judgment, but even for discovery. Here is the touchstone which detects the alloy of error. Here only we find positive conclusions which are undubitable. The sacred writings are a moral discipline, and promote holy states which are favourable to the apprehension and belief of

* "First Series of Christian Theology," p. 7. London, 1854.

truth. No one can fully estimate how much they prevent frivolous and aimless reasonings, by keeping the mind constantly in the presence of the greatest objects. The attainments here made belong to real knowledge ; and thus we have returned to the principal topic, which we discussed in the opening of these remarks.

What has been urged in the foregoing paragraphs, will, as we are fully aware, be little inviting to many an ambitious scholar. Genuine love of truth is not universal. Great numbers even of good men labour for knowledge of the vehicle ; books, cita-tions, masters, authority, learning as distinct from science. This has its subsidiary value, like the study of words ; but as an end, it belongs to inferior minds. The tendency may be detected by its shibboleths ; the talk of such scholars is alto-gether of verbal definitions, *sedes quæstionum*, debates controversial results, treatises, formularies, the bibliography of subjects. We would not undervalue these things, when kept among instru-ments. But this sort of research affords only knowledge to tell and to be talked of, to get benefit by ; ambitious knowledge, anything but knowledge for itself. The quality of such attain-ment is inferior ; it is shell, husk, integument. It is not fixed and permanent, but resting too much in words, being lost if the words be changed. Men of this school are presently gravelled, if pushed back a step or two, out of their authors and formulas, into the nature of things. Such a one will be found rehearsing formulas, or slightly varying them. The evil is fostered by setting inordinate value on mere reading, and by giving the rein to literary curiosity. Take a weak mind and inflate it with books, and you produce a pitiable theologian. Every one can recall some bookish man who is at the same time shallow. His glory is in citation. Where there is no determinate judgment, great knowledge tends only to vacillation, debility, concession when pressed, and frequent change of opinion. The entire mental furniture of such a scholar is a kind of nominalism. He is a treasury of arbitrary distinctions, classifications, common-places. His questions are, Who has said it ? Who has opposed it ? Where is it found ? How expressed ? This is the history of truth, rather than truth itself. Except in the sense of remembering, this person can scarcely be said to think without a book in his hand. We see to what extremes this sort of cortical or formal knowledge may run, in the case of Jewish scholars, Marsorites, and second-rate papists. All is textual. The disposition is encouraged by what university-men call *cramming*, and by all undigested learning.

It is possible that in our zeal to brand a prevalent evil, we have dwelt too much on the negative side. For there is another kind of knowledge, and another ministerial discipline. We sometimes find it in unlearned men; and always in those men in whom ponderous erudition has not smothered the native powers; such were Augustine, Calvin, Bacon, Owen, Horsley, and Foster. The learned man who comes to this, comes to it through and beyond his learning. He attains to the "clear ideas" of Locke. By patient thinking he disentangles the body of truth from its lettered and pictured integuments, of authority, treatise, and phrase. Perhaps a long period has been necessary, in order to learn terms, and read the tenets of other men; and here many rest, though genius sometimes shortens this period. But true science is not tied to certain phrases. The theologian, above all men, should possess insight. It should not be said of him, *Hæret in cortice*. The matter is not helped when weak but adventurous minds fly away from received formulas: the received formula may contain truth; the new formula may be as blindly and slavishly repeated as the old. The difference lies deeper than this. There is a discipline of mind which leads to genuine knowledge; which does not exclude erudition, but works through it to something higher. It is utterly remote from the idle musings of sundry, who absurdly boast that they are always thinking, but never read. It trains the mental eye to look through diction to essential truth; by which habit the student's notions become his own, and when afterwards expressed, however simply, bear the stamp of originality It conduces to sincere thirst for truth, as truth, in disregard of fame, of authority, of men and of consequences; and is, therefore, opposed to sectarian fire, bigotry, worship of masters, and pedantry. It ceases to swim with corks, and breaks away from the shallows of mere memory and rhetoric. Strength of judgment and firmness of conviction are its results. The mind thus taught does not allow doubts concerning unsettled things to agitate the foundation of things already proved, but maintains its conquests, and leaves no unprotected fortress in the rear. Such is the rare but attainable discipline, which we would covet for every minister of the word.

There is strong inducement to order one's studies in the way here recommended, in the further consideration that it leads directly to every good quality in the great work of preaching. The average of any man's sermons will be as the character of his general thinking. A good discourse is not so much the product of the week's preparation, as of the whole antecedent studies and discipline; it flows not from the pitcher, but the deep well. Hence that celebrated preacher spake a weighty thing, who, on being asked how long it took him to make a certain sermon, replied, " About twenty years."

The subject commends itself to a class, who constitute the strength of our American Church; we mean the rural clergy, dispersed through the length and breadth of the land, often in small parishes. The history both of England and of New England will evince, that some of the profoundest thinkers have become such in precisely these circumstances. It is a vulgar error to suppose that city pastors are in the most favourable situation for mental culture. Their labours are great, their public and executive duties are many, their interruptions are vexatious, and hence their time, especially for prolonged reflection, is little at their own disposal. No man can be so happily placed for mental culture as the pastor of a retired country parish. He may pursue the uninterrupted studies, which formed a Bochart, a Philip Henry, an Edwards, and a Dwight. Even worldly observers have looked with envy on such a seclusion.

The entire current of our remark has presupposed that the studies of the young pastor are sacred and biblical. Instances occur of clergymen who have devoted their strength to secular literature and science. Cardinal Wiseman, in his later series of Essays, delivers some severe blows at those Anglican dignitaries whose chief laurels have been won in mathematics, natural history, and the minute criticism of Greek plays. A well-known clergyman of our own country is remembered only as a consummate botanist. Such men are contributors to the stock of general knowledge, but they are scarcely to be accounted faithful to the imperative demands of an age and country like our own. " Our office," says Cecil, " is the most laborious in the world. The mind must be always on the stretch, to acquire wisdom and grace, and to communicate them to all who come near. It is well, indeed, when a clergyman of genius and learning devotes himself to the publication of classics and works of literature, if he cannot be prevailed to turn his genius and learning to a more important end. Enter into this kind of society—what do you hear? ' Have you seen the new edition of Sophocles?'—' No! is a new edition of Sophocles undertaken?'—and this makes up the conversation, and these are the ends of men who by profession should win souls. I received a most useful hint from Dr Bacon, then Father of the University, when I was at college. I used frequently to visit him at his living near Oxford. He would say to me, ' What are you doing? what are your studies?' —' I am reading so and so.'—' You are quite wrong. When I was young, I could turn any piece of Hebrew into Greek verse with ease. But when I came into this parish, and had to teach ignorant people, I was wholly at a loss; I had no furniture. Study chiefly what you can turn to good account in your future life.' " To which may be added the remark of a profound observer, Dr Witherspoon : " It is, in my opinion, not any honour to a minister to be very famous in any branch that is wholly unconnected with theology."* We cite these eminent authorities, in the full persuasion that they are not opposed to the most thorough acquaintance with worldly learning and philosophy as subsidiary to the defence and exposition of the gospel. But these are not so to usurp the time and heart as to make the Christian minister distinctively a man of science or letters. And

* Works, vol. iv. p. 19.

we admit, also, a valid exception in favour of such collateral pursuits as are for recreation, in the intervals of labour.

Valuable authorship has in every period of the Church been found among the parochial ministry. This should be borne in mind by the young pastor, in expectation of the day when he shall act upon Lord Bacon's oft quoted adage, that every man owes a debt to his own profession. New generations of men demand new books, even upon old subjects. No works of the pen are more honourable than those which disclose a sincere interest in the good of one's countrymen, and a desire to apply scriptural principles to national emergencies. Questions of true philanthropy continue to be safest in the hands of Christ's ministers. At the same time, the ordinary topics of theology and morals invite the attention of all whose hearts God hath touched, even though they dwell remote from city or college.

If we had not already trespassed on the reader's patience, we should take pleasure in examining the question how far the authorship of the Christian Church has resided among the working pastors. Let us say without fear of contradiction, the great and useful works of religious literature have not proceeded exclusively from professional *savans*, scholars, or university-men. The inquiry is a curious one, what causes have operated to give the preponderance in literary production sometimes to one and sometimes to the other class. It may be for the encouragement of diffident scholars, in distant and straitened fields, that some of the greatest productions of human genius have issued from retirement and poverty. Wealth has seldom stimulated to aught above the caprices of literature. The conditions of authorships, as shared between professors and private scholars, engaged the acute mind of the father of Political Economy ; whose remarks are worthy of all attention. Speaking of Europe, he observes, that where church-benefices are generally moderate, a university-chair will have the preference. In the opposite case, the Church will draw from the universities the most eminent men of letters. It is declared by Voltaire, that Father Porrée, a Jesuit of no great eminence in the republic of letters, was the only professor they had ever had in France whose works were worth the reading. The same remark is applicable to other Roman Catholic countries. After the Church of Rome, the Church of England is by far the best endowed in Christendom. In England, accordingly, says Smith, the Church is continually draining the universities of all their best and ablest members ; and an old college tutor, who is known and distinguished in Europe as an eminent man of letters, is as rarely to be found there as in any Roman Catholic country. "In Geneva, on the contrary, in the Protestant cantons of Switzerland, in the Protestant countries of Germany, in Holland, in Scotland, in Sweden, and Denmark, the most eminent men of letters whom those countries have produced, have, not all indeed, but the far greater part of them, been professors in universities. In those countries, the universities are continually draining the Church of all its most eminent men of letters." * These remarks have an application to the authorship of America, which we are compelled to leave to the reader's own mind.

But this whole subject of authorship is only incidental, and these remarks have trickled from the pen almost beyond our purpose. Even though the Christian pastor should never send a line to the press, he is continually engaged in literary production, and in a most important species of publication. There is no agency in the world which is more operative upon society than the faithful preaching of the gospel; there is none which demands more study, discipline, and wisdom. Hence every man who comprehends the greatness of his vocation will recognize the motives to unwearied exertion in the task of self-control, mental activity, and devoted inquiry after truth.

* Wealth of Nations, book v. chap. i.

THE MATTER OF PREACHING.

WITHIN a recent period, there has been much earnest discussion relative to the manner of preaching, in distinction from the matter of it. To a certain extent, the matter and manner of preaching interpenetrate and determine each other. All matter sensuous and intellectual must exist in some form, and, while it remains unchanged, is inseparable from that form; which is only saying, that any substance remaining what it is, is inseparable from the qualities which make it what it is. So far, to determine the matter is to determine the form. To determine that the matter of the human body is an animal organism, is so far forth to determine its form. To determine that the matter of a book shall be moral philosophy, geometry, or chemistry, is, so far, to determine its form. To settle the point that preaching shall be scriptural, philosophical, doctrinal, practical, Pelagian, Calvinistic, topical, or expository in its matter, is, so far, to determine its form. The discussions in regard to the manner of preaching to which we allude, have had respect to it, not in points wherein it is implicated in the matter, but to points which are independent of it. They admit of indefinite variation in proclaiming essentially the same matter, the same truths, thoughts, reasonings, in the same order of arrangement. They relate to elocution, gesticulation, the use of manuscripts in the pulpit, and whatever in style or delivery affects the vivacity and impressiveness of a sermon, which in substance and matter is essentially what it should be. Manner, in this sense, and as separable from the matter of preaching (while we by no means underrate its importance), it is no part of our present purpose to investigate. We inquire rather *what* it is the minister's duty to preach, and

how he shall do it, only so far as matter and form mutually interpenetrate and determine each other. This is the highest
question for the preacher to decide. It is of great consequence
how we preach. It is of still greater, what we preach, except so
far as the former involves the latter.

But is it, after all, a question, or at any rate, an open question,
among Christians, or if among Christians, among orthodox and
evangelical Christians, who acknowledge that the preacher's
commission is to preach the gospel, and that he fulfils his duty
only so far as he preaches the word, the whole word, and nothing
but the word? Can it be an open question among those who
accept the Reformed confessions as faithful summaries of the
teachings of revelation? In one sense, this is not an open question among any who can of right be called Christians. Still less
room for debate remains among those who agree in that interpretation of Scripture which makes salvation wholly of grace.
But even among these, there is a vast diversity, not merely in
the style of their preaching, but in the matter or substance of it.
This does not imply that they necessarily contradict one another.
It does not necessarily imply that any impugn, or even that
they do not confess and abide by every article of the Confession
in their discourses. But it implies something more than that
diversity of gifts, by which different men are endowed with
special qualifications for commending the same gospel to different
classes of minds. The difference lies in the different proportions, surroundings, applications in which they set forth the
different elements of the same body of truth ; in what they
signalize by frequent and emphatic iteration, and what they
omit or touch lightly and charily, and in the foreign matter with
which they illustrate, obscure, or encumber it. How else shall
we account for the fact that one preacher has power chiefly in
the aptness and force of his appeals to the impenitent; another,
in awakening devout feeling in the hearts of Christians ; a third,
in his lucid statement and unanswerable vindication of Christian
doctrines ; a fourth, in the enforcement of the moralities of the
gospel ; a fifth, in his extraordinary tact at working up occasional,
miscellaneous, and semi-secular sermons? Even among those

then, who acknowledge fealty to the great principle of preaching the word, it is still an open question, in what proportions, surroundings, applications, and other circumstances, this word and the various parts thereof shall be preached. And this question will bear long pondering by all who have assumed the awful, yet glorious office of watching for souls, and are bound to distribute to each a portion in due season. For who is sufficient for these things?

At the outset, we may safely postulate,—1. That the Scriptures themselves exhibit the various elements of divine truth in the relative proportions in which it is the preacher's duty to teach and enforce them.

2. That they are also an infallible guide as to the mutual relations and practical applications of these truths; and that, while the manner of exhibiting and illustrating them requires adaptation to the present circumstances and habits of thought among the people, they may not be intrinsically modified by alteration, suppression, or addition.

3. That the preacher fulfils his mission just and only as his preaching causes these truths to be known, and, through grace, operative among his hearers.

4. That all other acquirements, attractions, graces, or means of power and influence in a preacher, are legitimate and valuable in proportion as they subserve this end; and any sources of power in the pulpit, aside of this, no way contribute to the discharge of his mission. Their tendency is to supersede, and thus, in various degrees, to hinder or defeat it.

Finally: The great end of preaching is to glorify God and bless man, by bringing sinners to the " obedience of faith " in Christ, and promoting their sanctification, their knowledge, love, and adoration of God; their assimilation, conformity, and devotion to him, in thought, desire, word, and deed; their cordial and delighted communion with Father, Son, and Holy Ghost; their love, gentleness, meekness, patience, uprightness, and faithfulness towards their fellowmen. In a word, the great end of preaching, with respect to men, is to advance them "in all holy conversation and godliness."

Starting with these premises, which must be their own evidence to all who concede that our sole commission from Christ is to preach the word, it results :

1. That God should be the great, overshadowing object set forth in the preacher's message. All preaching that violates this precept must be vicious. This appears from every side and aspect in which the subject can be viewed. To say, as we shall say, that Christ should be the burden of the preacher's message, does not contradict, it re-affirms this principle. For Christ is God. In preaching Christ, we simply preach God in Christ reconciling the world unto himself, not imputing their trespasses. Whether we set forth the Father, the Son, or the Holy Ghost, either one of the Three, or the Three in One, we directly and immediately hold forth God, and none else. Now, if we look at the Bible or its inspired preachers as models, we find God always and everywhere in the foreground. Indeed the highest evidence of its divinity is the radiance of God upon it. He is the first and the last, shining in it, through it, and from it. Its words are not those which man's wisdom teacheth, and it speaks as never man spake. Another consideration is, that the word to be preached is the word of God. It emanates from him exclusively. It is to be enjoined in his name, and by his authority. It cannot be truly received, or produce its due saving effect, unless it be received "not as the word of man, but as it is in truth, the word of God, which worketh effectually in them that believe." 1 Thess. ii. 13. So the preacher is the ambassador of God. Can he then truly deliver his message, unless He in whose behalf he pleads be the prominent object in his inculcations ?

Still further : The truths which the Bible unfolds are truths relating to God, in his nature and attributes, his works and ways; or they concern us in our relations to him as our Creator, Preserver, Sovereign, Redeemer, and Judge ; or they respect the relations and obligations of men to each other, which in turn depend upon their common relation to the one God and Lord of all. Herein are contained all the doctrines, and hence arise all the duties of our religion. How then can they be adequately set forth in any form of sermonizing which does not make God all in all?

If we consider the duties or attainments required in the Bible, they all have God for their object and end. The love, the desires, the worship, the penitence, the sorrow, the self-renunciation, the devotion required, are no otherwise genuine than as they have supreme respect to God. Our duties to men have their strongest bond in his requirements, and are only acceptable when done as unto the Lord : "Not with eye-service, as men-pleasers ; but as the servants of Christ, doing the will of God from the heart." What better then than a mere counterfeit of Christian teaching can we have, when God is not made its Alpha and Omega?

Besides, all disposition, ability, efficiency, for attaining the favour or doing the will of God, are the gifts of his sovereign grace. Whatever we are, or have, or do, that is acceptable to God, or in the least meets his requirements, by the grace of God we are what we are. All is of God. All must come from God. To God belongs all the glory. To God we must look for every good gift and every perfect gift. When he withdraws, our comforts droop, and all our graces die. It is conceivable, then, that the religion of God can be inculcated, except as he himself is magnified? And is not this view thrice confirmed, when we consider that the declared end of the whole method of our salvation is that God may be glorified, the issue of the whole is to be, that God shall be visibly, as he is really, all in all?

Many, doubtless, will be ready to say that we have been vindicating a truism. We shall not dispute them. If it be so, it only proves our position the more impregnable. Is it one of those truisms that very many need to single out of their neglected and forgotten common-places, and to brighten it into its due lustre, and swell to its due proportions, by surveying it afresh, in its deep grounds and infinite reach of application. Coleridge says, in the first, if not best aphorism of his Aids to Reflection, that we can seldom be more usefully employed, than in "rescuing admitted truths from the neglect caused by the very circumstance of their universal admission. Extremes meet. Truths, of all others the most awful and interesting, are too often considered as *so* true, that they lose all the power of truth, and lie bed-ridden in the dormitory of the soul, side by side with the most despised and exploded errors." That there is a difference as to the extent to which God is magnified, and the whole texture of discourse saturated with the divine element, by different preachers, is undeniable. With some, a sense of his excellency and our own littleness and vileness; of the blessedness of his favour and the terrors of his wrath; of the importance of being prepared to meet him; of living for his service and glory: of dependence upon him for grace, salvation, and blessedness: of the impossibility of finding true felicity, except in the enjoyment of him forever, is the grand impression sought and effected. With others, the human, the worldly, the philosophic, social, and political, usurp the predominance. These are the great objective elements that loom up and secure an obtrusive, if not overshadowing prominence, in the preacher's unfoldings and inculcations. Man and the world appear so great, that God and heaven are scarcely greater. And in some cases the preacher himself is foremost in the group, and could hardly say with the Apostle, " we preach not ourselves, but Christ Jesus the Lord." *

If, then, the foremost object to be set forth in preaching is the Most High, in his being, infinitude, and perfection; in his works of creation, providence, and grace ; in his relations towards us as our Maker, Preserver, Benefactor, our Sovereign, Saviour, and Judge ; then that preaching is neither biblical, Christian, nor even religious, which is not so impregnated with this divine

---

* We have been credibly informed that two distinguished living preachers, when formerly stationed in the same Western city, had, for an occasional auditor, an irreligious officer of the army. This gentleman said to our informant, that he listened to the one with the greater pleasure; to the other with less satisfaction, but with greater respect and reverence, if not profit. Being asked to explain himself, he said, "The former exalts the dignity of man, and I always come away pleased with myself. The latter so magnifies God, that I seem nothing, and I always seem oppressed with a sense of my own insignificance and unworthiness." If preaching is to be estimated by the crowds it draws, we believe this man-exalting divine is now *facile princeps* among American preachers.

element, that God is not only its central, but pervading object;
over all, in all, through all, of whom, and through whom, and
to whom are all things, to whom be glory forever.

2. We are thus prepared to understand the attitude in which
man should be put by the preacher. As the Bible is addressed
to man, and aims to bring him to the salvation it proffers, *i. e.* to
spiritual life, holiness, and bless, this is a point of capital importance. But it is needless here to investigate anthropology. The
great object of the preacher should be to make him know and
feel that he is a dependent, rational, and accountable creature,
owing fealty to his Maker—that he was made to love, serve,
commune with, and enjoy him; that herein is life and bless, and
that alienation from God by sin is death and woe. These truths,
the more earnestly they are pressed, find a responsive attestation
in every conscience not sacred as with a hot iron. And they are
all the more felt, in proportion as God is apprehended in his
goodness and holiness, his sovereignty and omniscience. But
while this is fundamental and conditional to any religion whatever, it underlies another truth which is cardinal in Christianity.
We of course refer to man's fallen state, including sin, guilt,
misery, helplessness. In general it may be affirmed, that men
will realize all this, just in proportion as they see and feel what
God is. But in order to set forth God effectually for this purpose, his law, which mirrors his perfections in his requirements
of man, must be proclaimed in its spirituality and searching import, in its precept and penalty, line upon line, and precept
upon precept. The express law of God is but a formal republication of the law written by nature on the heart, although often
forgotten, disowned, and obscured under the mists of sin. But
still it is written there, although sin has blurred the record.
And when it is proclaimed in its full import and awful sanctions,
it finds an echo and witness in the conscience, that having been
drowsed into oblivion of it, is awakened to behold it. The
lightnings of Sinai bring out in visible distinctness the writing
before invisibly traced on the conscience. For " the conscience
meanwhile bears witness." They know the judgment of God,
that they which commit such things are worthy of death. With

all the world they become consciously guilty (ὑπόδικοι) before
God. We have reason to fear that too much of our current
preaching is more or less emasculated by a deficiency here. We
are no legalists. Neither are we antinomian. The law must
be proclaimed, not for the purpose of showing us how we can,
but that we cannot, obtain life, according to its requirements.
It is the grand instrument for producing conviction of sin. "By
the law is the knowledge of sin." It is only as the law, in its
breadth of precept and awfulness of penalty, is apprehended and
witnessed by the conscience, that conviction of sin is felt, that
self-righteous hopes are extinguished, or that men are driven
from all other refuges to Christ. None will thirst for or flee to
the Saviour till they see their case to be hopeless without him.
The whole need not a physician, but they that are sick. But
this conviction can be effected only by manifestation of the law,
which makes it evident that by violating its precept they are
subject to its curse, so it becomes a schoolmaster which leads to
Christ. Thus Paul was alive, i. e. confident of gaining eternal
life, without the law once. But when the commandment came,
sin revived, and he died. It slew him. Its manifestations under
the light of the law were the death of all his hopes. And he
further shows that this was accomplished only by a view of the
spiritual and heart-searching elements of the law. For he says,
"I had not known sin but by the law; I had not known lust
except the law had said, Thou shalt not covet." It is when the
law gleams and thunders, that sinners in Zion are afraid, and
fearfulness surprises the hypocrites. And it is only when thus
"pricked in the heart" by the sword of the Spirit, that they
will ask, What shall we do to be saved?

The law is no less indispensable, of course, as a rule of life to
Christians. It is the standard of excellence to which they
must aspire. They can neither have nor give evidence that
they are Christians, unless they are striving after conformity to
this perfect standard. The very end of their election, redemption, calling, is that they may be holy as God is holy—a
peculiar people, zealous of good works. In proportion as their
communion with God becomes perfect, they will be perfect in

holiness. But holiness is nothing else than conformity to the law of God. It is true that we do not thus seek a title to eternal life. But thus alone can that life, gratuitously bestowed, exist or manifest itself. Thus alone can we become attempered to, or capable of, the joys of heaven. Although released from the law as a condition of life, yet the Christian joyfully embraces it as a rule of living. He does so, because by the instinct of his gracious nature, he loves the law of God after the inward man, and because the adoption to sonship, which is freely given him in Christ, enables him and disposes him to obey it with filial freedom, love, and confidence. He is not without law to God, but under law to Christ. *Having these promises*, he cleanses himself from all filthiness of the flesh and spirit, perfecting holiness in the fear of God.

These commonplaces only need stating, so far as the principle involved in them is concerned. The chief questions which arise, respect the manner of carrying it out. It is here we judge that the most serious deficiency will be often found in preaching—a deficiency which too often dulls its edge and destroys its penetrative power. Many insist strenuously on the law, as the standard of goodness, which is evermore binding on all rational beings. They thunder its curses upon unbelievers. They insist upon all Christians making it the rule of life. Yet, after all, it fails of its due effect in alarming the unconverted, and purifying the hearts and lives of Christians. In short, it does not reach, enlighten, or awaken the conscience. Why? because it is not unfolded and defined in its import and applications to the manifold relations of our inner and outer life, and the modes of thinking, feeling, and acting therein required. No clear lines of discrimination are drawn, showing precisely where duty begins and ends, and where sin commences either in the form of omission or commission. It is one thing to denounce the curse of the law against the transgressor. It is another to denounce profaneness, or taking God's name in vain, as a heinous sin. But it is yet another, and a very different thing, to point out in clear and graphic delineation the various ways in which this command is violated in thought, word, and deed, and to show the criteria which distinguish the lawful from the profane treatment of things divine. This cannot be done, without giving the knowledge of sins before unknown or unheeded, while it relieves the conscience of the sincere believer, not only by defining his duty, but by showing what is not sin, and thus loosing him from the fetters of morbid scruples and groundless despondency. The latter object is often scarcely less important than the former. Many Christians go limping and halting all their days, in the fetters of a Judaical, Pharisaic, or ceremonial spirit; or of a superscriptural strictness and severity on some one or more points of Christian morality. This may make them harsh, sour, censorious, dejected, uncomfortable to themselves and their brethren. But such weights and consequent besetting sins must be laid aside, before they can run with patience and joy the Christian race. Instead of mounting up on wings as eagles, they grow weary, and their soul cleaveth to the dust. Those who undertake to be more righteous than God's law, in any respect, will be sure to compensate their work of supererogation by greater license in some other form of sin. We once knew a candidate for the ministry who denounced as a sin, eating meat, and drinking tea and coffee, and, if we remember right, any violation of Professor Hitchcock's prescriptions for avoiding dyspepsia. He ended with becoming the hierophant of a conventicle of free-love Perfectionists, and doing what he might, to turn temples into brothels. Take the law of the Sabbath, in regard to superiors and inferiors, indeed, the whole decalogue, and let it be so expounded, defined, and applied, that men must see not only what is, but what is not a violation of it—let the preaching of duty be clear, thorough, didactic, casuistic—and would it not oftener leave the arrows of the Lord sharp and rankling in the hearts of his enemies, and promote beyond measure the sanctification, the blamelessness, the usefulness of Christians? Is it not thus, and not otherwise, that the word becomes sharper than any two-edged sword, piercing to the dividing asunder of the joints and marrow, and a discerner of the thoughts and intents of the heart? So is it, and not otherwise, that it becomes profitable not merely for doctrine, but " for reproof, for correction, for instruction in righteousness, that the man of God may be perfect, thoroughly furnished unto all good works."

These principles, with regard to the inculcation of the law, apply of course, *mutatis mutandis*, to the whole sphere of evangelical duty; *i. e.* of duty as amplified in its scope, as modified in its source, rule and end, by the gospel. This is only saying that in summoning men to do their duty, we ought to explain and define so clearly, as to preclude all mistake, what duty is.* It is simply asserting the didactic element in preaching, which in the light of reason and scripture must needs be an integral and fundamental part of it. The commission given to preach the gospel to every creature, is given by another evangelist as a commission to teach all nations to do and observe Christ's commands. The instructions given to Timothy and Titus terminate very much in showing them whom, what, and how they shall teach.

We have dwelt the longer on this point, because we are persuaded that not a few are labouring under certain misconceptions regarding it, which impair their vigour and usefulness as preachers. It is a vulgar notion that all didactic preaching is dry and uninteresting. Hence many have deep prejudice against what

---

* It can hardly be necessary to enter a *caveat* against straining this maxim beyond the bounds of reason and even possibility. Even the applications of principles can be given by the preacher only in derivative principles of greater or less generality. He cannot go into the particular questions of fact, on which, in each case, the question of duty depends. To do so, would be to teach all knowledge, which is impossible, while the attempt to do it would be worse than ridiculous. Thus, that it is a duty to keep our promises, and to make none which are unlawful, or beyond our power to fulfil; and consequently that none ought to undertake the practice of law, medicine, statesmanship, or any calling, without competent qualifications to do aright, what they thus promise to do, is evidently within the province of the pulpit. But who will say, that it is within its province to teach law, medicine, politics, engineering, or bricklaying? Such knowledge, without which none can do their duty in these callings, must be learnt elsewhere. To lecture on Hydropathy and Allopathy, the merits of our various political parties, old line and new line, straight and crooked, on the right method of tailoring, or plastering, is not to teach or preach the gospel, and if done under colour thereof, it is simply a desecration.

they style doctrinal preaching. They crave warmth and life. They want earnest, hortatory discourse. They deem this practical and profitable. But let practice be urged in an instructive way, which displays its grounds, reach, and limits; which produces not merely some vague excitement, but shows them what they ought to be and do, and they stigmatize it as dull. didactic, and doctrinal. We do not dispute that there may be instructive preachers, who by their jejune style and frigid manner, are obnoxious to this complaint. This might happen, whatever the matter of the sermon. But in many cases the objection is aimed at the things said, not the manner of saying them. It is related of the late Professor Stuart, that, during his short but efficient pastorate, he dwelt much on certain doctrines of grace, which had been neglected or disparaged by his predecessor. The people were roused. Some said one thing and some another. The result, however, was, that his preaching was in the demonstration of the Spirit and of power; his church was filled with eager listeners; and experimental piety was greatly and permanently promoted. Some of his hearers, restive under a tone of preaching to which they were unused, begged him to give less doctrine, and more practical sermons. He complied with their request, and commenced delivering clear and thorough expositions of the divine law. In a short time, however, the same auditors waited upon him with a request that he would return to the doctrines. They had enough of practice. The truth is, aversion to legitimate preaching, whether of doctrine or practice, originates in one source. It is simply aversion to truth in its antagonism to corrupt nature, which, if doctrinal, requires a correspondent practice; if practical, has its roots in a correspondent doctrine. For truth is in order to goodness. Hence they prefer some transient and blind excitement of feeling, to that discovery of truth which alone can awaken sound evangelical feeling; which purifies while it quickens the heart, because it gives light to the understanding, and thus makes permanently wiser and better. We have said that preachers are in danger of being influenced by this vulgar prejudice, and to flatter themselves that they can benefit a large class most by imparting to

them heat without light.   We apprehend that such heat can be
but a momentary glow of sympathetic or animal excitement, as
flashy as its cause.   The rational soul can feel only in view of
what it first perceives.   Emotions must be founded on and determined by cognitions.   Christianity is not a religion of blind
feeling or capricious impulse.   It is a religion of truth.   It
sanctifies by the truth.   And the great duty of the preacher is,
"by manifestation of the truth to commend himself to every
man's conscience in the sight of God."   Our religion is not, as
some one has said, like the moon, giving light without heat, nor
like the stove, giving heat without light, but like the sun, giving
perennial light, and warmth, and life.

If there is any force in these views, they lead to the
conclusion, that the true interest, life, and power of preaching,
lie in the exhibition and enforcement of Christian truth and
duty; in the justness and force of the answers it gives to the
great questions, What shall I believe, what shall I love, what
shall I do, in order to lead a righteous, sober, and godly life;
and that when Christ appears, I also may appear with him in
glory?—in a word, in the Christian light it shed on the intellect
and conscience, to the end that it may mould the heart.   The
feeling awakened by such preaching will be salutary, Christian
feeling.   The greater the clearness, fervour, and vividness with
which such truths are set forth, and sent home, the better.   And
we may add, that all other sources of interest in a preacher and
his sermons, are aside of, if not athwart, the true aim of preaching.   That the preacher be admired ; that he fascinate by poetry
or oratory, by philosophy, or any excellency of speech or
wisdom, may answer a great many purposes.   But it may all
be, without preaching the gospel, or disturbing the thoughtless,
or guiding the anxious soul, or edifying the people of God.   We
by no means underrate a good report of them that are without.
We appreciate the importance of being in favour with all the
people, and giving no offence in anything, that the ministry be
not blamed.   But we know, too, that a woe is upon those who
preach not the gospel, and of whom all men at all times speak
well.   We should esteem the solemn awe, the deep thoughtful-

ness of the worldling, the alarm of the presumptuous, the ray of spiritual comfort stealing in upon the contrite soul, the devout feeling and holy purpose springing up in the breast of one and another, on leaving the sanctuary, a more precious testimony to the power and excellence of the discourse, than all the plaudits of graceless worldlings, and genteel professors, who are lovers of pleasure more than lovers of God. The self-searching, the humility, the tears of penitence, the sweet and confiding faith, the comfort of hope, the movement of the soul from self and the world, toward God in Christ, with which so many heard the preaching of a Nettleton or Alexander, are a thousand-fold higher attestations of pulpit power, than all the encomiums ever lavished upon merely magnificent oratory. It was a common question among the hearers of the famous Shephard of Cambridge (who was wont to say that all his sermons cost him tears), as they left church on the Sabbath, "Who was wrought upon to-day?" These are the best seals of the genuineness and apostolocity of a ministry: "By their fruits shall ye know them."

In the foregoing remarks, we have necessarily anticipated much that applies equally well to what follows. The effect of preaching the law faithfully, will not be to encourage men to attempt to gain life by keeping it, but to show them their utter inability to keep it, and their hopeless condemnation by it. Convincing them of their ruin, it fills them with a sense of their need of a Redeemer. This is the great central truth of revelation, and the foundation of true religion. For "other foundation can no man lay." Therefore, while, as we have shown, God must be set forth, first of all, and above all, in preaching, he must.

3. Be pre-eminently set forth as "God in Christ, reconciling the world unto himself, not imputing their trespasses." It were a poor and unworthy work to smite, and not to heal; to tear, and not bind up; to kill, and not make alive. Hence, since He, who by death overcame him that hath the power of death, alone can deliver us from sin, our paramount office is to declare Him, who is the way, the truth, and the life. As for us, our

mission is to " preach Christ and him crucified ; to the Jews as a stumbling-block, to the Greeks foolishness, but to them who are called both Jews and Greeks, Christ the power of God, and the wisdom of God." We need not labour to prove to the Christian, that

" Christ and his cross are all our theme."

All else converges towards him, or radiates from him. It tends to lead us to him, or flows from our union to him. All unfoldings of God in his perfections and glories ; all exhibitions of the character, condition, and duties of man ; all inculcations of doctrine and practice, if true and scriptural, lead the soul directly to the Lord Jesus Christ, for wisdom, righteousness, sanctification, and redemption. " Ye believe in God," says Christ, " believe also in me." True faith in God involves faith in Christ, as soon as he is set before the soul ; for in him all the fulness of the Godhead dwelt bodily. The first archangel never saw

" So much of God before."

We behold his glory in the face of Jesus Christ. Faith in God then is implicitly faith in Christ; it is a germ which will unfold itself as such, as soon as Christ is presented to it. The law slays, thus showing us that Christ is our only life. So every doctrine, every duty, all legitimate matter of preaching, of whatever sort, culminates in Christ, in whom all things shall be gathered into one, and who filleth all in all. All duty leads to him, to discharge the debt incurred by its non-performance, to obtain strength for its future fulfilment; while the wisdom, power, and love displayed in Christ, evoke the highest love and adoration, and incite, while they enable us to render grateful and devoted obedience.

But upon this general view there is no cause to dwell. Few Christians will deny that Christ should be the centre and substance of all preaching. It is only upon some of the consequences and bearings of this truth, that there is occasion for remark.

1. We apprehend that preachers are in little danger of excess

in setting forth Christ objectively to their hearers. He, God in him, is the great object towards which their faith, love, hope, obedience, and devotion, are to be directed. They are Christians only as they thus bow to that name which is above every name. They are complete in Him who is the Head of all principality and power. Without him they can do nothing. Life, faith, love, hope, come of looking to him, not to themselves, or to anything which they or other men can spin out of themselves. It should never be forgotten that Christianity, although working an inward renovation by the immediate operation of the Holy Ghost, developes this change in accordance with the laws of our rational and moral nature. No Christian affections can arise except in view of their proper objects. These objects are found in Christ, the God-man, our Saviour, in his person, offices, and works. Of course, we do not mean to advocate any monotonous repetition of any single or isolated truth in regard to him. There is no need of this. One of the most remarkable treatises in our language is that of Bell, showing how much of God is evinced in the human hand. A friend of ours has in contemplation a similar treatise in regard to the honey-bee. If these diminutive objects require volumes to show the extent of divine imprint upon them, can there be any lack of variety, and need of monotony, in exploring the infinite compass and relations of the Redeemer and his work? All life contains inexhaustible variety in unity which never tires by monotony. How much more He who is the Life, and combines in his own person a divine life, a human life, and the source of all life, out of whose fulness we all receive, and grace for grace! The endless sides and aspects in which he stands related to his people, enable us to view him in relations ever fresh and diversified, while yet he remains the same yesterday, to-day, and forever.

2. It hence follows, that the way and grounds of vital union to Christ should be thoroughly and abundantly set forth and cleared up in preaching. The nature of saving faith, as distinguished from all counterfeits of it; its simplicity, as distinguished from all the entanglements with which unbelief would

embarrass it; its naked essence, as simple trust in Christ and his righteousness, should be, in one form and another, a frequent theme of preaching, and habitually inwoven with the whole texture of our discourses. This must be done, even if it incur the danger of seeming repetitions. It is the grand requisite to the birth of the soul into the kingdom of God. Simple and rudimentary as it is in Christian teaching, free justification is an article in which men born under the covenant of works are dull learners. There always are those in every congregation who are thinking and inquiring on the subject of religion, but who have never known what it is to believe on Christ to the saving of the soul. There are always babes in Christ, and weak believers, who tremble and stumble in their Christian walk, because they have no adequate view of the free, gratuitous, and full justification which faith embraces and insures merely for the taking. At this point, too, not a few older Christians, " when, for the time, they ought to be teachers, have need that one teach them which be the first principles of the doctrine of Christ." Many ministers have been surprised, in conversations with the sick and dying, to find persons who have been their hearers all their days, in a mist on this simple and vital question, How can a sinner be justified before God? They know, indeed, in general, that it is not by their own, but by Christ's righteousness; yet, until the Spirit takes the scales from their eyes, they will be found, in some form, to be working up a righteousness of their own. They will think they must in some way make themselves better, before they can be fit to go to Christ, or he can receive them. Many believers often waver at this point. They doubt whether persons so unworthy have any warrant to appropriate to themselves the Saviour's righteousness. It is of great importance, that all inquiring, doubting, trembling souls be brought to see clearly the true nature of justification, which inures to those who believe on Him that justifieth the ungodly, that so they may stagger not at the promise, but be strong in the faith, giving glory to God. Nor can the preacher well expend too much of his strength here. All the liberty wherewith Christ maketh free; all filial confidence, love, and devotion; all holy

strength and courage to serve God without fear, in holiness and
righteousness, all the days of our lives; all that is sweet, genial,
and buoyant, in our spiritual state, depend upon it. Thus there
is peace and joy in believing. Thus we obtain righteousness,
peace, and joy in the Holy Ghost. Thus alone can we be
delivered from the spirit of bondage and slavish fear, or feel
ourselves in such a relation towards God as enables us to serve
him with a true heart and right spirit. To the carnal eye, it
indeed seems impossible that free justification should not encourage licentiousness. To the spiritual eye, it is the purifying
spring from which good works must flow, and cannot but flow.
We are not to get life in order to come to Christ, but to come to
Christ that we may have life.

There is a class of theologians and preachers who involve this
whole subject in perplexity, by the theory that love precedes
and is the spring of evangelical faith, and that none but peni-
tents are warranted to trust in Christ. The effect of this is to
make men feel that until they can find within themselves evidences of penitence and love, they must consider the mercies of
the gospel, as Boston says, "forbidden fruit," which it is unlawful for them to touch. On this subject, confusion of mind is the
easiest of all things, and the clear truth among the most important.
It is true, that no faith is genuine without repentance and love.
So faith without works is dead. It is also true, that faith,
although in the order of time simultaneous with commencing
love, repentance, and good works, is, in the order of nature,
before, conditional to, and causative of them. Love can only
arise from faith's perception and belief of the excellence and
glory of Christ and his cross, and of God as shining through
them. It arises, as they see

"What wisdom, power, and love,
Shine in their dying Lord."

But we must discern and believe in this loveliness before it
can excite our love. And when we believe and see it, it cannot
but draw the heart. Another consideration is, that until we
are in that friendly relation to God in which justifying faith
places us, we cannot confide ourselves to him. We feel that

our sins subject us to his righteous displeasure, and that we merit and must receive vengeance at his hands. Now love is impossible towards those whom we dare not trust because we are subjects of their righteous wrath. So faith is indispensable to love. And since all works not inspired by faith and love, are slavish, dead works, it follows, that although there be no faith without repentance, love, and holiness, yet faith is their antecedent and cause, as truly as the sun of its beams, and life of breath. We apprehend that a clear view of this point is of great moment in guiding inquiring souls. He is paralyzed in making the gospel offer, who cannot, without conditions, bid every thirsty soul come and welcome; who is constrained to tell sinners that they must get rid of their inward distempers and maladies before coming to Christ, instead of going to him at once for the removal of sin and guilt. This is preaching a fettered gospel, and it produces a fettered piety. It gendereth to bondage. It is alien from the sweet and simple faith, the filial confidence and freedom, the buoyant yet humble hope, the cordial love and genial devotion of the gospel; and which result from going at once to Christ for all, receiving all as a free gift from him, and thence giving all, in love and gratitude, to him. We think this view is sustained by the whole drift of scriptural representations. According to these, faith purifieth the heart: it works (exerts its energies) by love; it is the victory that overcometh the world. This view fully accords with the absolute necessity of love, repentance, humility, and good works, to salvation. Faith, which does not exert and evince itself in these, is not saving faith. Though we have all faith and have not charity, it profiteth nothing. Nor do the calls to repent, with the promise of pardon annexed, conflict with; they rather corroborate this view. On what is this pardon based? On Christ. How apprehended and applied? By faith. When the wicked are exhorted to forsake their way, and the unrighteous their thoughts, and turn to God, who hath mercy, and to our God who will abundantly pardon, it is only a form of teaching, that faith in God's pardoning mercy is prerequisite to true repentance. The definition of the Catechism is a true summation of scriptural teachings on this subject. " Repentance unto life is a saving grace, whereby a sinner, out of a true sense of his sin, *and apprehension of the mercy of God in Christ*, doth, with grief and hatred of his sin, turn from it unto God with full purpose of, and endeavour after new obedience."

The mistaken theory to which we have adverted, of deriving faith from love, and not love from faith, has, we are persuaded, a strong tendency to generate error on the subject of the sinner's inability. The preacher does not see his way clear to direct the sinner immediately to Christ for deliverance from this and all other evils and miseries of sin. If he cannot bid the sinner go out of himself at once to a strength which is made perfect in his weakness, nor till he has procured penitence, or love, or some other robe of clean linen with which to go, the question arises, How shall he get all this? How can he be incited to work and strive for it? The answer is, the preacher must be prepared to tell him he is able to accomplish it, or else he is hopelessly paralyzed, and can do nothing, but leave the inquirer passively awaiting the sovereign afflatus of the Spirit. Hence various fictions of natural, and we know not what other, ability, have been devised to bridge over this chasm. But the inability of the sinner, though moral, is real, and inconsistent with anything that can properly or safely be called ability. All modes of teaching which have any other effect than to lead men, under a sense of their own helplessness, to cast themselves on Christ for strength to lead a Christian life, are delusive and mischievous. We are not sufficient for anything, as of ourselves; our sufficiency is of God. When we are weak, then are we strong in the Lord and the power of his might. This is the whole theory of the Christian life. The just shall live by faith; not faith in their own ability, but of the Son of God who loved us and gave himself for us. The whole may be summed up by adding to the article of the Catechism on repentance, those on faith and effectual calling. " Faith in Jesus Christ is a saving grace whereby we receive and rest upon him alone for salvation, as he is offered to us in the gospel." " Effectual calling is the work of God's Spirit, whereby, convincing us of our sin and misery, enlightening our minds in the knowledge of Christ and renewing our wills, he doth persuade and enable us to embrace Jesus Christ, freely offered to us in the gospel."

3. A few words will suffice, after what we have already advanced, to show our views of doctrinal preaching. We can hardly conceive of a Christian discourse which does not implicitly contain, and, with greater or less explicitness, articulate a Christian truth or doctrine. Christian doctrines are but the truths of Christianity. The only real question then is, what Christian truths shall be preached, and in what relative proportions? Here the word of God is our true model and guide. But shall not certain doctrines be suppressed, although taught in the sacred oracles? Hear again our answer is, preach the word. "All scripture is profitable for doctrine," as well as other things, whoever may wish the ninth chapter of Romans, or any other part, expunged therefrom. Generally, the objection to preaching doctrines has reference to those doctrines which the objector dislikes. If he can prove them untrue or unscriptural, his objection is valid, not otherwise. All Christian affections and purposes are inspired by a view of Christian truth. They are otherwise impossible. And there is no Christian truth which, presented in its due proportions and surroundings, does not tend to nourish some holy affection. There can be no doubt, therefore, that it is a fundamental part of the preacher's vocation, to make these truths clearly understood, as the very condition of true faith, holy living, whatever is involved in right practice. The inculcation of doctrine is sometimes stigmatized as dull and unprofitable; as offering the mere dry bones to souls craving the nutritive milk and meat of the word. We do not deny that there may be doctrinal preaching obnoxious to this charge. We do not think sermons should be theological lectures, didactic or polemic. We think doctrine being clearly defined and established, should alway be developed in its practical and experimental bearings. So all Christian practice should be based on its correlate doctrines, and rooted in Christian principle, in order to be of that kind which accompanies salvation. As to fervid discourses which would stir the feelings without illuminating the understanding, we have already said enough. The attempt to

edify the Church without doctrinal instruction, is like the attempt to build a house without foundation or frame-work. Let any in derision call the doctrines " bones," if they will. What sort of a body would that be which was flesh and blood, without bones ? If any present them in skeleton nakedness, divested of their vital relations to life and experience, this is the fault of those who do it, not of true and proper doctrinal preaching, which on one of its sides is practical and experimental. In fact, the two should never be torn asunder, any more than the flesh and bones. They should ever blend with and vitally interpenetrate each other, and be pervaded by the unction of the Holy One. No sane man will contend for mere dogmatic abstractions in the pulpit. Much less should it be a theatre for philosophic or metaphysical disquisitions. But it should be a theatre for unfolding, illustrating, enforcing divine truth proved by the testimony of Him for whom it is impossible to lie, to be apprehended by the intellect, and vouched for by the conscience of man. We do not believe this truth so devoid of interest as seems to be supposed by many, who on this account studiously shun it. We believe it to be the only material on which most ministers, who have no coruscations of genius, with which to charm their hearers, can rely for awakening a permanent interest in their ministrations. While there is any religion in the world, he will hardly fail to interest his flock, who feeds them with knowledge and understanding. Dr Emmons, whose sermons were in a remarkably degree clear and icy metaphysical reasonings, far less attractive than the plain truths of Scripture, read off in the most passionless manner, always had an audience of eager listeners. He said in his laconic way, " I have generally found that people will attend, if you give them anything to attend to."

Polemical and controversial preaching is doubtless to be avoided, except so far as the preacher is called to combat the lusts and errors of hearers. In this sense, faithful ministers will always be obliged, like the apostle, to " teach the gospel with much contention." All preaching is immediately or remotely an assault upon the deceits of sin, and the refuges of lies in which it entrenches itself. And it may happen, when errorists are stealing the hearts of the people, that, with heavenly wisdom and prudence, ministers must dispute daily, as did Paul, the things of the kingdom. This is one thing. To bring the *odium theologicum* into the pulpit ; to be fond of holding up other bodies of Christians to reproach and derision ; to appear more anxious to gain the victory over our adversary, who has no chance to defend himself, than to save the souls of them that hear ; to display wrath, and bitterness, and clamour, and evil speaking, in a place that should be radiant with Christian benignity ; or, even without this, to be always thrusting out the horns dissevered from the body of Christian doctrine and practice, may accomplish a great many things. But we have never seen it productive of any signal fruits of faith, humility, penitence, love, and devotion. In general, it will be found, especially so far as the pulpit is concerned, that the positive and able inculcation of the truth is the best defence against error ; and that the more completely impersonal and uncontroversial it is, the less likely is it to arouse those carnal and malevolent feelings which always grieve the Spirit of God. This is the general principle. Cases may arise in which duty requires another course; but they should be exceptional and emergent.

4. In combating the errors and lusts of men, we do not believe that any great good is effected by abstract metaphysical and philosophical arguments. They are usually unintelligible to the common mind. They are the " wisdom of this world, which is foolishness with God," and which no preacher is commissioned to employ; and if he condescends to found his claims on his philosophy, one man's philosophy is as good as another's. He has a higher sanction for all that he proclaims, even the testimony of God, which shines in its own self-evidencing light throughout the Scriptures. Besides this, he has the witness of the consciousness of his hearers to attest what he affirms in regard to their moral state, their ill desert, their need of a Saviour, and their chief duties as Christians. Thus, for the principal parts of his message, he has proofs more effective, and exercising a far higher convictive power, than any ingenuity of speculation. And here he has an advantage which largely compensates for

the natural apathy and aversion of men to the gospel. He speaks by divine authority, and not as the scribes, if he is true to his trust. Their consciences meanwhile bear him witness. Any other basis of his teachings is of little efficacy in producing scriptural faith. For this is faith, not in any philosopheme or hypothesis of man, but in God and his word; and it must stand, not in the wisdom of men, but the power of God. It is beyond all doubt, then, that the preacher's discourse will be instinct with penetrating, convictive, spiritual, purifying energy, just and only in proportion as he appeals to the authority of God and the consciences of his hearers. This is wielding the sword of the Spirit; and when we use his sword, in devout dependence on him, we may look for his presence to give it an ethereal temper and penetrant edge. Such preaching, though it come not with excellency of speech or of wisdom, declaring the testimony of God, will doubtless be in demonstration of the Spirit and of power.

As the Spirit works the new creation not by any violation of, but in unison with, the nature and laws of the rational soul, as he persuades while he enables us to embrace Christ, and does this by giving efficacy to the external persuasions of the word read and preached, so the true method of bringing men to the knowledge and belief of the truth, is, as in all cases, to proceed from the known to the unknown. All moral and Christian truths are concatenated and interdependent, like the members of a living organism. Each one either supposes or is confirmed by all the rest. Had we adequate faculties, we should doubtless see, in regard to these truths, what we now see of some, that they involve all the rest ; just as the zoologist will tell from a tooth or a bone all the other parts of the animal to which it belonged. To a very great extent, this mutual connection of the various portions of moral and Christian truth is, or ought to be, known to the preacher, and is a chief element in his reasonings and pleas with all classes of hearers. Few are so totally imbruted, as to be blind to the simplest moral truths. In the light of these, the evidence of higher truths to which they have been blind and indisposed, may be made to appear—as surely as from the letters of the alphabet we may syllable out words, sentences, discourses, all literature. The recognition of the distinction between moral good and evil, cannot be developed without revealing sin, guilt, the need of repentance and redemption, and from these first principles of the doctrine of Christ we must go on unto perfection. As sin is deceitful and blinding, so we must strive to dispel its bewilderments. As it is madness, we must use the fragments of truth and sanity still left, for the restoration of so much of reason as is shattered or lost. In this view, a sound and prayerful discretion is to be used, as to the time and circum-- stances for declaring the various portions of the counsel of God, the whole of which we may not shun to declare at a proper time. Otherwise, though we give each one his portion, we may fail to do it in due season, and may oppress with meat, by them indigestible, those babes in Christ, who are not as yet able to bear it. It may indeed be the preacher's fault that they are such as have not their senses exercised to discern between good and evil, and are still such as have need of milk and not of meat ; yet in forwarding their growth in knowledge, he must, like all other skilful teachers, adapt himself to their stage of spiritual attainment.

5. Here arises the question, as to the extent of which prudential considerations, and the principle of expediency are legitimate in determining the matter of preaching. We are met by two classes of scriptural instructions, which in sound are contradictory, but in sense are perfectly coincident. The first are those which demand the fullest regard to the dictates of prudence and expediency. They teach us to refrain from lawful things which are inexpedient, to please our neighbour in order to his edification, to become all things to all men, if by any means we may save some. Here the strongest sanction is given to the principle of expediency. We are taught with still greater emphasis, " though we or an angel from heaven preach any other gospel, let him be accursed ;" that we may not shun to declare the whole counsel of God ; that we may not do evil that good may come ; that we must be faithful to the testimony of Jesus, and the truth of his word even unto death, if we would receive the crown of life. There is no question that our duty is to preach the truth, the whole truth, and nothing but the

truth. All seeming discrepancy here disappears, if we have recourse to the familiar ethical classification of actions as good, bad, and indifferent. In regard to acts in themselves morally right or wrong, no license is given to neglect the one or do the other, out of regard to any considerations of expediency. We are not to lie or blaspheme, or refuse to confess Christ and his gospel, though we might thus save our own lives, or prevent the crush of worlds. No instance can be found in which Paul did or sanctioned such things, strenuous as he was for expediency. On the other hand, in regard to things indifferent, *i. e.*, in themselves neither morally good nor evil, expediency is the governing principle. And, by expediency, we mean tendency to promote what is morally good, or prevent what is morally evil. To give a familiar example. As to whether we shall worship God and abjure idols, there is no option. But as to the style of dress and equipage I shall adopt, this is a matter to be determined wholly by its relation to my ability to discharge my just obligations, and my influence for good or evil upon my fellow-men. For intrinsically, linsey-woolsey and satin sparkling with diamonds are on the same moral footing. We think that the application of these principles to preaching is not difficult or obscure.

1. The minister has no discretion as to setting forth the whole body of divine truth in the course of his inculcations. He may not add to, or take from the word of God.

2. He may not, with a good conscience, when in any way questioned or put to the test, disown, or give it to be understood that he does not believe, what he does believe to be the truth in Christ, on any consideration or pretext whatsoever.

3. But since he cannot, in any one discourse, or in any limited period, traverse the whole circle of divine truth, he must exercise his own conscientious discretion as to the times and occasions, when each respective part is to be brought forth as to divide to each his portion in due season.

4. As to all matters indifferent, whether of act or word, private and public, they are to be regulated by the single aim of giving the truth more facile and effective access to the souls of men ;

whether we eat or drink, or whatsoever we do, all must be done to the glory of God and the edification of souls.

5. With regard to rightly dividing the word of truth, in the foregoing cases, as well as all others, much must doubtless be left to Christian prudence ; a want of which, more frequently than any other fault, impairs the usefulness of clergymen, and ejects them from their positions. Dr Dwight says, that by far the larger part of the forced dismissions of pastors within his know-ledge were attributable to this cause. There is, however, a general principle in regard to the distribution of the different portions of divine truth, which results from all that we have advanced, is plainly enunciated in the Bible, is enforced by the example of prophets, apostles, and Christ himself, and which no man can safely disregard. In a religion which mercy and truth, righteousness and peace, are met together, men must be made to behold both the goodness and severity of God. Great evil results from the disproportionate or exclusive exhibition of either the stern and awful, or the benignant and alluring aspects of the divine character. One class should not be suffered to overshadow the other. The soul's welfare requires that neither should be forgotten or ignored : " For the better understanding of this matter, we may observe, that God, in the revelation that he has made of himself to the world by Jesus Christ, has taken care to give a proportionable manifestation of two kinds of excellencies or perfections of his nature, viz. those which speci-ally tend to possess us with awe and reverence, and to search and humble us ; and those that tend to win, draw, and encourage us. By the one, he appears as an infinitely great, pure, holy, and heart-searching judge ; by the other, as a gentle and gracious father, and loving friend. By the one, he is a pure, searching, and burning flame ; by the other, a sweet refreshing light. These two kinds of attributes are, as it were, admirably tempered together in the revelation of the gospel. There is a proportion-able manifestation of justice and mercy, holiness and grace, gentleness, authority, and condescension. God hath thus ordered that his diverse excellencies, as he reveals himself in the face of Jesus Christ, should have a proportionable manifesta-

tion, herein providing for our necessities. He knew it to be of great consequence, that our apprehensions of these diverse perfections of his nature should be duly proportioned one to another. A defect on the one hand, viz. having a discovery of his love and grace, without a proportionable discovery of his awful majesty, his holy and searching purity, would tend to spiritual pride, carnal confidence, and presumption; and a defect on the other hand, viz. having a discovery of his holy majesty, without a proportionable discovery of his grace, tends to unbelief, a sinful fearfulness, and a spirit of bondage."*

We shall bring these observations to a close, by a few suggestions relative to the extent of the preacher's obligations to give instructions to men in respect to worldly relations and interests, economic, social, and political.

1. With regard to all that is commonly understood by the moral and worldly virtues; *i.e.* virtues which often exist without piety, and are commanded by the natural conscience, and the code of worldly respectability, as well as by the gospel, such as temperance, chastity, honesty, veracity, fidelity, kindness, &c., it is needless to say that they are of self-evident obligation; that if they may exist without piety, piety cannot exist without them; and that they should be enjoined as they are in the Bible. They should be enforced, not merely by natural and worldly, but by spiritual and evangelical motives. Yet they ought not to fill any large or overshadowing place in preaching. This should be mainly occupied with the glorious gospel of the blessed God, and its heavenly truths and requirements; and with these subordinately, as its subordinate, though indispensable fruits. Such is the uniform course of the New Testament preachers; such is the most effective way of promoting morality. It makes the tree good; so the fruit must be good. Unless it be a very distempered and unevangelical type of religion, the most religious men are the most moral individuals and communities, in all countries and all ages. Those who have laid out their chief strength in preaching worldly morality, have had but slender success. Without the fascination of genius, they can

* Edwards' Works. New York edition, vol. iv. pp. 224, 225.

seldom keep a congregation together. The mightiest preachers
of the everlasting gospel, who have done most to bring men to
the obedience of faith, have produced the greatest moral refor-
mations. Dr Chalmers's experience is a remarkable instance of
"philosophy teaching by example." He relates, that in his
earlier ministry, he plied his congregation with enthusiastic
discourses on the moral virtues, and made it his chief labour thus
to effect a reformation of their morals. They loved the preacher,
and were charmed with the magic of his eloquence. But they
did not reform their morals. He at length felt the hollowness
of mere morality, and was brought to the cross for pardon and
peace. He at once altered the whole matter of his preaching. In
place of splendid moral essays, he gave them clear and fervid
discourses on sin, guilt, and retribution; on salvation by the
Redeemer's blood and righteousness; on spiritual regeneration,
faith, repentance, holy living, heaven, and hell. Multitudes
were awakened and converted to the Lord. And not only so,
but there was a thorough, wide-spread, and permanent reformation of morals. *Ex uno disce omnes.* The pools of worldly
morality will stagnate, unless vitalized by streams from the
fountain of life.

As we have said that morality should be taught not so as to
crowd out the supremacy of the gospel, but as its necessary
subordinate fruit, so, the less immediate and direct, the more
distant and inferential the duty, the more distant and chary
should the pulpit be in treating it. " At the last extremity of a
branch, it is difficult to retain a view of the stem. Represent to
yourself, for example, sermons on neatness, politeness, &c.
Some topics of this sort, doubtless, may be approached, but it
must be done incidentally; they should never furnish the subject
for a sermon." *

2. With respect to the social and civil relations, and all
interests merely worldly, Christianity insists on the exercise of
religious principles, and all the virtues of our holy religion in
every sphere of life and action. There can be no doubt that
God will honour those that honour him in all the spheres and

* Vinet's Homiletics, translated by Dr Skinner, pp. 82, 83.

offices of life. They will be blessed in their basket and store, their going out and coming in. Society is elevated and purified, individuals and families are prospered, every worldly interest of man thrives in proportion as religion, pure and undefiled before God and the Father, prevails. This is its inherent tendency, as it exalts the whole man, and restrains those corrupt passions that blight the body as well as the soul, and destroy both in hell. It is a blessing, also, often conveyed in honour of his religion by the undercurrents, and secret prospering gales of his gracious providence. But it is often withheld in his wisdom, or prevented by counteracting causes. How often has persecution hunted the people of God to the dens and caves of the earth, while faith has enabled them to take joyfully the spoiling of their goods, and to count not even their own lives dear, knowing that in heaven they have a better and more enduring substance? In all cases, they that will live godly in Christ Jesus must suffer persecution, and endure chastening. The promise will be fulfilled, that through much tribulation they shall enter the kingdom of God. Their worldly prosperity, so far as it is vouchsafed, follows their religion as the shadow follows the substance. But it is not the substance—it is not that with which religion concerns itself, otherwise than in ways incidental and subordinate. On the contrary, its effort is to raise the soul to a sublime superiority above the transient and worldly. It puts no value upon these further than as they may be linked with and subserve our eternal welfare—than as the scaffolding to the edifice. We are surely not mistaken here. We are charged to take no thought what we shall eat, what we shall drink, or wherewithal we shall be clothed; to look not at things seen and temporal, but at things not seen and eternal; if we are called, being servants, to care not for it; but, if we may be free, to choose it rather; but always to seek first the kingdom of God and his righteousness, with the promise that all other things shall be added unto us, which our true well-being demands. Of the whole doctrine of Scripture on this subject, the Apostle gives the following beautiful summation:—" But this I say, brethren, that the time is short. It remaineth, that both they that have wives be as though they had none; and they that weep, as though they wept not: and they that rejoice, as though they rejoiced not; and they that buy, as though they possessed not; and they that use this world, as not abusing it; for the fashion of this world passeth away."

In correspondence with all this, it is evidently no part of the preacher's commission to make the promotion of men's worldly interests any prominent object of his inculcations. On the contrary, such a course is clearly discountenanced in the Bible as not only repugnant to religion, but suicidal; for, by displacing the divine and eternal element, it fails of its benignant fruits for this world. For these bear not the root, but the root beareth them. So far as we have observed, those who most signalize worldly interests in preaching, so far from eternizing the temporal, merely secularize the spiritual. "No man that warreth entangleth himself with the affairs of this world." With respect to those who would encourage servants to be restive under the yoke, or contemptuous of their masters, Paul denounces them as "men of corrupt minds, supposing that gain is godliness; from such withdraw thyself. But godliness with contentment is great gain. For we brought nothing into the world, and it is certain we can carry nothing out." We think that the same principle holds in this matter, which Christ propounds in regard to individuals. "He that findeth his life shall lose it, and he that loseth his life for my sake shall find it." Preachers who spend their strength in efforts at worldly amelioration, usually spend their strength for nought. Those who spend it in promoting godliness, usually build up every interest of man, temporal, spiritual, eternal, individual, and social. "Godliness is profitable unto all things, having promise of the life that now is, and that which is to come." All forms of mistaking gain for godliness, betray a radical misconception of the whole nature and scope of the gospel. Says John, "they are of the world, therefore speak they of the world, and the world heareth them. We are of God. He that heareth God, heareth us; he that is not of God, heareth not us. Hereby know we the spirit of truth, and the spirit of error."

It being thus clear that worldly amelioration, however it may be a consequence, is not the direct object of the preacher's inculcations, it follows, that the pulpit, in proportion as it is engrossed with interests less than those of the soul, God, and eternity, usually suffers loss itself, and thus indirectly damages what it undertakes to promote. Let a preacher devote his pulpit to any questions social or civil, which respect simply their better or worse condition in regard to the good things of this life, and he will generally accomplish less for their temporal, to say nothing of their eternal welfare, than if he had devoted himself to the promotion of that godliness which, with contentment, is great gain.

As, however, religion has its development and sphere of action in the world, and includes all social and relative duties, simply because it includes all duty, and requires us to do all things to the glory of God; it, of course, requires us to act in all good conscience in reference to our country and government; to do what we may consistently with paramount obligations, to make our officers peace, and our exactors righteousness; to procure just and salutary laws; to sustain their authority and execution; so there can be no question as to the propriety of inculcating these great, and (among Christians) undisputed principles, from the pulpit. Indeed, as Christ taught us to render unto Cæsar the things that are Cæsar's, and unto God the things that are God's; as Paul enjoined obedience to the powers that be, not only for wrath, but for conscience' sake, so he expressly charges ministers to " put them in mind to be subject to principalities and powers, to obey magistrates, to be ready to every good work." Of course this means a real, an authorized magistrate, not a pretender or usurper; and demands obedience to laws enacted by a competent authority, not by a mob, or any unauthorized assemblage. And it further means obedience to real rulers, as to all other superiors, so far, and so far only, as they do not require us to disobey God. In this case, we are clearly taught we ought to obey God rather than man. To obey a magistrate who requires us to blaspheme, is simply to abet him in his rebellion against God. In such a case, our only course is to sustain the law, not by obeying its precept, but, if need be, by enduring the penalty. It is no strange thing, to be required to witness a good confession at the cost of martyrdom.

We have no reference here to those great and abnormal emergencies which speak for themselves, when the people, in the exercise of their own *vis medicatrix naturæ*, by the sudden violent throes of revolution, cast off a government intolerable or outgrown, for one suited to their wants. We only mean to say that the foregoing principles are proper, and at times necessary to be inculcated in the pulpit. But when we pass from these principles, which must commend themselves to every enlightened conscience, to the details of their concrete application, in actual politics, other considerations have place. There is no question that men ought to regard it, and to be taught to regard it, as a duty to promote the elevation to office of the most faithful and competent men, as well as the enactment of just and equal laws. But few sane men would deem it safe or edifying for the pulpit to discuss the respective merits of different candidates; or whether the tariff, or sub-treasury, or statutes enfranchising and making voters of foreigners were just and salutary. Similar embarrassments may exist, however firm the preacher's personal convictions, as to whether a given man, or set of men are the legal officers they claim to be. It is not so much on first principles, which few men possessing a moral sense will dispute, as the application of these principles to the vast and complex affairs of nations and communities, that the angry questions of party politics arise." And here, imperfect knowledge, interest, prejudice, party predilections so distort and bewilder, that however strong our own personal convictions, we see vast numbers earnestly enlisted on opposite sides, whose piety cannot be questioned. We do not undertake to say that these questions may not sometimes have an ethical or religious side too obvious and urgent for the pulpit to neglect. But we do say, as the result of considerable observation, that we never knew the pulpit throw itself into the issues that divide political parties, without contracting a stain and a wound upon its sanctity and spiritual power. It inevitably soils itself by such association with the unworthy passions which embitter and disgrace political conflicts. We have not known any instance in which political harangues from the pulpit aided the party espoused, or gained a voter, or did anything more than give intolerable offence to partisans of the opposite side. Others may have witnessed better results. " As to patriotic and political sermons, they are rather to be avoided, and yet in certain grave circumstances, we may be obliged to touch upon such subjects in the pulpit. . . . We must beware, least we inflame on this hearth, the passions of the natural man. How shall we now speak of politics without taking a side ? We must remark, also, the utilitarianism which for the most part is concealed in these subjects. It is better for the preacher, as it is for the navigator, to keep himself in the high sea ; it is in the neighbourhood of coasts that shipwrecks are most frequent."—*Vinet's Homiletics*, pp. 86–7. And it may be added, that with the ample sources of political information afforded by a free press, exigencies can rarely occur which call for its dissemination from the pulpit. Its office should rather be to moderate the fierceness of these violent conflicts, by holding up the contrasted greatness of the Infinite and Eternal.

NOTE.— The above article, by Professor ATWATER, of Princeton, was inadvertently inserted; but as it so admirably compliments the matter of this work, with the consent of the author it is retained.

EXPOSITORY PREACHING.

THE pulpit discourses of Roman Catholics as well as Protestants, during several centuries, have been, for the most part, founded on short passages of Scripture; commonly single verses, and oftener less than more. This has become so prevalent, that, in most treatises upon the composition of sermons, all the canons of homiletics presuppose the treatment of an isolated text. We are not prepared to denounce this practice, especially when we consider the treasury of sound doctrine, cogent reasoning, and mighty eloquence, which is embodied in productions formed on this model, and call to mind the instances in which such discourses have been signally owned of God in the edification of his church. But there is still another method, which, though less familiar to ourselves, was once widely prevalent, and is recognized and approved in our Directory for Worship, in the following words : " It is proper also that large portions of Scripture be sometimes expounded, and particularly improved for the instruction of the people in the meaning and use of the sacred oracles." * And it may not be out of place to mention here, that in the debates of the Westminster Assembly. there were more than a few members, and among these the celebrated Calamy, who maintained with earnestness, that it was no part of the minister's duty to read the Scriptures in public *without exposition.*†

It is not a little remarkable, that in an age in which so much is heard against creeds and systems as contradistinguished from the pure text of Scripture, and in which sacred hermeneutics

* Directory for Worship, chap. vi. § 2.
† Lightfoot's Works, vol. xiii. p. 36.

hold so high a place in Theological education, we should have allowed the methodical and continued exposition of the Bible to go almost into disuse.* What our predecessors practised under the name of lectures is almost banished from the pulpit. It is against this exclusion that we now propose to direct our argument. And in what may be offered in the sequel, we ask attention to this statement of the question as limiting our purpose. Far be it from us to decry the mode of discoursing which prevails in our churches. We freely acknowledge its many excellencies, and rejoice in its gracious fruits ; but we plead in behalf of another and an older method, which we lament to see neglected and forsaken. With this preface, we shall proceed to give some reasons why a judicious return to the expository method of preaching seems to us to be desirable.

1. The expository method of preaching is the most obvious and natural way of conveying to the hearers the import of the sacred volume. It is the very work for which a ministry was instituted, to interpret the Scriptures. In the case of any other book, we should be at no loss in what manner to proceed. Suppose a volume of human science to be placed in our hands as the sole manual, text-book, and standard, which we were expected to elucidate to a public assembly: in what way would it be most natural to go to work ? Certainly not, we think, to take a sentence here, and a sentence there, and upon these separate portions to frame one or two discourses every week. No interpreter of Aristotle, of Littleton, Paffendorf, or of Paley, ever dreamed of such a method. Nor was it adopted in the Christian church, until the sermon ceased to be regarded in its true notion, as an explanation of the Scripture, and began to be viewed as a rhetorical entertainment, which might afford occasion for the display of subtilty, research, and eloquence.

2. The expository method has the sanction of primitive and ancient usage. In the Israelitish, as well as the Christian

* Although the subject of this essay may, in certain particulars, run very naturally into that of critical interpretation, the writer begs leave to disclaim any special right to dwell upon this topic, as his pursuits have not led him into the field of hermeneutics, any further than the performance of ordinary ministerial duty required.

church, preaching was an ordinary mode of religious instruction. In both it was justly regarded as a means of conducting the hearers to the knowledge of revealed truth. As early as the time of Ezra, we find that the reading of the law was accompanied with some kind of interpretation. In the synagogues, after the reading of the law and the prophets, it was usual for the presiding officer to invite such as were learned to address the people. Our Lord Jesus Christ availed himself of this opportunity to deliver one of his most remarkable discourses; and this was an exposition of a prophetic passage. The apostle Paul seems also to have made portions of Scripture the basis of his addresses in the synagogues. But it is not to be expected that the preaching of the apostolic age, when the speakers were divinely inspired, should be in all respects a model for our own times. It was their province to communicate truth under inspiration; it is ours to interpret what has thus been communicated. The early Christian assemblies naturally adopted the simple and rational methods of the Jewish synagogues; in conformity with which it was an essential part of the service to read the Scriptures. Manuscripts were rare, and the majority of believers were poor; and hence the church assemblies must have long continued to be the chief, if not the only, sources of biblical knowledge. Justin Martyr, who is one of the earliest authorities on this subject, informs us that the public reading of the text was followed by addresses adapted to impress the subject on the minds of the hearers.* According to Neander, who may be considered as an impartial judge on this topic, it was at first left to the option of the bishop what portions of Scripture should be read; though it was subsequently made necessary to adhere to certain lessons, which were judged appropriate to times and seasons. Bingham also concedes that the lessons were sometimes arbitrarily appointed by the bishops at discretion. Augustine declares that he sometimes ordered a lesson to be read which harmonized with the psalm which he had been expounding.†

* Apolog. 2.
† Aug. in Psalm xc. Serm. ii.—Bingham, Antiq. B. xiv. c. iii. § 3.

As this is a point of history concerning which there is little room for question, we shall content ourselves with the diligent, and, as we believe, impartial deductions of Bingham and Neander. It is not to be denied, that there were, even in the early ages, several different modes of preaching, and that some of these approached very nearly to that which now prevails; yet there was no period during which the expository method was not highly prized and extensively practised. These discourses were very frequent, and often flowed from the intense feeling of the moment. Pamphilus, in his Apology for Origen, represents this great teacher as discoursing extempore almost every day. The same frequency of public address is recorded of Chrysostom, Augustine, and other fathers. Their sermons were taken down by stenographers, and in such of them as are extant we have repeated evidences of their familiar and unpremeditated character. Chrysostom, for instance, thus breaks forth, in one of his homilies on Genesis : "I am expounding the Scriptures; yet you are all turning your eyes from me to the person who is lighting the lamps. What negligence ! to forsake me, and fix your minds on him ! For I am lighting a fire from the holy Scriptures, and in my tongue is a burning lamp for instruction." Augustine also tells us, in one of his homilies, that he had not thought of the subject on which he actually preached, until the reader chanced to read it of his own accord in the church.[*]

The two greatest preachers of the Greek and Latin churches, respectively, afford striking examples of the value set upon exposition. Augustine has left homilies upon the Psalms, the Gospel of John, and other whole books of Scripture. Chrysostom, in like manner, expounded at length the book of Genesis, the Psalms, the Gospels of Matthew and John, and all the Epistles of Paul. His homilies consist usually of a close interpretation, or running commentary, followed by an Ethicon, or practical application. That biblical exposition was recognized as the end of preaching seems clear from some declarations, as the following : " If any one assiduously attend public worship, even without reading the Bible at home, but carefully hearken-

* Bingham, Book xiv. chap. iv. § 4.

ing here, he will find a single year quite sufficient to give him
an intimate acquaintance with the Scriptures." *   And indeed
this is so natural a result of the catholic belief that the Scriptures are the great storehouse of saving truth, as to leave us in
some surprise at the neglect into which this direct exposition of
the authentic records has fallen.

When we look into the history of England during the thirteenth
century, we find that two modes of preaching were in use,
neither of these being that which we now employ.   In the first
place, that of *Postillating*, which was identical with the expository method; secondly, that of *Declaring*, in which the discourse
was preceded by a declaration of the subject, without the citation of any passage of Scripture.   When about the beginning of
the thirteenth century, the method of preaching from insulated
texts, with subtile divisions of the sermons, was introduced, it
was zealously adopted by the younger clergy, and became extensively popular; while it was as warmly opposed by some of
the best theologians of the age, as " a childish play upon words
—destructive of true eloquence—tedious and unaffecting to the
hearers—and cramping the imagination of the preacher."   Among
others, it found an able opponent in the great Roger Bacon; a
man whom we can never mention without amazement at his
philosophical attainments, and veneration for his character.
" The greatest part of our prelates," says he, " having but little
knowledge in divinity, and having been little used to preaching
in their youth, when they become bishops, and are sometimes
obliged to preach, are under the necessity of begging and borrow--
ing the sermons of certain novices, who have invented a new
way of preaching, by endless divisions and quibblings, in which
there is neither sublimity of style nor depth of wisdom, but
much childish trifling and folly, unsuitable to the dignity of the
pulpit.   May God banish this conceited and artificial way of
preaching out of his church; for it will never do any good, nor
elevate the hearts of his hearers to anything that is great or
excellent." †

* Hom. 28, in Job. —Neander, Der heilige Chrysostomus.
† R. Bacon, apud Henry's Hist. iv. 366.

" The opposition to this new method of preaching," says Dr
Henry in his History of England, " continued through the whole
of the fourteenth, and part of the fifteenth century. Dr Thomas
Gascoigne, Chancellor of the University of Oxford, tells us that
he preached a sermon in St Martin's Church, A.D. 1450, without a text, and without divisions, declaring such things as he
thought would be useful to the people. Amongst other things
he told them, in vindication of this ancient mode of preaching,—
' that Dr Augustine had preached four hundred sermons to the
clergy, and people, without reading a text at the beginning of
his discourse ; and that the way of preaching by a text, and by
divisions, was invented only about A.D. 1200, as appeared from
the authors of the first sermons of that kind.' "

It is no part of our business to enter further into this investigation, or to determine critically at what point of time the
method of preaching from insulated verses became exclusively
prevalent in the church. Whatever excellencies it possesses,
and there are many, can derive no additional dignity from the
origin of the method, which is referable to a period by no means
the most glorious of Christian history. When the light of divine
truth began to emerge from its long eclipse, at the Reformation,
there were few things more remarkable than the universal return
of evangelical preachers to the expository method. Book after
book of the Scriptures was publicly expounded by Luther, and
the almost daily sermons of Calvin were, with scarcely any exceptions, founded on passages taken in regular course as he
proceeded through the sacred canon. The same is true of the
other reformers, particularly in England and Scotland.

To come down to the times of the Nonconformists ; while it
is undoubtedly true that they sometimes pursued the textual
method even to an extreme, preaching many discourses on a
single verse, it is no less true, that exposition in regular course
was considered a necessary part of ministerial labour. Hence
the voluminous commentaries on single books with which the
press groaned during that period. Let us take a single instance,
as late as the latter half of the sixteenth century, in the person
of Matthew Henry, whom it is difficult to refer exclusively to

the era of the elder or the later Nonconformists. We may suppose his practice in this particular to be no extreme case. Mr
Henry was an able and laborious preacher from single texts, but
it was by no means to the exclusion of the expository plan. On
every Lord's day morning, he read and expounded a part of the
Old Testament; on every Lord's day afternoon a part of the
New; in both instances proceeding in regular order. During
his residence in Chester he went over the whole Bible in this
exercise, more than once.* Such was the custom of our forefathers; and in the prosecution of such a plan we need not
wonder that they found the body of their hearers constantly
advancing in scriptural attainments. The sense of change, and
change without improvement, is unavoidable when we come
down to our own times; in which, within our immediate knowledge, there are not a dozen ministers who make the expounding of Scripture any part of their stated pulpit exercises. Nay,
although our Directory for Worship declares expressly that "the
reading of the Holy Scriptures in the congregation, is a part of
the public worship of God, and ought to be performed by the
ministers and teachers;"—that the preacher, " in each service,
ought to read at least one chapter, and more, when the chap-
ters are short or the connection requires it; " yet it is undeniably
the common practice to confine this service, which is treated as
something almost supererogatory, to the Lord's day morning.
Now while we are zealous in maintaining, that the Christian
minister should not be bound down by any imperative rubric or
calendar as to the portion which he shall read, we cannot but
blush when we compare our actual performances in this kind
with those of many sister churches who have chosen to be
guided by more strict liturgical arrangements.

3. The expository method is adapted to secure the greatest
amount of scriptural knowledge to both preacher and hearers.
It needs no argument, we trust, to sustain the position that every
minister of the gospel should be mighty in the Scriptures;
familiar with the whole text; versed in the best commentaries;
at home in every portion of both Testaments; and accustomed

* Williams, Life of Henry, c. x.

to grapple with the most perplexing difficulties. This is the appropriate and peculiar field of clerical study. It is obvious that the pulpit exercises of every diligent minister will give direction and colour to his private lucubrations. In order to success and usefulness in any species of discourse, the preacher must love his work, and must have it constantly before his mind. He must be possessed of enthusiasm which shall never suffer him to forget the impending task. His reading, his meditation, and even his casual trains of thought, must perpetually revert to the performances of the Sabbath. And we take pleasure in believing that such is actually the case with a large proportion of clergymen.

Now it must not be concealed that the popular and prevalent mode of sermonizing, however favourable it may be to professional zeal of this kind, and to the cultivation of mental habits, does by no means lead in any equal measure to the laborious study of the Scriptures. The text, it is true, must be a fragment of the word of God; and it may be confirmed and illustrated by parallel or analogous passages. But where no extended exposition is attempted, the preacher is naturally induced to draw upon systematic treatises, philosophical theories, works of mere literature, or his own ingenuity of invention, and fertility of imagination, for such a train of thought as, under the given topic, may claim the praise of novelty. We are aware that with many it is far otherwise, and that there are preachers who are wont to select such texts as necessarily draw after them a full interpretation of all the foregoing and following context; and such sermons are, to all intents and purposes, expositions. But we also know, that to compose a sermon upon a text of Scripture, with very little reference to its position in the word of God, and a very little inquiry as to the intent of the Spirit in the words, is a thing not only possible, but common. The evil grows apace, wherever the rhetorical aspect of preaching attracts undue attention; and the desire to be original, striking, ingenious, and elegant, supersedes the earnest endeavour to be scriptural.

This abuse is in a good degree precluded by the method of exposition. The minister who from week to week is labouring to elucidate some important book of Scripture, has this kept

forcibly before his mind. It will necessarily be the chief
subject of his studies. Whatever else he may neglect, he
will, if a conscientious man, sedulously peruse and ponder those
portions which he is to explain ; using every auxiliary, and
especially comparing Scripture with Scripture. Suppose him to
pursue this regular investigation of any one book, for several
successive months, and we perceive that he must be acquiring a
knowledge of the very word of truth, vastly more extensive,
distinct, and profound, that can fall to the lot of one who, perhaps
for no two discourses together, finds himself in the same part of
the canon. Two men practising upon the two methods, each in
an exclusive manner, may severally gain an equal measure of
intellectual discipline and real knowledge, but their attainments
will differ in kind. The one is driven from the variety of his
topics to a fitful and fragmentary study of the Bible ; the other
is bound down to a systematic and unbroken investigation of
consecutive truths. Consider, also, how much more of the pure
teachings of the Spirit, accompanied with suitable explanation,
necessarily occupies the mind of the preacher in one method than
in the other.

If such is the influence, with respect to the preacher himself,
who, under any system, is still free to devote his mind to scriptural study, how much greater is it not likely to be with respect
to the hearers, whose habits of investigation almost always receive their character from the sermons to which they listen ?
Perhaps none will deny that every hearer should be made as
fully acquainted with the whole word of God, as is practicable.
But where, by the mass of Christian people, is this knowledge
to be obtained, except at church ? The truth is, the scriptural
knowledge possessed by our ordinary congregations, amidst all
our boasted light and improvement, bears no comparison with
that of the Scottish peasantry of the last generation, who, from
very infancy, were taught to follow the preacher, in their little
Bibles, as he expounded in regular course. If long habit had
not prepossessed us, we should doubtless agree at once to the
proposition, that all the more cardinal books of Scripture should
be fully expounded in every church, if not once during the life

of a single preacher, certainly once during each generation; in order that no man should grow up without the opportunity of hearing the great body of scriptural truth laid open. And considering the Bible as our only authentic document, this method seems so natural, that the burden of proof may fairly be thrown on such as have well nigh succeeded in excluding it. There is something beautiful in the very idea of training up a whole congregation in the regular study of the holy Scriptures. And if we were called upon to devise a plan for inducing people to read the Bible more diligently, we could think of none as likely to attain the end. When hearers know that a certain portion of Scripture is to be explained on the ensuing Lord's day, they will naturally be led to examine it during the week, and will thus be prepared to listen with greatly increased advantage to what may be offered. This is precisely the exercise which Chrysostom recommends to his hearers in his first homily on Matthew.* The same father seems also to have sometimes thrown out to his hearers difficult questions, in order that they might be stimulated to inquiry. "Wherefore," he says, "have I presented the difficulty and not appended its solution? Because it is my purpose to accustom you, not always to receive food already prepared; but often to search for the explanation yourselves. Just as it is with the doves, which as long as their young remain in the nest, feed them from their own bills; but as soon as they are large enough to be fledged and leave the nest, cease to do thus. For, while they bring them corn in their bills, they only show it to them; and when the young ones expect nourishment, and draw nigh, the mother lets it fall upon the earth, and the little ones pick it up."† If Scripture difficulties are in our day often started in the pulpit, and often left unresolved, we are not prepared to say whether it is exactly with the motive avowed by this great preacher. Certain it is that the able elucidation of dark places, and the reconciling of seeming contradictions occupy far less

* Ὥστε δὲ εὐμαθέστερον γενέσθαι τὸν λόγον, δεόμεθα καὶ παρακαλοῦμεν, ὅπερ καὶ ἐπὶ τῶν ἄλλων γραφῶν πεποιήκαμεν, προσλαμβάνειν τὴν περικοπὴν τῆς γραφῆς, ἣν ἂν μελλῶμεν ἐξηγεῖσθαι, ἵνα τῇ γνώσει ἡ ἀνάγνωσις προσεδοποιοῦσα (ὁ καὶ ἐπὶ τοῦ εὐνούχου γέγονε, πολλὴν παράσχοι τὴν εὐκολίαν ἡμῖν.

† Vol. iii. p. 103.

room in the sermons which we now-a-days preach, than they did in those which have come down to us from a former age. Not many clergymen adopt the method of Bishop Horsely, who was accustomed to select difficult texts, in order that his preaching might be in the highest possible degree, an aid to the inquiries of his hearers. And unless scriptural doubts are resolved from the sacred desk, it is plain that the great body of our congregations are likely to remain in darkness as long as they live. But he who proposes to analyse and interpret any considerable portion of the Bible, in regular order, cannot evade this labour, but must repeatedly confront the most difficult passages, and prepare himself to make them intelligible. It would be easy to expatiate on this topic, but enough has been said to awaken some doubt as to the expediency of banishing formal exposition from the church assembly.

4. The expository method of preaching is best fitted to communicate the knowledge of scriptural truth in its connection. The knowledge of the Bible is something more than the knowledge of its isolated sentences. It includes a full acquaintance with the relation which every proposition sustains to the narrative or argument of which it is a part. This is particularly true of trains of reasoning where everything depends on a cognizance of the links which connect the several truths, and the order in which those truths are presented. Large portions of holy writ are closely argumentative and can be understood in their true intention only when the whole scope and sequence of the terms are considered. This logical connection is no less the result of inspiration than is any individual statement. In some books of Scripture the argument runs from beginning to end, and the clew to the whole is to be sought in the analysis of the reasoning. As instances of this we may cite the epistles to the Romans and to the Hebrews, of which no man can have any adequate conception who has not been familiar with all their parts as constituting a logical whole. This, however, is so universally conceded as a first principle of hermeneutics, that it is needless to press it further. But it is not so generally perceived, that in the other methods of preaching this great advan-

tage is sacrificed. It is true that a man may announce as his text a single verse or clause of a verse, and then offer a full and satisfactory elucidation of the whole context; but, so far as this is done, the sermon is expository, and falls under the kind which we recommend. But this species of discourse is becoming more and more rare. In the sermons of the Nonconformists this was usually the plan of proceeding. In modern sermons, there is, for the most part, nothing which resembles it. A text is taken, usually with a view to some preconceived subject; a proposition is deduced from the text; and this is confirmed or illustrated by a series of statements which would have been precisely the same if any similar verse, in any other part of the record, had been chosen. Here there is no interpretation, for there is no pretence of it. There may be able theological discussion, and we by no means would exclude this, but where a method merely textual or topical prevails, there is an absolute forsaking of that which we have maintained to be the true notion of preaching. We can conceive of a hearer listening during a course of years to every verse of the epistle to the Hebrews, laid open in connection with as many sermons of the popular sort, without obtaining thereby an insight into the grand scope and intricate contexture of that wonderful production. Now we say that the method which makes such an omission possible is unfit to be the exclusive method.

As a remarkable instance of what is meant, we may adduce the sermons of the Rev. William Jay, who is justly celebrated as one of the most fascinating and instructive preachers of Great Britain. In these sermons we find many valuable scriptural truths, many original and touching illustrations, much sound argument, pungent exhortation, and great unction. In themselves considered, and viewed as pulpit orations, they seem open to scarcely a single objection; yet as expositions of the Scripture, they are literally nothing. They clear up no difficulties in the argument of the inspired writers; they give no wide prospects of the field in which their matter lies; they might be repeated for a lifetime without tending in the slightest degree to educate a congregation in habits of sound interpretation. The same remark applies to the majority of Amĕrican discourses, and most of all to those which conform to the prevailing taste of New England. In occasional sermons, and monthly collections, where we have access to a number of printed discourses, we are often forcibly struck with the absence of all logical concatenation. The text is a sign or motto, after announcing which the preacher glides into a gentle train of common-places, or a series of thoughts which, however ingenious and interesting and true, have no necessary connection, " continuous in their discontinuity, like the sand-thread of the hour-glass."

The mental habits of any Christian community are mainly derived from the preaching which they hear. It is fair to ask, therefore, from what source can the Christians of our day be expected to gain a taste and ability for interpreting the Scripture in its connection ? Certainly not from the pulpit. Among the ancient Scottish Presbyterians the case was different. Every man and every woman, nay, almost every child, carried his pocket-Bible to church, and not only looked out the text, but verified each citation ; and as the preaching was in great part of the expository kind, the necessary consequence was, that the whole population became intimately acquainted with the structure of every book in the Bible, and were able to recall every passage with its appropriate accompanying truths. The genius of Protestantism demands that something of this kind should be attempted. Where the laity are not expected to search the Scriptures, or in any degree to exercise private judgment, it may answer every purpose to give them from the pulpit the mere *results* of exposition ; but more is needed where we claim for all the privilege of trying every doctrine by the word of God ; and sermons should therefore be auxiliaries to the hearers in their investigation of the record. And we earnestly desire a general return on the part of our preachers to a method which will necessarily tend, from week to week, to open the Scriptures, and display what is by no means their least excellency, the harmonious relation of their several portions.

5. The expository method affords inducement and occasion to the preacher to declare the whole counsel of God. No man,

who selects his insulated texts at random, has any good reason to be satisfied that he is not neglecting the inculcation of many important doctrines or duties. This deficiency is prevented in some good measure, it must be owned, by those who pursue a systematic course of doctrines in their ordinary ministrations. But usually the indolence or caprice which renders any one averse to the expository method will likewise withhold him from methodical series of any kind in his discourses. There is perhaps no man who has not an undue fondness for some one circle of subjects: and this does not always comprise the whole of what he is bound to declare. But the regular exposition of a few entire books, well selected, would go far to supply every defect of this nature.

It is the province of the minister to render plain the difficulties of the Bible, and this is not likely to be done extensively, as we have elsewhere hinted, in an exclusive adherence to single texts.

There are some important and precious doctrines of revelation which are exceedingly unwelcome to the minds of many hearers : such, for instance, are the doctrines of predestination and unconditional election. These, the preacher is tempted to avoid, and by some they are never unfolded during a whole lifetime. It is obvious that no one could expound the Epistle to the Romans, without being under the necessity of handling these points.

Moreover, it is unquestionable that many doctrines are abhorrent to the uninstructed mind, when they are set forth in their naked theological form, which are by no means so when presented in their scriptural connection. Here, again, is a marked superiority on the side of exposition.

There is, we suppose, no pastor who has not, in the course of his ministerial life, found himself called upon to press certain duties, or inveigh against certain sins, which it was exceedingly difficult to dwell upon, either from the delicacy of the theme itself, or from its relation to particular classes or individuals in his congregation. Now when such topics naturally arise in the regular progress of exposition, all hesitation on this score is removed at once. The most unpopular doctrines may be stated and enforced, the most prevalent vices denounced, and the most daring offenders chastised, while not even the censorious or the sensitive can find room for complaint. For these and similar reasons, we conceive the expository way of preaching to supply a grand deficiency in our common pulpit ministrations.

6. The expository method admits of being made generally interesting to Christian assemblies. We are aware that the vulgar opinion is just the reverse of this, and that there are those who refrain from this way of preaching, under the belief that it must necessarily prove dry and repulsive to the hearer. To this our reply is, that the interpretation of the Scriptures *ought* to be interesting to every member of a Christian community: if it is not so, in fact, the cause of this disrelish is an evil which the church should not willingly endure, and which can be remedied in no other way than by bringing the public back to the assiduous study of the Bible. It is not every sort of exposition, any more than every sort of sermon, which is interesting. He who hastily seizes upon a large portion of the text, in order to furnish himself with ample material for an undigested, desultory, and extemporaneous address, cannot expect to awaken and maintain attention. With all their blindness in certain matters, the public are very sagacious in discovering when the minister gives them that which costs him nothing. But let any man devote equal labour to his lectures as to his sermons, and unless he be the subject of some idiosyncrasy, the former will be equally interesting.

The observation is very common that expository preaching is exceedingly difficult. Yet the writers on homiletics, as if it were the easiest thing in the world, and taught by nature, almost without exception, dismiss the whole subject with a few passing remarks, and lay down no rules for the conduct of a regular exposition. We are persuaded that if equal pains were taken to prepare for one as for the other, and if the one were as often practised as the other, this complaint would have no place.

As a matter of fact, we have observed no lack of interest in such exercises, on the part of intelligent hearers. The truth is, the Bible is made for the common mind, and as it is the most

interesting book in the world, so its interpretation, well conducted, is always to be found highly and increasingly agreeable
to the majority of hearers. On the other hand, there are few
instances of any man's interesting large congregations, for any
length of time, by discourses which were void of scriptural
statements, however elegant they might be in a rhetorical point
of view. The effect of mere ethical preaching has been sorely
felt in Germany, where, in the greater number of places, the
ancient services of the Sunday afternoon and during the week
have gone into desuetude, and there are whole classes of persons
whom one never expects to see in church, such as merchants,
military officers, and savans. Teller once preached a sermon to
a congregation of just sixteen persons, the intent of which was
to warn them against setting too high a value on going to
church. " Let any man," says Tholuck, " imagine a modern
preacher—as was common in former days—to direct his congregation to bring their Bibles with them, and that they might be
assured that he declared not man's word, but the word of God,
at every important point, to look out the passage cited: the
remark of all elegant gentlemen and ladies would be, ' O, this
is too simple !' *Dies ist doch allzu naiv !"* But in the days when
this simple practice was in vogue, every one was interested in
exposition ; and it will be so again, whenever the public taste
shall have been reformed by a return to what was good in the
ancient methods. We rejoice to know of at least one instance,
even in Germany, serving to show that ordinary Christians may,
with proper care, be led back into the old paths, and that highly
to their satisfaction. " I know but one preacher," says a writer
in the Evangelical Church Journal, " in my native country,
where there are more than four hundred churches, who practises
biblical exposition with success. In his country parish, which
comprises several hamlets, he is accustomed to visit each of
these in turn once a month (perhaps oftener in winter), and to
lecture in the school-house. The hearers bring their Bibles, and
even aged and infirm persons, who cannot go to church, repair
hither with eagerness and delight. They receive neither mere
fragmentary and superficial remarks on single words or clauses,

nor a merely edifying address on a scripture passage; but the
connected exposition of some whole book, developing as well
the specialties of language and matter, as the entire scope
according to its contents. The lecturer begins, at every meeting,
where he left off at the previous one. In the next hamlet he
interprets another book, as large numbers come in from the
neighbouring villages to enjoy the additional privilege." Would
that we could witness the same thing in every congregation in
America!

There is one advantage of expository lectures, in respect to
interest, which must not be omitted. Nothing is more evident
than that the attention and sympathy of an audience are best
ensured by a rapid transition from topic to topic. This cannot
always be secured in the common method. The preacher, from
a sort of necessity, hammers with wearisome perseverance upon
some one malleable thought, in order to keep within his preconceived task. But where he has before him a number of connected scriptural propositions, he is not only allowed, but
constrained, to make precisely such quick transitions from each
point to the next, as gives great variety to his discourse, and
keeps up the unwearied attention of the hearer. With faithful
preparation and assiduous practice, there is probably no minister
who might not find this happy effect from weekly lecturing.

7. The expository method has a direct tendency to correct, if
not to preclude, the evils incident to the common textual mode
of preaching. It is an ordinary complaint that the sermons of
the present day, as compared with those of the seventeenth
century, are meagre, and often empty of matter; we think the
charge is founded in truth. No one can go from the perusal of
Barrow, Leighton, Charnock, or Owen, to the popular writers
of our time, without feeling that he has come into an atmosphere
of less density. In the mere form of the pulpit discourse, in an
æsthetical point of view, we have unquestionably improved upon
our model. The performances of that day were too scholastic
and complicated. "The sermons of the last century," says
Cecil, "were like their large unwieldy chairs. Men have now
a far more true idea of a chair. They consider it as a piece of

furniture to sit upon, and they cut away from it everything that embarrasses and encumbers it." But we have gone on to cut away until we have, in too many cases, removed what was important and substantial. The evil is acknowledged, but it is worthy of inquiry, how far the superficial character of modern sermons is derived from the exclusive use of short texts. We certainly do not assert that the Puritans' themselves did not carry this very method to an extreme, by preaching many sermons on the same text; but it is well known that they almost universally pursued some variety of regular exposition in conjunction with this. Still less do we contend that all the evils of sermonizing are to be imputed to the exclusive use of brief texts; the source of the evil is more remote, and must be sought in the spirit of the age. But still there is good ground for the position that the prevailing method gives easy occasion to certain abuses, to which direct exposition is not liable; and hence we argue that the exclusion of the latter mode is greatly to be deprecated. This is the extent of our demand. Some of the abuses to which we refer may be indicated.

It is by no means uncommon to hear sermons which are absolutely devoid of any scriptural contents. The text indeed is from the Bible, and there may be interspersed, more for decoration than proof, a number of inspired declarations; but the warp and the woof of the texture are a mere web of human reasoning or illustration. Sometimes the subject is purely secular; and often, where it is some topic of divine truth, it is maintained and urged upon natural grounds, independent of the positive declarations of the Word. It is not merely among the Unitarians of Boston that this style prevails. There are various degrees of approach to it in many orthodox pulpits of New England. The expository method renders this exceedingly difficult: being professedly an explanation of the Bible as the ideas are there set forth. In point of fact, this evil seldom occurs in exposition, as it is both natural and easy for the preacher to open clause after clause in its true sense and its revealed order. Expository discourse can scarcely fail to be largely made up of the pure biblical material.

A still greater abuse is that of wresting texts from their genuine meaning by what is called accommodation. This is the extreme refinement of the modern method. As if there was a lamentable paucity of direct scriptural declarations, to be used as the subjects of discourse, we have proceeded to employ sacred words in a sense which never entered into the minds of their inspired writers. This is the favourite trick of many a pulpit haranguer, and deserves to be classed with the sesquipedalian capitals of play-bills, and the clap-traps of the theatre: in both cases the object is to attract attention or awaken astonishment. There can scarcely be found, on the other hand, a single man, however unbridled his imagination, who could fall into such a fault in the process of formal and professed exposition. Common reverence for the Word of God must needs forbid any one, while in the very act of interpreting its successive statements, to exhibit as the true intent of any passage, sentiments which no fair exegesis can extract from it.

But even where the text is understood in its literal and primary sense, the avidity for something new, and a regard for the "itching ear" of modern auditories, seduce the preacher into such a mode of treating his subject as renders the sermon too often a mere exercise of logical or rhetorical adroitness. Where the æsthetics of sermonizing have been cultivated with overweening regard, and the exquisite partition of the topics has been exalted to the first place, we see everything sacrificed to ingenuity. The proper basis of every discourse is some pregnant declaration of the Scripture. But in the elegant sermons which are occasionally heard, the real basis is an artificial division, or "skeleton," commonly tripartite, and frequently of such structure as to offer a pretty antithetic jingle of terms, and at the same time to remove out of sight the true connection and scope of the text. When this is the case, far too much stress is laid upon the division, however ingenious. This abuse has grown from age to age. It was the natural consequence of exclusive textual preaching. Among the French divines it may be said to have prevailed, but it has reached its acme among the Germans, who have almost defeated our object in these remarks by playing the same tricks of fancy with long passages. Thus the excellent Tholuck, in the ninth of his second series of University Sermons, has contrived from Acts i. 1-14, to produce a division not merely in forced antithesis, but actually in rhyme! The partition being as follows :

1. Die Stätte seines *Scheidens*, die Stätte seines *Leidens ;*
2. Verhüllet ist sein *Anfang*, verhüllet ist sein *Ausgang ;*
3. Der Schluss von Seinem *Wegen* ist für die Seinen *Segen;*
4. Er ist von uns *geschieden*, und ist uns doch *Geblieben ;*
5. Er bleibt *verhullet* den Scinen, bis er wird klär *erscheinen.*

But as a discourse is not made expository by having prefixed to it a connected passage of Scripture, we still maintain, that genuine exposition removes in great measure the temptation to these refinements. It deserves consideration that we treat no other subjects but those of religion in this way. In all grave discussions of human science, all juridical arguments, and all popular addresses, the logical or natural partition of the subject commends itself to the common sense of mankind. Such is the judgment of unbiassed men on this point. It may not be improper here to cite the opinion of Voltaire himself, because through his sneer we discern something like the aspect of reason. " It were to be wished," says he, " that in banishing from the pulpit the bad taste which degraded it, he (Bourdaloue) had likewise banished the custom of preaching upon a text. Indeed, the toil of speaking for a long time on a quotation of a line or two, of labouring to connect a whole discourse with this line, seems a play unbecoming the gravity of the sacred function. The text becomes a species of motto, or rather an enigma, which is unfolded by the sermon. The Greeks and Romans had no knowledge of this practice. It arose in the decline of letters, and has been consecrated by time. The habit of always dividing into two or three heads subjects which, like morals, demand no partition whatever, or which, like controversy, demand a partition still more extensive, is a forced method, which P. Bourdaloue found prevalent, and to which he conformed."

But there is another evil incident to the modern method of preaching which is still more to be deprecated ; namely, emptiness. Next to the want of truth, the greatest fault in a sermon is want of matter. It is not the province of any mere method, as such, to furnish the material, but the ordinary mode of handling Scripture in the pulpit affords great occasion for diffuseness, and has brought leanness into many a discourse. A man of little thought, it is true, whether he preach from a verse or a chapter, will necessarily impress the character of his mind upon his performance; yet the temptation to fill up space with inflated weakness is far greater under the modern method; and where this method is universal will overtake such as are undisciplined in mind. We conceive it to be no disparagement of the Word of God to say that it is not every verse even of sacred writ upon which a long discourse can be written without the admixture of foreign matter. In too many instances, when a striking text has been selected, and an ingenious division fabricated, the preacher's mind has exhausted itself. Perhaps we mistake, but our conviction is, that far too much stress has been laid upon the *analyses* of sermons. Essential as they are, they are the bare plotting out of the ground. The *skeleton*, as it is aptly called, is an unsatisfactory object, where there is not superinduced a succession of living tissues; it is all-important to support the frame, but by no means all-sufficient, and they who labour on this, in the vain hope of filling up what remains by extemporaneous speaking or writing, " quite mistake the scaffold for the pile."

We regard the diffuseness of many ministers, however perspicuous, as even worse than obscurity. The labour of the preacher's thought is too often intermitted upon the conception of a good analysis. Our fathers of the last century used to throw out masses, sometimes rude, and sometimes fantastically carved and chased, but always solid and always golden; we, their sons, are content to beat the bar into gold leaf, and too frequently to fritter this into minute fragments. Defect of thought is a sad incentive to laboured expansion, when a man is resolved to produce matter for a whole hour. In such cases, the effort is to fill up the allotted number of minutes. Too many moments of sacred time are thus occupied in adding water to the pure milk of the word. The dilute result is not only wanting in nutritive virtue, but often nauseous. Under an admirable partition, we find sermonizers offending grossly, and this in a two-fold way. One preacher will state his topic, and then, however plain it may be, pertinaciously insist upon rendering it plainer. In this instance the heads of discourse may be likened to milestones on a straight and level highway, from each of which the traveller is able to look forward over a seemingly interminable tract. Another will, in like manner, announce his topic, and then revolve around it, always in sight, but never in proximity, until the time of rambling being spent, he chooses to return and repeat his gyrations about a new centre. There is little progress made by the haranguer, though his language or his embellishment be unexceptionable, *qui variare cupit rem prodigialiter unam.* This paucity of such matter as is germane to the subject in hand is sometimes betrayed in the attempt to indemnify for the meagreness of the argumentative part by an inordinate addendum in the shape of improvement, inference, or application.

The expository method, if judiciously intermixed with the other, offers a happy corrective to this fault. Here the preacher is furnished with abundance of matter, all-important, and fertile of varied thought. He is placed under compression, and compelled to exchange his rarity of matter for what is close and in the same proportion weighty. We could give no better receipt for the cure of this tympany of sermonizers, than a course of expository lectures.

One word must be added, before we leave this copious topic, upon the avidity with which both preachers and hearers seek for novel and striking texts. The most common and familiar texts have become such, for the very reason that they are the most important. It is unworthy of the minister of Jesus Christ to be always in search of fragments which have never before been handled. The practice militates against the systematic and thorough development of the whole counsel of God. We need not pause a moment to show that this is an evil that cannot exist under the method which we are solicitous to recommend.

It forms no part of our plan, in these remarks, to lay down

rules for the conduct of an expository discourse, though the subject is quite as deserving of being treated in detail as any other
connected with homiletics. No mistake could be more injurious
to the character of such exercises, than to suppose that they demand less method or less assiduity than the most finished sermons of the ordinary kind. They are not to be used as a means
of retreat from the labours of the closet, and he who thus
employs them will soon find his pulpit services empty and un-
successful. In the present state of society, when the public
mind, especially in our own country, is trained by the discipline
of reading and hearing the highest specimens of forensic and
deliberative eloquence, it is vain to expect that any congregation
can long be interested in unpremeditated addresses. We may
apply to this whole subject the words of our Directory for
Worship: "The method of preaching requires much study,
meditation, and prayer. Ministers ought, in general, to prepare
their sermons with care; and not to indulge themselves in loose,
extemporary harangues; nor to serve God with that which cost
them naught."* We have met with no instance in which permanent usefulness has followed the practice of delivering
unstudied sermons. The preacher who attempts this is sure to
fall into empty declamation, objurgatory invective, or tedious
repetition. Undigested discourses are commonly of tiresome
length and proportionate dulness. Wherever we hear frequent
complaints of a preacher's prolixity, we are sure ourselves that
he leaves much of the filling up of his outline to the hour of
actual delivery. Without being himself aware of it, such a
preacher falls into a routine of topics and expressions, and is
perpetually repeating himself, and becoming more and more
uninteresting to his charge; while, at the same time, he is
perhaps wondering at the diminution of his hearers, and attri-
buting his want of success to any cause but one within himself.
The assiduous study of the Bible, with direct reference to the
services of the pulpit, is indispensably necessary, whatever
species of preaching may be adopted.

We plead at present for no more than a discreet admixture of

* Chap. vi. § 3.

biblical exposition with the other methods of discourse. In entering upon such a course, it is not necessary that the minister should introduce his first experiments into the principal service of the Lord's day : he might make trial of his gifts in less frequented meetings, or in some more familiar circle called together for this special purpose. And even where the expository method is exclusively adopted, as some may see cause to do, the pastor is to beware of that extreme which would always present very long passages. The expository plan, wisely conducted, may be said to include the other. Where, in due course, a verse or even a part of a verse occurs, so important in its relations and so rich in matter as to claim a more extended elucidation, it should be taken singly, and be made the basis of a whole sermon or even more.

As a model of familiar exposition we would cite the Lectures of Archbishop Leighton on the First Epistle of Peter. The great excellency of these is their heavenly unction, which led Dr Doddridge to say that he never read a page of Leighton without experiencing an elevation of his religious feelings. " More faith and more grace," says Cecil, " would make us better preachers, for *out of the abundance of the heart the mouth speaketh.* Chrysostom's was the right method: Leighton's Lectures on Peter approach very near to this method." —" Our method of preaching," says the same writer, " is not that by which Christianity was propagated ; yet the genius of Christianity is not changed. There was nothing in the primitive method set or formal. The primitive bishop stood up and read the gospel, or some other portion of Scripture, and pressed on the hearers with great earnestness and affection a few plain and forcible truths, evidently resulting from that portion of the divine word : we take a text, and make an oration. Edification was then the object of both speaker and hearers ; and while this continues to be the object, no better method can be found." *

Such a mode of preaching is less adapted than its opposite to make the speaker a separate object of regard, and might be

* Cecil's Works, vol. iii. p. 312.

selected by many on this very account. It is now some years
since we enjoyed the privilege of listening to the late pious and
eloquent Summerfield, the charm of whose brilliant and pathetic
discourses will never be forgotten by those who heard them.
After having, on a certain occasion, delivered a deeply impressive sermon on Isaiah vi. 1–6, he remarked to the writer of
these pages that, in consequence of having been pursued by
multitudes of applauding hearers, he had been led to exercise
himself more in the way of simple exposition, as that which
most threw the preacher himself into the shade, and most illus-
triously displayed the pure truth of the Word.

The same idea was expressed by the late Dr Mason in circumstances which no doubt drew from him his sincerest convictions and most affectionate counsels. The words are found
in a sermon preached in Murray Street Church, December 2,
1821, on the occasion of resigning the charge of his congregation;
and we earnestly recommend to every reader this testimony of
one who, it is well known, was eminently gifted in the very
exercise which he applauds.

In suggesting to his late charge the principles upon which
they should select a pastor, he says: " Do not choose a man
who always preaches upon insulated texts. I care not how
powerful or eloquent he may be in handling them. The effect of
his power and eloquence will be to banish a taste for the Word
of God, and to substitute the preacher in its place. You have
been accustomed to hear that word preached to you in its connection. Never permit that practice to drop. Foreign churches
call it *lecturing;* and when done with discretion, I can assure
you that, while it is of all exercises the most difficult for the
preacher, it is in the same proportion, the most profitable for
you. It has this peculiar advantage, that in going through a
book of Scripture, it spreads out before you all sorts of character,
and all forms of opinion ; and gives the preacher an opportunity
of striking every kind of evil and of error, without subjecting
himself to the invidious suspicion of aiming his discourses at
individuals." *

* Mason's Works, vol. i. p. 366.

With these remarks we may safely leave the subject, commending it to the careful and impartial investigations of all who are interested in the propagation of divine truth, and particularly to ministers of the gospel, who, of all men living, should be most solicitous to direct their powers in such channels as to produce the highest effect.

SKETCHES OF THE PULPIT IN ANCIENT AND IN MODERN TIMES.

IT admits of little question that preaching took its rise from the public reading of the Scriptures. No one needs to be informed how regularly this formed a part of the synagogue service. The case of our Lord's expositions in this way is too familiar to bear recital. The apostles, and Paul in particular, seem to have followed the same method. Indeed, this may be taken as the rule, while free utterances, like that at Mars' Hill, are considered as the exceptions. Little has come down to us, in regard to the precise form taken by the discourses of Christian teachers in the early and less rhetorical period. The celebrated passage of Justin Martyr points towards the familiar harangue or exhortation, rather than the elaborate comment on Scripture. This we apprehend arose in part from the fact—now very much neglected, though significant—that inculcation of doctrine was carried on chiefly in the classes of catechumens, while the public assembly was more employed for lively addresses to the Christian people. Justin expressly declares that the writings of the prophets and apostles were read to the assembly. The Apostolical Constitutions doubtless report a well-known usage, when they say that the congregation reverently stood, while the reading took place; of which some churches retain a vestige, in the custom of rising, when the little fragment by synecdoche, called the *Gospel*, is recited. Liberty was given to the aged and infirm to remain seated. In our times, when people refuse to stand even in prayer, such a usage would prove burdensome in the extreme.

There is good reason to believe, that the portions of Scripture for public reading were at first left to the free choice of the presiding minister. After a while, when festivals and fasts became numerous, ingenuity was exercised to affix certain passages to the subject of commemoration. From this it was an easy step to a programme of regular lessons, for all Sundays and great days. But these were far from being uniform or immutable. Thus we find that the Churches in Syria read at Pentecost from the Acts of the Apostles, while those of Spain and Gaul read the Revelation. In Syria they read Genesis in Lent, but at Milan, Job and Jonah. In Northern Africa the history of our Lord's passion was appropriately read on Good Friday; at Easter, the account of the resurrection; in both cases from Matthew. When we come down to the days of Augustine, we find the lessons somewhat fixed; and it would be easy to make numerous citations from his works to this point. Antiquaries refer the first collection of lessons, called Lectionaries, in Gaul, to about the middle of the fifth century; the oldest known being the celebrated *Lectionarium Gallicanum*. In the eighth century it was still necessary for the imperial authority of Charlemagne to enforce uniformity in the portions read.

When matters had gradually assumed their rubrical settlement, the Church customs became fixed. The reading was by a reader, or lector, who stood in the elevation known as the *ambo*. He began with the words, "Peace unto you," to which there was a response by the people, such as is familiar to us in modern service-books. The gospels had the precedence, as they still have in the Missal, and were frequently read by the deacon. This we suppose to have been a very ancient custom, and one which might well have a place in modern liturgies, where the voice of the minister is often overtasked, in oppressive seasons and times of ill-health. The sermon was pronounced sometimes from the bishop's cathedra, before bishops had ceased to preach, or from the steps of the altar, when this had taken the place of the communion table; in some instances, however, from the *ambo*, which reveals a connection of the discourse with the lesson of Scripture.

In attempting to gather some notices of early preaching, we have to grope amidst darkness, most of our authorities belonging to a corrupt and ritualistic period. The preacher began with the *Pax omnibus* to which the audience responded. We find Augustine asking them sometimes to help him with their prayers. "The lesson out of the Apostles," he says, in one place, "is dark and difficult;" and he craves their intercession. And elsewhere: *Quemadmodum nos, ut ista percipiatis, oramus, sic et vos orate, ut ea vobis explicare valeamus.* The preacher sat, while the people stood; as no seats were furnished for the worshippers. Augustine speaks of this, in apologizing for a sermon longer than usual, and contrasts his easy posture with theirs.

Every one must be persuaded that early preaching was without the use of manuscript. It was in regard to expression extemporaneous. Here we might again quote Justin. Socrates tells us indeed, concerning Atticus, Bishop of Constantinople, that he committed to memory at home such things as he was about to deliver in the church; but afterwards, he says that he spoke from the impulse of the moment. Sidonius, addressing himself to Faustus Rejensis, writes thus: "Prædicationes tuas nunc repentinas, nunc cum ratio præscripsit elucubratas, *raucus plosor audivi.*" The allusion is to the audible applause given to popular orators. Pamphilus relates of Origen, that the discourses, which he delivered almost daily in church were *extempore*, and that they were taken down by reporters, and so preserved for posterity. We find Chrysostom changing his subject, in consequence of tumults in the street on his way to the public assembly. His discourses, as now extant, contain many observations which plainly arose from the circumstances in which he stood during the delivery; such as the clapping of hands, the shouts heard from the neighbouring hippodrome, and the entrance of attendants to light the lamps. In one instance we find Augustine suddenly taking up a passage which the lector, who it seems was a boy, had read by mistake, instead of the one which the preacher had premeditated. The whole air of his *Sermones* is that of the extemporaneous preacher. Again and again he descants on the psalm which has just been sung. He throws in such remarks as this : " You see, beloved, that my sermon to-day differs from what is usual ; I have not time for all," etc.   And we may here observe that the four hundred sermons of this father afford the richest treasure for any one who wishes to study the peculiarities of ancient Latin preaching.   Gregory the Great says in one place : " I understand some hard passages now, *coram fratribus*, which I could not master *solus*."   " In the earliest times," says Thiersch, " it is certain the free outpouring more prevailed, the nearer we get to primitive simplicity, and the liberal manifestation of the *charismata*."   According to Guericke, the reading of sermons occurred only as exceptional.   For example, Gregory says in one of his Homilies on the Evangelists : " It has been my wont to dictate many things for you ; but since my chest is too weak for me to read what I have dictated, I perceive some of you are hearing with less displeasure. Hence, varying from my usual practice. . . . I now discourse *non dictando, sed colloquendo*."   It should seem, perhaps from the same infirmity, that hè sometimes wrote sermons which were read to the people by the lector.

If any should inquire how we come to have so many extant sermons of the Christian fathers, the reply must be, that they were taken down by reporters ; the revision and emendation of the author being added in some instances, then as now.   Great preachers in every age have been accustomed, also, to write out at their leisure, the discourses which they had delivered extempore.   It would be a great historical error to suppose that shorthand reporting was unknown to the ancients.   There were many causes which operated to bring it into general use.   The enthusiastic admiration of eloquence, which prevailed among the Greeks and Romans, furnished a motive for seeking to preserve what had electrified the populace.   The extraordinary amount of manuscript, in ages before the invention of printing, led to a facility in the penman's art, which we probably undervalue.   The use of uncial or separate characters, in place of a cursive or running-hand, in rapid writing, would naturally prompt, first to such ligatures and contractions as we observe in many manuscripts, and then to still greater abridgments, condensations, and

symbols, by means of which a whole word or even a whole sentence was denoted by a single mark.   Specimens of these, from
ancient remains, may be seen appended to some editions of Cicero.
But as to the details of the methods, we are altogether unin-
formed.   The result show that full reporting was as such relied
upon by them as by us.   Those orations of Greek and Roman
orators, which were produced on the spot, were thus taken down;
and as soon as Christian eloquence began to be regarded from
its worldly and literary side, the same mode was applied.   Eusebius assures us that the discourses of Origen were thus written
by stenographers.   Reference has already been made to the case
of Gregory the Great.   Almost all the sermons of Augustine
which remain to us, are due to this method.   Many, doubtless,
receive their fitness for this work from acting as amanuenses.
Thus, Augustine writes feelingly of the death of a boy who was
his notary.*   In the Ecclesiastical Acts, concerning the designation of Eraclius as his successor, we find Augustine thus
addressing the assembly : " A *notariis ecclesiæ*, sicut cernitis,
excipiuntur quæ dicimus, excipiuntur quæ dicitis ; et meus
sermo, et vestræ acclamationes in terram non cadunt." †   But
the authorities on this head are innumerable ; indeed, some of
our most valuable patristical treasures were thus preserved.
Modern times and our own days have seen the same means employed.   The expositions of Calvin on the Old Testament are
from reports of this sort, which contain the very prayers which
he offered.   The Commentary on the Ephesians, by M'Ghee,
one of the most admirable evangelical works of the age, was delivered by the author at a little weekly lecture in Ireland, and
reported in stenography.   Some of the greatest sermons of
Robert Hall were never written till after the delivery; and some
of these were "extended" from the notes of Wilson, Grinfield,
and Green.   But we need look no further than to the orations
of Webster, Clay, Russell, Palmerston, Cobden, Thiers, and
Montalembert, to escape all doubts as to the practicability of
what has been supposed.

With the secular advancement of Christianity, the argumen-

* Ep. clviii.   † Ep. ccxiii,

tation of assemblies, and the accession of learned men and orators, the simple and ardent addresses of apostolic times gave place to all the forms of Grecian rhetoric. The house of worship, no longer a cavern or an upper chamber, became a theatre for display. This is apparent more among the Greeks than the Latins, and was not inconsistent with much ardour of piety and edification of the faithful ; yet the change was very marked, and in the same proportion we observe the art of homiletics assuming a regular shape. It is impossible to condemn what we here discern, without at the same time censuring the pulpit of our own day in the most refined portions of Christendom : but we are not sure that a universal advancement in the spiritual life of the Church would not instantly put to flight many adventitious glories of the sermon, and restore a more natural and impassioned species of sacred oratory. The ancient preacher was frequently interrupted by bursts of applause, clapping of hands, and acclamations of assent. Chrysostom says :—" We need not your applause or tumultuous approbation," and asks for silence. These tokens of admiration are to be compared, not with the devout exclamations of the Methodists, in their more illiterate assemblies, but with the cheers of our anniversary meetings, if not with the turbulent praise of the House of Commons. The great preacher last named, found it necessary, therefore, to remind the Christians of Antioch that they were not in the theatre. Yet such signs of sympathy in the people, when moderate and decorous, were expected and approved. For example, Augustine thus closes a sermon : " *Audistis, laudastis ; Deo gratias.*"

In early times, public preaching was by no means confined to the Lord's day ; and its frequency indicates a great interest in divine things on the part of the public. It is necessary only to look through a number of consecutive sermons of Augustine, particularly at the beginning and end of each, to learn that he was accustomed to preach very often, and during sacred seasons for several days in succession, and at times more than once in the same day. Seasons of extraordinary religious emotion are always signalized by this avidity for the word. So it was at the

Reformation. Luther preached almost daily at Wittemberg, and Calvin at Geneva, as did Knox and Welsh in Scotland. And so it will be again when religion is greatly revived in our own land.

As a matter of course, the great body of ancient sermons has passed into oblivion; but enough remains to give us a very complete notion of the way in which the fathers treated divine subjects before the people. Of the Greeks, we possess discourses of Origen, Eusebius of Cæsarea, Gregory Thaumaturgus, Athanasius, Basil, the Gregories of Nyssa and Nazianzen, Cyril, Macarius, Amphilochius and Chrysostom. In all these the traces of Gentile rhetoric are visible. Of the Latins, none are so remarkable as Ambrose, Augustine, and Leo the Great. To gain some fair conception of the manner adopted, it would be well for every student acquainted with the ancient languages, to peruse a few discourses of Basil, Chrysostom, and Augustine. He will discover amidst all the elegance of the golden-tongued Greek, an admirable simplicity in the exposition of Scripture in regular course, as, for example, in the numerous sermons on the Romans; and a fidelity of direct reproof, worthy of imitation in all ages. What are called the *Sermones* of Augustine are not only shorter—perhaps from abridgment by the notary—but in every respect more scattering, planless, and extemporaneous, but at the same time full of genius, full of eloquence, full of piety, all clothed in a Latinity, which, though not Augustan, and sometimes even provincial and Punic, carries with it a glow and a stateliness of march, which oftener reminds us of the Roman orator than the elaborate exactness of Lactantius, the "Christian Cicero." If, sometimes he indulges in a solecism, for the sake of the *plebs Christiana* of Carthage, it is not unconsciously; and we seem to see him smile when he says in apology, "Dum omnes instruantur, grammatici non timeantur." He even begs pardon for the form *fenerat;* though this is used by Martial and occurs continually in the Digests. And of a blessed neologism he thus speaks: "Christ Jesus, that is *Christus* SALVATOR. For this is the Latin of JESUS. The grammarians need not inquire how Latin it is, but the Christians how true. For *salus* is a Latin noun. *Salvare* and *salvator*, indeed, were not Latin, before the

Saviour *(Salvator)* came ; when he came to the Latins he made this word Latin." * But we check our hand, on a subject, which from its tempting copiousness, is better fitted for a monograph. On this period of patristical eloquence much remains to be written. There are good things in Fénélon, Maury, Gisbert, Theremin, and above all in Villemain ; but we have reason to long for a work of research and taste, which shall present the modern and English reader with adequate specimens and a complete history and criticism of the great pulpit orators of the Greek and Latin Churches.

Pursuing our ramble among old Churches, we leap without further apology into the middle age, in order to say that in this period, about which there is so much dispute and so little knowledge, preaching could not but suffer a great decadence, when sound letters and taste fell as low as religion. When every other description of oratory became corrupt, it is not to be expected that sacred eloquence should abide in strength. Among the Greeks, it sank under the influence of superstition, frigid rhetoric, tinsel, and bombast. In the Latin Church, plagiarists and abridgers took the place of genuine preachers. The method of postillating came in ; that is, of uttering a short and jejune discourse after the lesson ; *post illa (*sc. *verba Domini)* hence the name *postill.* The diction and style of Latin preaching decayed with the general language. Preaching in the vernacular was not unknown in the West, but grew less and less impressive. At times of great popular excitement, when crowds were flocking after crusading captains, or trembling before the invading Turk, there were vehemently passionate harangues, and we have instances of street and field-preaching. What great revivals are with us, were those simultaneous awakenings of religious emotion which sometimes stirred the entire population of large districts. These engendered a sort of eloquence which in degree was high enough, but of which few records appear in our books of history. Among the most extraordinary actors in these moving dramas were the *Flagellantes, Giesseler,* or Whippers, of the fourteenth century. We find an account of the entrance of these

* Serm. ccxcix.

penitentiary fanatics into Strasburg, in the year 1349. The universal panic in expectation of invasion, and even of the judgment-day, prepared the people for singular impressions. About two hundred entered the city, in solemn procession, singing those ghastly hymns which were chief instruments of their work. Their flaunting banners were of the costliest silk and satin. They carried lighted tapers, and all the bells of the country sounded at their approach. Their mantles and cowls bore red crosses, and as they chanted together, they would sometimes kneel and sometimes prostrate themselves. Multitudes joined themselves to their number, for purposes of penance, and subjected themselves to the fearful lacerations of self-flagellation, from which the order took its name. The discourses delivered by these sombre itinerants were in every way fitted to harrow up the consciences, and beget the religious fears in which middle-age popery had delighted.

Every reader of Church history is familiar with the preaching friars, as they were called. The same enthusiasm, and the same successes, attended their progress from land to land. That branch of the Franciscan Minorites, called the Capuchins, is well known, even in our day, to every traveller in Europe. The bare head, filthy robe, and tangled beard, occur in many a picture. The cant of these holy beggars has received the distinctive title of *capucinade*, a vulgar but impressive sort of preaching, which was found very serviceable to the Church of Rome. In the *Lager* of Wallenstein, the most comic and at the same time the most Shakspearian of Schiller's productions, the camp-sermon of the Capuchin is one of the most felicitous parts. It was, evidently, in the mind of Scott, when he depicted, in exaggerated burlesque, the fanatic preacher of the Covenant in Old Mortality. As to preaching before the Reformation, it needs scarcely be repeated here, that as a part of regular religious worship in churches, it had fallen very much into desuetude. The great preachers of Popery were raised up as the result of a reaction against Protestant reform.

The modern pulpit really dates from the Reformation. With few exceptions the Reformers were mighty preachers, and some of them wielded an influence in this way which far surpassed all their efforts with the pen, and was felt over half Europe. In the British isles the power of the Word was particularly felt. Cranmer, Latimer, and Jewell, in their several varieties of eloquence, awakened an interest in the new doctrines which nothing was able to allay. The fearless tongue of John Knox, even against princes, has been noted as fully by foes as friends. In the recorded specimens of his sermons, if we translate them out of the atrocious Scotch spelling, and the fetters of the uncouthest dialect ever pronounced, there are apparent both power and elegance. From that day to this, the Presbyterians of Scotland have been, above all people, lovers of the preached Word.

Some of the more prominent characteristics of the Scottish pulpit are familiarly known. It was at once expository, doctrinal, methodical, and impassioned. For ages it was without book, as it still is in a great degree; for the country parishes retain all their ancient contempt for the "paper-minister;" notwithstanding the eloquent examples of reading by such men as Chalmers, Irving, Candlish, and Hamilton. The citation of Scripture passages, and the custom of "turning up" the same in the little Bible of the hearer, have given a peculiarly textual character to Scottish sermons. The great stress laid upon strong and tender emotion at the Lord's Table, the meeting of several ministers and multitudes of people on sacramental occasions, and the continuance of these services during several days, have contributed to an unction and pathos which have been extended to our own churches, among the purer settlements of strict Presbyterians. The power of the pulpit has, therefore, been nowhere more manifest. No public authority has ever availed to silence this mode of popular agitation and rebuke.

In the sermons of the Scottish Church two very unlike tendencies are clearly distinguishable; one is the fondness for scholastic method and minute subdivision, derived from the dialectical turn of the people, and the familiarity of the preachers with the severe manuals of Calvinistic theology; the other is the disposition to give outlet to high religious feeling. In some portions of the Kirk both have been active throughout the entire period; there have been manifest the acumen and ratiocinative precision, as well as what Buchanan calls the *ingenium perfervi-dum Scotorum*. This has been diversified by the constant practice of lecturing in the forenoon service, which has maintained expository preaching for three hundred years, and done much to mould the religious temper of the nation. There was indeed a period in the eighteenth century, when the chill of Moderatism fell upon public discourses, in a part of the Church, producing the tame literary elegance of Robertson and Blair. But the same age produced the Erskines of the Secession, in one school of homiletics, and Walker and Witherspoon in another. The Ecclesiastical Characteristics and the Corporation of Servants, did much to stigmatize the unfaithfulness of the frigid preachers, and even to open the way for those triumphs of principle which have since resulted in the strength and fervour of the Free Church. It would carry us beyond all due limits to enlarge on the new modes of pulpit discourse which have owed their origin to the brilliant but sometimes misleading example of Chalmers and his imitators. This great preacher, admirable as he appears in his printed works, can never be fully comprehended by those who never heard him. The cool reader has time to pause over sole-cisms of language and excesses of amplification, which were put utterly beyond the hearer's sense by the thunder of his delivery. When Dr John M. Mason, on his return from Scotland, was asked wherein lay Chalmers's great strength, he replied, " It is his blood-earnestness."

The free course of our remarks has led us somewhat further than we intended, and we must go back to gather up a few observations respecting the English pulpit, more, however, in the way of desultory observation than of historical detail. From the very beginning of Reformation times, the pulpit has been a potent engine of popular impression in England. Indeed, we suppose that at no time has preaching been more powerful in its influence on the people, than before the rise of those corruptions which rent the Aglican Church, and drew off some of its greatest minds to the side of Puritanism. When this rupture took place,

it is just to say, that in many of the greatest qualities of preaching, the true succession was in the line of non-conformity. But
it is impossible to ignore the fact, that in some important attributes, the Anglican pulpit is the greatest of which the press has
given any record. As the movement party was characterized
by great warmth, extemporaneous flow, and assault on the
religious passions, it became at once a necessity and a fashion for
churchmen to cultivate a species of discourse which was more
learned, more accurate, and more sedate. We do not mean to
admit the force of the vulgar taunt, that the Puritans, as a body,
were deficient in learning. The first generation of Dissenters
numbered among them some of the most profound scholars in the
Christian world. Yet, as the lines diverged, and the Non-conformists were excluded from the great seats of learning and all
the emoluments of the Church, the difference in this particular
became more marked; and notwithstanding some brilliant
exceptions, it must be acknowledged, that in point of erudition
and elegant letters, the dissenting ministers of England, as a body,
are inferior to the established clergy. The latter, indeed, vaunted
of this difference much beyond any substantial ground, and
sometimes made the pulpit a place for dogmatic discussion and
patristic lore, to a degree which was unseasonable and offensive.
In its more favourable manifestations, the learning of the Anglican Church has been nobly brought out in defence of the truth;
especially against the Freethinkers, the Unitarians, and the
Papists. A body of divinity might be compiled solely from the
sermons of great English divines; a library might be filled with
the elaborate dissertations which they have preached.

No one could reasonably expect us, in an article of such
limits and character as this, to recite the splendid roll of English
preachers; but there are a few whom we would earnestly commend to the notice of every theological student. Omitting
entirely the great names which occur in an earlier period, it is
important to mention the four bright luminaries, Barrow, Taylor,
South, and Tillotson, each so unrivalled in his way, and all so
unlike. Barrow was an extraordinary man, as a traveller, a
philologist, a mathematician, and a divine. He read Chrysostom

at Constantinople before he was made Greek Professor at Cambridge. He was predecessor of Sir Isaac Newton in the mathematical chair. Both pursuits tended to make him the eloquent reasoner. It was the age of long periodic sentences, such as appal modern lungs, and Barrow knew how to give a sonorous swell and climacteric advance to his Demosthenic passages. Many is the period in his pages, which for matter might fit out the whole fifteen minutes' sermon of a dapper Oxonian of our times. He abounds in high argument, which is more inflamed by passion than coloured by decoration. His noblest passages leave us thrilling with his passion, rather than captivated by his imagination. He is sometimes too abundant, and sometimes unwieldy; but not dull, not weak, not quaint. A ponderous earnestness and a various wealth, strike you in every page. With Barrow, multitude of words is never verbosity, and length of discussion is never diffuseness; it is massive strength without brevity. Hence, we do not wonder that the great Chatham should have taken him as a model, reading over some of his sermons as much as twenty times. " In his sermons," says Mr Grainger, " he knew not how to leave off writing, till he had exhausted his subject; and his admirable discourse on the duty and reward of bounty to the poor took him up three hours and a-half in preaching." His bust in Westminster Abbey will be fresh in the recollection of all clerical travellers.

How abrupt is the transition to the " Shakspeare of the pulpit!" Bishop Taylor, in his own manner, has had a few imitators, but never a competitor. If we except the great dramatist, no man can be named in any department of literature, who stands more clearly alone. Never were there sermons, we suppose, which purely for intellectual pleasure have been read with such satisfaction. In everything but the outward guise, they are often the highest poetry. Imagination has no flights more lofty and adventurous, than many which have been quoted again and again. He soars in a grand similitude, with a boldness of preparation and a sustaining power of wing, and then descends to the earth with a graceful undulation and gentle subsidence, which are absolutely without a parallel. The voluptuous melody of the rhythm gives a charm to his diction. Interwoven with these brilliant strands of fancy, there is often a subtle thread of argumentation which wins your assent before you are aware; often, unfortunately, to worse than semipelagian laxity; for Taylor was very remote from the orthodoxy of his day. Along with all this, there is poured out upon us a profusion of learning as from a golden horn of plenty. No preacher of our day would venture to quote as much Greek, during his whole life, as Jeremy Taylor sometimes brings out in a single sermon. But the reminiscences and allusions of classic learning spin from him spontaneously in every paragraph. While his invective is sometimes of a scalding heat, he is often tender and pathetic; and there is a scholarly negligence in the style which charms while it baffles all attempts at imitation. It must now be admitted that with all these claims to our wonder, Taylor seldom makes prominent the peculiarly gracious doctrines of the evangelical system. There is a saintly calm about his ethics, which reminds us of the purer class of Romish preachers, but the ascetic directions and the exaltation of human merit belong to the blemishes of the same school. The amplitude of his comparisons, sometimes conducted with a sameness of display which runs into mannerism, did not escape the censure even of his contemporaries, and was plainly struck at by the following sentences of the austere and caustic South : " Nothing here [namely in Paul's preaching] of the ' fringes of the north star ;' nothing of ' Nature's becoming unnatural ;' nothing of the ' down of angel's wings,' or the ' beautiful locks of cherubims :' no starched similitudes, introduced with a ' *Thus have I* seen a cloud rolling in its airy mansion, and the like.' "*

---

* Compare the famous passage from Taylor : " For so have I seen a lark rising from his bed of grass, and soaring upwards, singing as he rises, and hopes to get to heaven, and climb above the clouds ; but the poor bird was beaten back with the loud sighings of an eastern wind, and his motion made irregular and inconstant, descending more at every breath of the tempest, than it could recover by the libration and frequent weighing of his wings ; till the little creature was forced to sit down and pant, and stay till the storm was over ; and then it made a prosperous flight, and did rise and sing,

But a single perusal of any one of those beautiful passages, of which the above is so clever, and so cruel a travesty, will instantly obliterate the criticism from the mind of any tasteful reader. Though it would end in ludicrous disaster for any one now to try to preach like Jeremy Taylor, we are persuaded that the study of his works would be an excellent regimen for young clergymen, especially for such as labour under the diseases of coldness and lethargy. It would at least stimulate them to warmer effusions, and would show them that logic and immensely fertile learning are compatible with a flow of elegance and an exuberant illustration, such as we commonly seek only in verse.

We speak of the "witty South," as familiarly as of the "judicious Hooker," and with less fear of any exception. But we despise the man, while we admire the genius. South was a veritable Vicar of Bray, trimming his sails to every gust of popular or royal favour. It is amusing to find this scourge of dissent beginning his career at Oxford, with a paper of Latin verse in eulogy of Cromwell. He afterwards had rich livings and stalls and high diplomatic places. When it was no longer profitable to truckle to the Stuarts, he took the oath of allegiance to William and Mary.

We are now fairly beyond the region of fancy, pathos, or eloquence, in its ordinary sense. South is clear, strong, saturnine, and truculent. He is a cogent reasoner, always observing

as if it had learned music and motion from an angel, as he passed sometimes through the air, about his ministries here below : so is the prayer of a good man ; when his affairs have required business, and his business was matter of discipline, and his discipline was to pass upon a sinning person, or had a design of charity, his duty met with infirmities of a man, and anger was its instrument, and the instrument became stronger than the prime agent, and raised a tempest, and overruled the man ; and then his prayer was broken, and his thoughts were troubled, and his words went up towards a cloud, and his thoughts pulled them back again, and made them without intention ; and the good man sighs for his infirmity, but must be content to lose the prayer, and he must recover it when his anger is removed, and his spirit is becalmed, made even as the brow of Jesus, and smooth like the heart of God ; and then it ascends to heaven upon the wings of the holy dove, and dwells with God, till it returns, like the useful bee, loaded with a blessing and the dew of heaven."

an exact method, and establishing his point by the most effective reasoning. He seldom quotes, never displays his reading, and always advances with directness, brevity, and a sort of bull-dog fierceness to his purposed end. Where his terrible prejudices do not come into play, he commands our highest respect, as in some of his masterly arguments for divine predestination; but in other places he bends his tremendous powers against the other doctrines of grace. It would be difficult to find in any language such insufferable rebukes of worldly indulgence, as in certain sermons of South. But his dark and bitter sarcasm is chiefly expended on the Puritans; and he leaves any subject to deal a blow at these enemies, when no longer in power. It is difficult to speak of his style without danger of exaggeration. It combines some of the highest excellencies of human language. Being always sourly in earnest, he never makes ornament or elegance an object of study, though he often attains them. Rotundity and periodicity in sentences are not sought. But he is perpetually clear, energetic, vivacious, and memorable. He strikes us as far before his age in English writing, as having by the prerogative of genius seized upon the imperishable part of the language, and as having attained the excellencies of such prose as that of Pope and Warburton. The antithetic character prevails throughout, and this always ensures brevity, and gives opportunity for that tremendous sting which makes the end of many a paragraph like the tail of a scorpion. This venom is for the most part distilled on the Non-conformists. A few quotations will not only exemplify his manner, but illustrate the homiletics of that day, by showing what were the charges brought against the Puritan pulpit. Speaking of falsehood, he says: "But to pass from that to fanatic treachery, that is, from one twin to the other: how came such multitudes of our own nation, at the beginning of that monstrous rebellion, to be spunged of their plate and money, their rings and jewels, for the carrying on of the schismatical, dissenting, king-killing cause? Why, next to their own love of being cheated, it was the public, or rather prostitute faith of a company of faithless miscreants that drew them in and deceived them. And how

came so many thousands to fight and die in the same rebellion?
Why, they were deceived into it by those spiritual trumpeters
who followed them with continual alarms of damnation, if they
did not venture life, fortune, and all, in that which wickedly
and devilishly those impostors called the *cause of God.*" In his
two sermons " against long extemporary prayer," he thus distills
his gall: " Two whole hours for one prayer, at a fast, used to
be reckoned but a moderate dose; and that for the most part
fraught with such irreverent, blasphemous expressions, that to
repeat them would profane the place I am speaking in; and
indeed they seldom ' carried on the work of such a day,' as
their phrase was, but they left the church in need of a new
consecration. Add to this, the incoherence and confusion, the
endless repetitions, and the insufferable nonsense that never
failed to hold out, even with their utmost prolixity; so that in
all their long fasts, from first to last, from seven in the morning
to seven in the evening, which was their measure, the pulpit
was ever the emptiest thing in the church; and I never knew
such a fast kept by them, but their hearers had cause to begin a
thanksgiving as soon as they were done." " The consciences of
men," he says again, " have been filled with wind and noise,
empty notion and pulpit-tattle. So that amongst the most
seraphical *illuminati*, and the highest Puritan perfectionists, you
shall find people of fifty, three-score and four-score years old,
not able to give that account of their faith, which you might
have had heretofore of a boy of nine or ten. Thus far had the
pulpit (by accident) disordered the church, and the desk must
restore it. For you know the main business of the pulpit, in
the late times, was to please and pamper a proud, senseless
humour, or rather a kind of spiritual itch, which had then seized
the greatest part of the nation, and worked chiefly about their
ears; and none were so overrun with it, as the holy sisterhood,
the daughters of Zion, and the matrons of the New Jerusalem,
as they called themselves. These brought with them ignorance
and itching ears in abundance; and Holderforth equalled them
in one, and gratified them in the other. So that whatsoever
the doctrine was, the application still ran on the surest side; for

to give those doctrine and usemen, those pulpit-engineers, their
due, they understood how to plant their batteries, and to make
their attacks perfectly well; and knew that by pleasing the
wife, they should not fail to preach the husband in their pocket."
Our own day might learn a lesson from the fling at the prophetic preachers, who interpreted Scripture, " as if, forsooth,
there could not be so much as a few houses fired, a few ships
taken, or any other calamity befall this little corner of the
world, but that some apocalyptic ignoramus or other must presently find and pick it out of some abused martyred prophecy of
Ezekiel, Daniel, or the Revelation." It was South, who, in a
sermon said of Milton, " as the Latin advocate, who, *like a blind
adder*, has spit so much poison upon the king's person;" and
who says of the opposition to liturgies : " I question not, but
that fanatic fury was then at that height, that they would have
even laughed at Christ himself in his devotions, *had he but used
his own prayer*." But one grows weary of malice, however
epigrammatic. When the same edge is turned against prevailing sins, especially among courtiers, it does great execution.
We would send no man to South for gentle, persuasive,
melting, spiritual instruction ; but the scholar may gain from
him many lessons of dialectic force, of directness and pungency,
of earnest, indignant invective, and of pithy, apothegmatic
declamation. The vice of his method is indicated by one of
his own sayings : " That is not wit, which comporteth not with
wisdom."

It is refreshing to turn from such a malignant, to the sweet
and gentle Tillotson. The good archbishop's father was a York-
shire clothier, a stern Calvinist; perhaps this may account for
the son's mildness towards dissent. But in Kneller's great portrait at Lambeth, we discern the unmistakable lineaments of
holy peace, joined with everything that a wise churchman might
wish in the personal presence of a primate. In this, though for
other reasons we might compare the picture with that of Bossuet,
which ennobles the gallery of his native Dijon. Burnet testifies
of Tillotson, after long acquaintance, that " he had a clear head,
with a most tender and compassionate heart ; he was a faithful

and zealous friend, but a gentle and soon conquered enemy; his
notions of morality were fine and sublime, his thread of reasoning was easy, clear, and solid; he was not only the best preacher
of the age, but seemed to have brought preaching to perfection;
his sermons were so well liked, that all the nation proposed him
as a pattern, and studied to copy after him." Such was the
judgment of contemporaries. After his death, there was found a
bundle of bitter libels, which had been published against him,
preserved, and endorsed with his own hand as follows : "I forgive the authors of these books, and pray God that he may, also,
forgive them." When the Huguenot Refugees sought the
prayers of the Church, Beveridge, with genuine Episcopalian
etiquette, scrupled to read a brief to this effect, in Canterbury
Cathedral, because it was against some rubric. "Doctor, doctor," replied the wiser, greater Tillotson, "Charity is above
rubrics." We are not to suppose, however, because the. archbishop was good and gentle, that he was either feeble in
argument or tame in controversy. Against both infidels and
papists, his sermons afford some of the most powerful apologetic
treatises which have ever been composed. His argument on
Transubstantiation would singly be sufficient to make the fortune
of a common disputant. Vulgar minds so commonly think that
what is very clear must be very shallow, that reasoners of great
simplicity and perspicuity are in danger of losing credit; and
such, we believe, has been the case with Tillotson, in our day.
He was so little offensive to Dissenters, being indeed the friend
of John Howe, that his works would have been widely read and
long preserved in our churches, if the stature of his theology had
not fallen far below the mark which Evangelical Calvinism fixes
as a standard. But there is a boundless store of wealth in all
those discourses which treat of Natural Religion, the difficulties
of infidelity, the absurdities of Popery, and the neglected circle
of Christian duties. The style of Tillotson is gracefully negli-
gent, sometimes even flat, but generally agreeable, invariably
perspicuous, and at times eminently happy, from his idiomatic
English ; it is well known that Addison took him as a model.
For studied ornament, and the glow of oratorical passion, he

will never be quoted ; but a better model of didactic or practical discourse could scarcely be chosen.

If our object had been to go fully into the history of the Anglican pulpit, we should have inserted many other names ; but then we should have written a volume. Among these we should have found a place for Atterbury, a man of worldly character, but great force, and often superior to Tillotson in the elaborate graces and warmth of oratory. We could not have omitted Bull and Waterland, whose learned and profound vindication of Athanasian truth will abide as a venerable and unequalled monument, as long as our language shall be the vehicle of sound theology ; Samuel Clarke, the friend and interpreter of Newton ; Secker and Ogden, smooth, judicious, and instructive sermonizers;

ently, Butler, Warburton, and Horsley, giants in theological conflict. But these and many others must be left unrecorded. The perusal of all will only serve to evince more fully the justice of our statement, that the predominant quality of the Anglican pulpit, has been learned and extensive instruction. A manner corresponding to this has prevailed even till our day. Sermons have been read from the manuscript, with little elevation of voice, little action of body, and no fervour of delivery. As the liturgy has become the crowning part of public services, the sermon has become more attenuated in matter and curtailed in length ; until, in many a fashionable church and chapel, there is a cold essay of fifteen minutes. The mode just now is to cultivate what is called a " quiet manner ; " by which is meant a *nonchalant* utterance, such as may persuade the hearer that preaching, after all, is almost a work of supererogation. There have indeed been Simeons, Melvilles, and M'Neiles; but these are *raræ aves* in the Anglican flock. Though a Scotchman, Blair was in all respects a sermonizer after the English heart, and his discourses had immense currency south of the Tweed. No manly critic can read without contempt his pretended survey of the British pulpit, in his Lectures. Amply has the truth been avenged by John Foster's strictures on the once famous sermons of Blair himself. " After reading five or six sermons," says Foster, " we become assured that we must perfectly see the whole compass of his powers, and that, if there were twenty volumes, we might read on through the whole, without once coming to a broad conception, or a profound investigation, or a burst of genuine enthusiasm. A reflective reader will perceive his mind fixed in a wonderful sameness of feeling throughout a whole volume; it is hardly relieved a moment, by surprise, delight, or labour, and at length becomes very tiresome; perhaps a little analogous to the sensations of a Hindoo while fulfilling his vow, to remain in one certain posture for a month. A sedate formality of manner is invariably kept up through a thousand pages, without the smallest danger of once luxuriating into a beautiful irregularity. A great many people of gayety, rank, and fashion, have occasionally a feeling that a little easy quantity of religion would be a good thing; because it is too true, after all, that we cannot be staying in this world always, and when one gets out of it, why, there may be some hardish matters to settle in the other place. The Prayer-book of a Sunday is a good deal to be sure toward making all safe, but then it is really so tiresome; for penance, it is very well, but to say one likes it, one cannot for the life of one. If there were some tolerable religious things that one could read now and then without trouble, and think it about half as pleasant as a game of cards, it would be comfortable. One should not be so frightened about what we must all come to some time. Now nothing could have been more to the purpose than these sermons; they were welcomed as the very thing. They were unquestionably about religion, and grave enough in all conscience, yet they were elegant; they were so easy to comprehend throughout, that the mind was never detained a moment to think; they were undefiled by Methodism; they but little obtruded peculiar doctrinal notions; they applied very much to high life, and the author was evidently a gentleman; the book could be discussed as a matter of taste, and its being seen in the parlour excited no surmise that any one in the house had lately been converted. Above all, it was most perfectly free from that disagreeable and mischievous property attributed to the eloquence of Pericles, that it 'left stings behind.'"

If we retrace our steps to the last point of departure, in order to consider the preaching of the Non-conformists, we shall find abundant cause to believe, that even after being politically defeated and overthrown at the Restoration, they continued to possess learning, eloquence, and piety, such as were worthy of that great Church of England, of which they were really though not nominally a part. It is somewhat remarkable, that, notwithstanding the extraordinary theological interest which characterized the Puritans and the voluminous works which proceeded from their great men, these less frequently took the precise form of sermons, than was the case with their churchly oppressors. Most of them, it is true, left numerous sermons, but the great mass of their religious writings were given to the public in the shape of treatises and protracted works. This did not certainly arise from any undervaluing of the pulpit ; indeed, an over-estimate of this instrument was universally laid to their charge ; they preached more frequently, more fervently, and at greater length, than the beneficed divines, and these exercises were attended by greater throngs of animated hearers. But the sermon, as a species of literary creation, was less an object of separate regard. They were more accustomed to the effusion of thought and feeling in language suggested at the moment of delivery ; and even when they studied for successive months and years on particular books of Scripture, or heads of theology, and preached constantly of the same, the utterances of the church were not identical with the labours of the study, and the latter continued to retain that form which we now observe in their published works. Of some great treatises we know assuredly, and of others we have the strongest presumption, that they contain the substance of a series of pulpit discourses. This we suppose may be affirmed concerning the greatest works of the most eminent Puritan divines. We need scarcely add, that they had among them some of the mightiest preachers whom the Church has ever seen. Whether we judge by extant remains, or by the testimony of coevals, Richard Baxter was one of these. In our judgment, the English language was never more dexterously wielded by any writer. The thing most observable is, that it is the language of the common people, that which does not grow obsolete, that which is racy with idiomatic anomaly, that which obeys every impulse of the heaving mind, that which goes direct to the heart. His perspicuity is absolutely cloudless. When he chooses to inveigh against sin, or to thunder from the legal mount, or to depict the doom of sinners, or to awaken the slumbering sinner, he is terrific and irresistible. In graceful description he paints without a superior. And for melting pathos, such as soothes the soul and opens the hidden spring of tears, what can be compared to some passages of the Saint's Rest? Baxter was often betrayed by his native subtlety and his familiarity with the schoolmen, into an intricacy of excessive distinctions which mars all the beauties of his style ; and though this occurs more in his controversies than his pulpit labours, we should never think of setting up his sermons as the greatest of his works. The eminent piety which breathes through his practical writings makes him a model for the preacher and pastor of every subsequent age.

The number of distinguished Puritan preachers is so great that we should not dare to attempt enumeration ; and if we used selection, we should name those who are familiar to our readers. Of Owen and his works, we have lately written, at some length, in a separate article. In connection with the argumentative force and profound experience of this greatest of the Puritans, the student of theology will remember the silver current and figured diction of Bates ; the sweet and simple eloquence of Flavel; the sententious brilliancy of Charnock, like the iridescence of crystals on the surface of a massive rock ; and, perhaps, above them all, the majestic strength of Howe, a grave and stately bearing of mind, which looks down on the quaint antitheses and foreign images of his contemporaries. In John Howe we meet a writer who seems entirely free from the vicious passions of his day, in thought and language. He even shuns the conventional phrases of the Calvinistic schools, while he teaches their theology. But he was a great Christian philosopher, imbued with the choicest literature of the ancients, and trained, by long meditation, to expatiate in tracts of spiritual truth, where superficial minds will never follow him. His

manner is said to have been in a high degree engaging and impressive. If any one will collate his sermon on the " Vanity of
Man as mortal," with the famous discourse on the same topic by
Robert Hall, who profoundly admired him, he will find the
germs of the latter in the former; yet, in everything but the
exquisite finish of Hall's style, we think the palm must be given
to the older divine.

The succeeding generations certainly manifest a decline in
regard to the annals of the dissenting pulpit. Even before we
come down to the latter half of the eighteenth century, and leaving entirely out of view the lamentable defection from the faith
of many Independents, and of most called Presbyterians, it must
be admitted that the age of great English preachers was past.
That title we unhesitatingly give to Watts and Doddridge.
Both, in our opinion, have undeservedly fallen into the shade.
For fertility, facility, graceful fluency of thought, charms of
illustration, and delightful variety, we know no one who excels
Watts, in any period. His theological whimsies are well known,
and he is not what we denominate a great doctrinal preacher;
but the warmth of love, and the play of sanctified imagination,
give a stamp to most of his sermons which we would gladly
recall to the notice of the younger ministry. Doddridge was a
safer and a graver mind, and, according to all canons, a better
builder of sermons. Some of his discourses come near being
master-pieces; they instruct the mind and elevate the heart;
those addressed to youth, and those on Regeneration, have been
reprinted again and again, and have won the admiration even of
severe judges. They labour sometimes under a fault of style
belonging to a particular school of Dissenters at that period, and
which, for lack of a better phrase, we may call a sort of genteel
affectionateness, or a tenderness of endearing blandishment; but
this is forgotten amidst the great amount of saving truth, expressed in language which is always clear and pleasing. It does
not fall within our plan to enumerate the celebrated dissenting
preachers of a later day and of our own times.

To those who have a facility in the language, we commend
the careful study of the French pulpit; for to speak of preach-

ing, and not to name the times of Louis the Fourteenth, would
be like discoursing of sculpture without allusion to the age of
Pericles. Considered as a product of literary art, the sermon
never attained such completeness, beauty and honour, as at this
period. Our remark must not be taken apart from our limitations. We do not say it was most apostolic, most scriptural, or
most fitted to reach the great spiritual end of preaching; the
results show that such was not the fact. But viewed in relation
to letters, logic, and eloquence, as a structure of genius and
taste, the French sermon, in the hands of its great orators, had
a rhetorical perfection as distinctly marked as the Greek drama.
We are constrained to look upon it in much the same light. The
plays of Corneille and the victories of Turenne were not more
powerful in penetrating the public mind, than the oratory of
Notre Dame. Rank and fashion, including royalty itself,
thronged the church, as if it were a theatre, wondering and
weeping. Madame de Sevigné, the best painter of her age,
speaks of a *belle passion*, as the Good Friday sermon was called,
just as she speaks of the Cid. The greatest scholars and critics
of the Augustan era of France, saw their ideal of faultless composition realized in the pulpit. The culmination of the art was
rapid, and the decline soon followed. No one will claim more
than a few names for the catalogue of masterly French preachers;
Bourdaloue, Bossuet, Fenelon, Massillon, Fléchier. Many who
had a temporary vogue in their day, have been forgotten; but
these sustain the ordeal of time. We shall offer a few remarks on some of them, but chiefly on the unapproachable
triumvirate.

To Bourdaloue is unhesitatingly given the honour of having
raised the French pulpit at once to its greatest height. The
judgment of our day is coming more and more to acquiesce in
the decision which ranks him clearly first. We may see in La
Bruyère how degenerate preaching had become before his day.
It was florid, quaint, affected, perplexed with divisions, and
overlaid with impertinent learning. He restored it to reason
and to nature. No misapprehension can be greater than that
which imagines Bourdaloue to have been a man of show, a

gaudy rhetorician, or a declaimer. He was, of course, a strenuous Papist, he was even a Jesuit; but assuming his Church to
be right, there never was a more unanswerable reasoner in her
behalf. It is reasoning, above all things else, which is his
characteristic. Seldom does he utter even a few sentences
without a connected argument. The amount of matter in his
discourses, which are sometimes very long, is truly wonderful.
His power of condensation, his exactness of method, his singular
clearness, and his animated force, enable him to throw an elaborate argument into a single head. The glory of his art is his
magical ability to clothe the subtlest reasoning, in diction so
beautiful, as to captivate even the unthinking. In our view, his
sermons are a study for the young logician. Even when he is
defending the extremest errors of Rome, as in his discourse on
the saving merit of alms, we feel that we are in the hands of a
terrible antagonist. Amidst passages of incomparable fire he
seems constrained to indulge his propensity for laying a train of
proofs. Thus in his passion-sermon, on the power of the cross,
he inserts in the first and greatest part, a series of admirable
arguments for the truth of Christianity.

In some points which concern the outward form of the discourse, Bourdaloue left much to be reformed by his great
successors. His divisions are bold and numerous, and are
stated not only with openness, but with a repetition which we
have seen nowhere else. So far from hiding the articulations
of his work, he is anxious that they should be observed and
never forgotten; but he so varies the formulas of partition, and
so beautifies the statement of transitions, by ingenious turns,
that the mind is gratified by the exquisiteness of the expression.
It had been the fashion to quote the Fathers very largely.
Bourdaloue retains this practice. He even seems to wish that
his whole performance should rest on citations; and some of
them look like centos from Chrysostom, Ambrose, Augustine,
and Gregory. But his management of this is graceful and
masterly. And it is entertaining to observe with how rich and
eloquent an amplification he will paraphrase and apply one of
these little Latin sentences, often bringing it in again and again

to close some striking period, and making it ring on the ear
with happy vehemence at the climax of a paragraph.

If the observation be modified by our protest against the
enormities of Popish falsehood, we are willing to say that
Bourdaloue was eminently a spiritual, warm, and edifying
preacher. Upon the sufferings of Christ, the love of God, the
vanity of the world, and the delights of heavenly contemplation,
he speaks with a solemnity and an unction, which explain to us
the admiration felt for him by Boileau and other Jansenists.
The manner in which Bourdaloue pronounced his discourses
must have had a power of incantation to which even their
greatness as compositions gives us no key. It was his remarkable
custom to deliver his sermons with his eyes closed; and he is
so represented in his portrait. On coming from the provinces,
to preach in the Jesuit Chapel in Paris, he was at once followed
by crowds of the highest distinction; and his popularity increased
to the very close. For thirty-four years he was equally admired
by the court, by men of letters, and by the people. To the
Christian visitor in Paris, there is something solemn in the
church of St Paul and St Lewis, to approach the tablet with
the simple inscription, HIC JACET BOURDALOUE.

Bossuet was a greater man, but not a greater preacher than
his eloquent contemporary. The reputation derived from his
vast learning, his controversial ability, his knowledge of affairs,
and his strength of will, we very naturally transfer to his
preaching, which was nevertheless of consummate excellence.
As an author, especially as a master of style, he surpasses them
all, if indeed he does not surpass all who ever wrote in French.
The power of that somewhat intractable language was never
more fully brought out than by Bossuet, to whom the crown of
eloquence is, therefore, given by Voltaire. He was the orator
for courts, and we suppose no prince in ancient or modern times
ever had a nobler panegyrist. To learn his argumentative
eloquence, we must look to his other works; but in his celebrated Funeral Orations, we have unequalled examples of
sublime and original conceptions, arrayed in a diction majesti-
cally simple and yet triumphantly splendid. The term which

characterizes the discourses of Bossuet is magnificence. We believe it to be admitted by French critics that his style is as faultless as that of any writer in any tongue.

There are those who consider Massillon the greatest of French preachers; and the award is just, if we confine our regards to simple elegance of style, traits of nature, strokes of pathos, perfect contexture of the entire performance and irresistible command of assemblies, and in elocution. Being thirty years younger than the men we just named, he represents a different school, but it is one which he founded himself. When Father Latour, on his arrival at the capital, asked him what he thought of the great orators, he replied, " I find them possessed of genius and great talent; but if I preach, I will not preach like them." Great clearness of thought, perfect sobriety of judgment, profound knowledge of the human heart and of manners, a fund of tender emotion, novelty of illustration, copiousness of language, perspicuous method, and unerring taste, are the characteristics of Massillon. He simplified the divisions of the sermon, and reduced its length, conforming the whole treatment to the most classic models. He is sparing in his citations and unobtrusive in his array of argument. Beyond all competitors, he dissects the heart, reveals the inmost windings of motive, and awakens the emotions of terror, remorse, and pity. In the ethical field, he excels in depicting vice and awakening conscience, in pursuing pride, avarice, and self-love, to their retreats, and in exposing and stigmatizing the follies of the great. When the aged Bourdaloue heard him, he pointed him out, as he descended from the pulpit, saying, " Hunc oportet crescere, me autem minui " Baron, the great actor, said of him to a companion, " My friend, here is an orator; as for us, we are but actors." Whole assemblies were dissolved in tears, or started to their feet in consternation. When he preached the funeral sermon of the King, on the words, " Lo, I have become great;" he commenced by repeating them slowly, as if to recollect himself: then he fixed his eyes on the assembly in mourning; next he surveyed the funeral enclosure, with all its sombre pomp; and, lastly, turning his eyes on the mausoleum erected in the midst of the

cathedral—after some moments of silence, exclaimed, *Dieu seul
est grand, mes frères*. " My brethren, God alone is great!" The
immense assembly was breathless and awestruck. Voltaire
always had on his table the *Petit-Carême* of Massillon, which he
regarded as the best model of French prose.

There are discourses of Masillon, which, with the omission of
the *Ave Maria*, and a few superficial forms, might be delivered
to any Protestant assembly. The union of simple elegance and
strong passion has given his sermons a formative influence in
every language of Europe; and they stand at the head of what
may be called the modern school of preaching.

Space would fail us, if we were to enlarge upon Fenelon,
Fléchier, Bridaine, and other pulpit orators of less note.
Chastely beautiful as is the style of Archbishop Fenelon, it is not
exactly that which belongs to eloquence. The saintly gentleness
of his temper, as well as the doctrines of Quietism which he had
embraced, were not the best preparations for passionate oratory.
Among his numerous and often delightful works, the number of
sermons is not very large. One reason of this may be, that he
favoured the extemporaneous method, of which, in his Dialogue
on Eloquence, he is the ablest vindicator. There is a sermon of
Fenelon's on Foreign Missions, which is full of fine thoughts, and
worthy of examination.

The Protestant Churches of France, and of the Refugees,
produced some great preachers, of whom the most famous are
Claude and Saurin. For solid doctrinal discussion, elaborated
into the ·form of eloquent discourse, the preacher last named
continues to be admired. In our own day, there has been a
revival of Protestant eloquence, in such men as Vinet, Grand-
pierre, and Adolphe Monod; and Parisian crowds still follow
Lacordaire, Ravignan, Felix, and de Courtier.

The subject has grown upon our hands and must be dismissed,
though we leave untouched the preaching of Germany and
Holland, of the contemporary Churches of Great Britain, and
the inviting field of the American pulpit.

An enterprising publisher might benefit himself and the
Church by issuing, under wise direction, a few volumes of

sermons, which should contain none but master-pieces. There
are a few such, in each period, which stand out with great prominence, as exhibiting the highest characteristics of their respective authors. In such a selection would be found Bourdaloue's
Passion Sermon; Bossuet's Funeral Oration on Turenne; Massillon on the Small Number of the Elect; Barrow's Discourse
on the Death of Christ; Jeremy Taylor's Marriage Ring;
Maclaurin's Glorying in the Cross; Edwards on "Their feet
shall slide in due time;" Davies' Bruised Reed; Mason's
Gospel to the Poor; Hall's Modern Infidelity; Chalmers'
Expulsive Power of a New Affection; and Monod's "God is
Love;" with others, perhaps as worthy, which need not now
burden our pages. It has sometimes been made a question how
far it is desirable for a preacher to collect and study the written
labours of others. There is a use, or rather an abuse, of other
men's compositions, which is slavish and dishonourable. No
young man of independent mind and high principle will go to
books for his sermon, or for its method, or for any large continuous portion. There is a tacit covenant between preachers
and hearers, in our Church and country, which makes it a
deception for any man to preach that which is not original.
Pulpit larceny is the most unprofitable of all frauds; it is almost
certain of detection, and it leaves a stigma on the fame even
beyond its intrinsic turpitude. But surely an honest soul may
wander among valuables without any necessity of thieving.
Some have excluded books of sermons from their libraries, and
by a "self-denying ordinance" have abstained from perusing
them, lest, forsooth, they should damage their own originality.
This is about as wise as if an artist should refrain from looking
at the frescoes of the Vatican, and the galleries of Florence,
Dresden, and the Louvre. We have seen the works of a
Western painter, who is said to have acted on such a maxim;
he would see no Raffaelles or Van Dycks, lest he should spoil
his native manner. He has certainly succeeded in avoiding all
that one beholds in these great masters. But in all labours, to
the success of which, judgment, taste, and practice must com-
bine, the highest capacity of production is fostered by studying

the works of others; and we see not why this is less true in homiletics than in the arts. If a man may not read good sermons, we suppose he may not hear them. The wise student will, with the utmost avidity, both read and hear all that is accessible of the greatest achievements in the declaration of God's truth. At the same time, he will sit down to his labours as if he had known no performances but his own. He will borrow no man's plan; he will shun all repositories of skeletons and what are ironically named " Preachers' Helps;" and will be himself, even in his earliest and faintest efforts.

In any retrospect of the work of preaching in successive ages, there is one snare which the young minister of Christ cannot too solicitously avoid; it is that of looking upon the utterances of the pulpit with a mere literary eye, as objects of criticism upon the principles of rhetoric and taste. Extensive scriptural knowledge, solid thought, sound judgment, thorough inward discipline, and bursting spiritual emotions, will frame for themselves as a vehicle such a discourse as shall be truly eloquent. In this way, and in this way only, does a discourse on divine subjects come to be subjected to the rules of art. But no rules of art can ensure a sermon which shall please God; and every rule of art may seem to be observed, while yet the result shall be as " sounding brass and a tinkling cymbal." The best sermons are not those which most approach to classical perfection. As preaching is a universal function of the ministry, and intended for the whole race, that property which only one man in a million attains cannot be indispensable to its exercise; yet such a property is eloquence. If we could have revealed to us which were the thousand sermons which had most honoured Christ and most benefited men, we should perhaps find among them not one of those which have been held up as models from the desk of professors. " That is a good sermon," says Matthew Henry, " which does thee good." The greatest effects have been produced, in every age, by discourses which sinned against every precept of the schools. The sermon of John Livingstone at the Kirk of Shotts, which was the means of awakening not less than five hundred persons, was never written at all, and if we may judge by what remains to us of his writings, was in a manner exceedingly rude and homely. Yet it was kindled by the fire of God. The more profoundly we are impressed with the utter inefficacy of all intellectual construction and oratorical polish, and feel our absolute dependence on the Spirit of God in preaching, the more likely shall we be to come before God's waiting people with performances, which, however defective or anomalous, as measured by critical standards, shall answer the great end of preaching, being carried to their result by the irresistible demonstration and persuasion of the Holy Ghost.

ELOQUENCE OF THE FRENCH PULPIT.

THE age of Louis XIV. has ever been considered the most brilliant era for France. Under the conduct of the most renowned generals, it attained the highest pitch of military glory; under the encouragement given to philosophy, the most valuable discoveries were made in science; under the liberal patronage bestowed upon the fine arts, taste and genius achieved the most splendid triumphs. It was an age of truly great men—of warriors, politicians, philosophers, poets, historians—of such men as Condé and Turenne, Corneille and Racine, Descartes and Fontenelle, Montesquieu and Malebranche, Rochefoucauld and Pascal, Boileau and Rollin, and hundreds of others whose works still yield improvement and delight. It was a period, too, when eloquence of the highest kind lived and flourished. Not the eloquence of the bar; for its celebrated pleaders, in judicial contests, and the application of the law, seldom went beyond the strain of dry and logical reasoning. Not the eloquence of popular assemblies; for there were no such assemblies there to nourish the genius of liberty. Nothing of that kind existed, as in ancient Greece and Rome, and as in our own country, where the assembled people are brought under the influence of the art of speaking; where the public affairs are transacted; where those who compose the nation and make the laws can be convinced and persuaded by direct appeals to their interests and passions; where continued struggles for rights and power rouse the genius of every citizen, force to exertion every talent, inspire with enthusiasm every council, and give to orators all that can qualify them for the sublimest eloquence. There was no room for such eloquence in France at the period to which we refer.

" She sat as a queen, and said, I shall see no sorrow." After a combat of many years with the rest of Europe, she beheld provinces conquered, and kings humbled before her; she owned no superior; she feared no rival; she saw the arts and sciences raised to the highest splendour, and the most refined taste and erudition in all the walks of polite literature; she beheld all her people vying with each other in the increase and enjoyment of national glory—while the " grand monarque " sat in his palace proclaiming, "I am the government." In such circumstances, we cannot suppose that *that* high, manly, forcible eloquence, which, as an instrument of power, mingles with the busy scenes of public life, could find an existence. But all this is perfectly consistent with another kind of eloquence—the eloquence of the *Pulpit.* To be truly eloquent, the speaker must feel on a level with his auditors—at times even exercise a kind of dominion over them. The sacred orator, speaking in the name of God, can do this under any government; in the most arbitrary monarchy, he can display the same lofty freedom which the equality of citizens gives to a speaker in the active scenes of a republic. Hence, in a country where no civil freedom was enjoyed, there was an eloquence of the loftiest kind, which long flourished, which was carried to the greatest height, and which is still the object of warm admiration.

Some eloquent preachers existed in France, previous to the times of which we now speak, but whatever reputation they may have had at the time, few have attained any celebrity. They were eclipsed like tapers placed in the rays of a meridian sun.

Bossuet lived when the French language had reached a degree of maturity, and was advancing towards perfection. He first appeared in Paris in 1659; was soon invited to be one of the preachers of the court; for ten years passed through a most brilliant career; and then was promoted to the bishopric of Condom, and afterwards to that of Meaux.

He has been termed the " French Demosthenes," and well does he deserve the title; for he, of all his contemporaries, bears the greatest resemblance to the Athenian orator. He was regarded as the former, in Europe, of the eloquence of the pulpit;

and his works were directed to be studied as classic works, as men repair to Rome to improve their taste by the master-pieces of Raphael and Michael Angelo. Time, that great destroyer of ill-founded reputation, instead of impairing, has from age to age added fresh lustre to his glory.

He was devoted to the study of the Fathers, particularly of Chrysostom and Austin, from whom he drew profound maxims and convincing arguments ; and to the frequent reading of Demosthenes and Homer, to imbibe the vehemence of the one, and the imagination of the other. But he was specially sedulous in the study of the Holy Scriptures. From that divine book he drew forth the richest treasures ; in this inexhaustible mine he found the sublimest thoughts, the strongest expressions, the most eloquent descriptions, the most pathetic images. There he found history, laws, moral precepts, oratory, and poetry.

If eloquence consist in taking strong hold of a subject, knowing its resources, measuring its extent, and skilfully uniting all its parts ; in causing ideas to succeed each other, so as to bear us away with almost irresistible force ; if it consist in painting objects in such a manner as to give them life and animation ; if it consist in such a power upon the human mind as leads us to be carried along with the speaker, and to enter into all his emotions and passions, then the Bishop of Meaux is eloquent. But let us not mistake the nature of his eloquence. He was not content with gratifying his audience, or leaving their minds in a state of satisfied tranquillity, but aimed at thoroughly convincing and agitating their souls, and making such an impression as could not be easily obliterated. Everything is simple and natural— there is no affectation of pomp, no visible desire to please, no disposition to withdraw attention from the subject to the author —all is related and described in such a manner as to conceal all art. In everything there is nature, both its order and its irregularity—sometimes rising to the mountain-top, and sometimes descending to the valleys—sometimes the winding and transparent rivulet, and sometimes the mighty cataract which astonishes and overwhelms.

Few of his sermons that have come down to us received his

finishing hand.   The greater part are sketches—full and perfect as far as they go, and filled up at the time of delivery.   They were such, too, as he never repeated, after he left Paris; for when he became bishop, though he preached much, yet he wrote not his sermons, but trusted to the occasion for language, after profoundly studying his subject.   But though they are the productions of his youth, and in a state of comparative imperfection, yet they bear the marks of a mighty genius; they present thoughts strong and original, in a corresponding style of energy and majesty; they show the author powerfully affected by what he writes, and when the subject requires it, warmed by imagination, and heated by passion; they impress and captivate the reader, and animate him with the same admiration, love, fear, and hatred with which the orator is inspired.

We shall present, in a free translation, a few quotations from some of his sermons, fully sensible how much is lost in such translation, and how a resort to the original can alone discover their beauties.

One of the best sermons is on the *Truth and Perfection of the Christian Religion*, from Matt. xi. 5, 6.—" Preached before the king."   It is, throughout, convincing and eloquent.   We make the following extract:

* " Truth is a queen who may be said to inhabit her own ex-cellence; who reigns invested with her own native splendour, and who is enthroned in her own grandeur, and upon her own felicity.   This queen condescending to reign in our world for the good of man, our Saviour came down from above to establish her empire upon earth.   Human reason is not consulted in the establishment of her empire.   Relying on herself, on her celestial origin, on her infallible authority, she speaks and demands belief; she publishes her edicts, and exacts submission; she holds out to our assent the sublime and incomprehensible union of the most blessed Trinity; she proclaims a God-man, and shows him to us extended on a cross, expiring in ignominy and pain, and calls upon human reason to bow down before this tre-mendous mystery.

* "La vérité est une reìne qui habite en elle-même," &c., &c.

" The Christian religion, not resting her cause upon the principles of human reason, rejects also the meretricious aid of human eloquence. It is true the apostles, who were its preachers, humbled the dignity of the Roman fasces, and laid them at the foot of the cross ; and in those very trials to which they were summoned as criminals, they made their judges tremble. They conquered idolatry, and presented their converts as willing captives to the true religion. But they accomplished this end, not by the artifice of words, by the arrangement of seductive periods, by the magic of human eloquence—they effected it by a sacred persuasive power which impressed—more than impressed—which captivated the understanding. This power being derived from heaven, preserves its efficiency, even as it passes through the lowly style of unadorned composition ; like a rapid river, which, as it courses through the plain, retains the impetuosity which it acquired from the mountain whence it sprung, and from whose lofty source its waters were precipitated.

" Let us then form this conclusion, that our Saviour has revealed to us the light of the Gospel by means worthy of the Giver, and at the same time by means the most consonant with our nature. Surrounded as we are by error, and distressed with uncertainty, we require not the aid of a doubting academician, but we stand in absolute need of a God to illuminate our researches. The path of reason is circuitous, and perplexed with thorns. Pursuit presupposes distance, and argument indecision. As the principle of our conduct is the object of this inquiry, it is necessary to have recourse to an immediate and immutable belief. The Christian finds everything easy in his faith ; for though the doctrines of which Christ proposes to his acceptance are too immeasurable for the narrow capacity of his intellect, yet they may be embraced by the expansive submission of his belief.

" Let us dwell on a theme so interesting ; let us direct our view to those divine features which proclaim the heavenly origin of our religion. When she first descended from above, did she not come as an unwilling visitant ? Rejection, hatred, and persecution met her in every step ; nevertheless she made no appeal to human justice, no application to the secular power; she enlisted defenders worthy of her cause, who, in attachment to her interests, presented themselves to the stroke of the executioner, in such numbers that persecution grew alarmed, the law blushed at its own decree, and princes were constrained to recall their sanguinary edicts. It was the destiny of truth to erect her throne in opposition to the kings of the earth. She called not for their assistance, when she laid the foundation of her own establishment—but, when the edifice rose from its foundation, and lifted high its impregnable towers, she then adopted the great for her children; not that she stood in need of their concurrence, but in order to cast an additional lustre on their authority, and to dignify their power. At the same time, our holy religion maintained its independence; for when sovereigns are said to protect religion, it is rather religion that protects them, and is the firmest support of their thrones. I appeal for the ascertainment of this fact to the history of the church. The world threatened, but the Christian religion continued firm; error polluted the stream, but the spring retained its purity; schism wounded the holy form of the church, but the truth remained inviolable; many were seduced, the weak overcome, the strong shaken, but the pillar of the sacred edifice stood immovable.

"—You that think yourselves endowed with a sagacity to pervade the secrets of God, approach, and unfold to us the mysteries of nature—the whole creation is spread out before you. Choose your theme—unravel what is at a distance, or develope what is near; explain what is beneath your feet; or illustrate the wonderful luminary which glitters over your head. What! does your reasoning faculty stagger on the very threshold? Poor, presumptuous, erring traveller, do you expect that an unclouded beam of truth is to illuminate your path? Ah! be no more deceived. Advert to the dark, tempestuous atmosphere, which is diffused over that country through which we are travelling; advert to the imbecility of our reasoning powers; and until the Omniscient God shall remove the obscuring veil that hangs between heaven and earth, let us not reject the solitary aid and soothing intervention of a simple faith."

In the sermon *on the Crucifixion*, from Gal. vi. 14, the influence of Christianity in destroying idolatry is strikingly exhibited :

* " Religious truth was exiled from the earth, and idolatry sat brooding over the moral world. The Egyptians, the fathers of philosophy, the Grecians, the inventors of the fine arts, the Romans, the conquerors of the universe, were all unfortunately celebrated for perversion of religious worship, or gross errors, which they admitted into their belief, and the indignities which they offered to the true religion. Minerals, vegetables, animals, and elements, became objects of adoration ; even abstract visionary forms, such as fevers and distempers, received the honours of deification ; and to the most infamous vices and dissolute passions altars were erected. The world, which God made to manifest his power, seemed to have become a temple of idols, where everything was God but God himself. The mystery of the Saviour's crucifixion was the remedy which the Almighty ordained for this universal idolatry. He knew the mind of man ; and he knew that it was not by reasoning that an error could be destroyed, which reasoning had not established. Idolatry prevailed by the suppression of the rational faculty ; by suffering the senses to predominate, which are apt to clothe everything with qualities with which they are affected. Men gave the Divinity their own figure, and attributed to him their vices and passions. It was a subversion of reason, a delirium, a frensy. Argue with a man who is insane—you do but the more provoke him, and render the distemper incurable. Neither will such argumentation cure the delirium of idolatry. What has learned antiquity gained by her elaborate discourses—her disputations so artfully framed ? Did Plato, with that eloquence which was styled divine, overthrow one single altar, where those monstrous divinities were worshipped ? Experience has shown that the overthrow of idolatry could not be the work of reason alone. Far from commissioning human wisdom to cure such a malady, God completed its confusion by the mystery of the cross. When that was raised, and displayed to the world an agonized Re-

* La vérité religieuse étoit exilé sur la terre, &c.

deemer, incredulity exclaimed, it was *foolishness*—but the darkened sun—nature convulsed—the dead arising from their graves, said, it was *wisdom*."

Many fine thoughts are found in the sermon on *the Name of Jesus*, from Matt. i. 21.

* "I cannot observe without an emotion of astonishment the conduct of the Son of God. I observe him through the course of his ministry displaying, even with magnificence, the lowliness of his condition, and when the hour approaches which is to terminate in his death, the word *glory* dwells on his lips, and he discourses with his disciples of nothing but his greatness. On the eve of his ignominious death, when the traitor had just gone from him, big with his execrable intention, it was then that the Saviour of the world cried out, with a divine ardour—' Now is the Son of man glorified.' Tell me in what manner he is going to be glorified? What means the emphatic word—*now?* Is he at once to rise above the clouds, and thence to advance vengeance on his foes? Or is the angelic hierarchy, seraphs, dominions, principalities, and powers, to descend from on high, and pay him instant adoration? No! he is going to be degraded; to submit to excruciating pain; to expire with malefactors. This is what he denominates his *glory*; this is what he esteems his triumph! Behold his entrance into Jerusalem, ' riding on an ass.' Ah! Christians, let us not be ashamed of our Heavenly King—let the sceptic deride, if he please, this humble appearance of the Son of God; but I will tell human arrogance that this lowly exhibition was worthy of the king who came into this world, in order to degrade and crush beneath his feet all terrestrial grandeur. Behold what a concourse of people, of all ages and of all conditions, precede him, with branches of palm trees, in the act of exultation—how the air resounds with the acclamations: ' Hosannah to the Son of David—blessed is he that cometh in the name of the Lord.' Whence this sudden change, so opposite to his former conduct? Whence is it that *he* now courts applause, whom we see in another part of the gospel, retiring to the summit of a solitary mountain to escape the

* Certes je ne puis voir sans étonnement dans les Ecritures Divines, &c.

solicitations of the multitudes assembled from the neighbouring cities and villages for the purpose of electing him their king? He now listens with complacency to the people who accost him with that title. The jealous Pharisees endeavour to impose silence; but the Saviour cries, 'If these should hold their peace, the stones would immediately cry out.' I ask again, whence is this abrupt change? why does he approve of what he lately abhorred, and accept of what he lately rejected? Entering Jerusalem now for the last time, it is in order to die; and agreeably to his sentiments, to die is to reign; to die, in his estimation, is to be 'glorified.' How dignified was his conduct through the whole process of his passion! How dignified his deportment at the tribunal of Pilate! The Roman President asked, 'Art thou a king?' The Son of God, who had until that time been silent, no sooner heard his title to royalty mentioned, than he abruptly replied, 'Thou sayest that I am a king; to this end was I born, and for this cause came I into the world.' Yes! gracious Saviour, I comprehend thee—it is thy glory to suffer for the love of thy people; and thou wilt not claim the sceptre, until, by a victorious death, thou deliverest thy subjects from eternal slavery!

"Let heaven and earth burst forth into a song of praise, for Jesus Christ is a King. To those who have been regained and subdued to his protection at so high a price, he is a most liberal monarch—through him they not only live, but have the hope of reigning themselves—for such is the munificence of our celestial King, that in every court, every brow is to be encircled with a diadem. Listen to the beautiful hymn of the twenty-four elders —representing most probably the assemblage of the faithful under the Old and the New Testament—the one half representing the twelve patriarchs of the Jewish church; the other half, the twelve apostles of the Christian Church. Observe that the elders are crowned, that they fall prostrate in humble adoration before the Lamb, singing, 'Thou hast made us kings.' Let me ask if human grandeur dare for a moment to enter into competition with this celestial court? Cyneas, the ambassador of Pyrrhus, in speaking of ancient Rome, said that he beheld in that imperial city as many kings as senators. But our God calls us to a more resplendent exhibition; in this court, this nation of elected kings, this triumphal city, whose walls are cemented by the blood of Christ, I not only affirm that we shall behold as many kings as senators, but I assert that there will be as many kings as inhabitants. The King of the world admits to the participation of his throne all the people whom he has redeemed by his blood and subdued by his grace."

There are some similar thoughts in his second sermon " pour le premier dimanche de l'avent;"—in which there is a beautiful contrast between Jesus Christ and Alexander—presented with great simplicity, by an allusion to authentic history.

* " Hear how the author of the first book of Maccabees speaks of the great king of Macedonia, whose name seemed to breathe nothing but victory and triumph. ' It happened that Alexander, son of Philip, reigned over Greece, and made many wars, and won many strongholds, and slew the kings of the earth, and went to the ends of the world, and took spoils of many nations, insomuch that the earth was quiet before him.' What a grand and magnificent beginning!—but hear the conclusion. ' After these things he fell sick, and perceived that he must die; wherefore he called his servants, and parted his kingdom among them. So Alexander reigned twelve years, and he died.' To this fate is suddenly reduced all his glory; in this manner the history of Alexander the Great terminates. How different the history of Jesus Christ! It does not indeed commence in a manner so pompous—neither does it end in a way so ruinous. It begins by showing him to us in the sordid manger—then leads him through various stages of humiliation—then conducts him to the infamy of the cross—and at length envelopes him in the darkness of the tomb—confessedly the very lowest degree of depression. But this, instead of being the period of his final abasement, is that from which he recovers, and is exalted. He rises—ascends—takes possession of his throne—is extending his glory to the utmost bounds of the universe, and will one day come with great power to judge the quick and the dead."

* " Ecoutez comme parle l'Histoire," &c. &c.

In his addresses to the king, there is a noble and manly freedom which we cannot but admire—an apostolic fidelity which shows a marked dislike and careful avoidance of adulation. The following is a specimen :

* " While your majesty looks down from that eminence to which Providence has raised you ; while you behold your flourishing provinces reaping the harvest of happiness, and enjoying the blessings of peace ; while you behold your throne encompassed with the affections of a loyal people what have you to fear ?   Where is the enemy that can injure your happiness ? Yes ! sire, there is an enemy that can injure you—that enemy is yourself—that enemy is the glory that encircles you. It is no easy task to submit to the rule that seems to submit to us.   Where is the canopy of sufficient texture to screen you from the penetrating and searching beams of unbounded prosperity ?   Let me entreat you to descend in spirit from your exalted situation, and visit the tomb of Jesus ; there you may meditate on loftier subjects than this world with all its pomp can offer ; there you may learn that by our Redeemer's resurrection from the grave, you may be entitled to a crown of immortal glory.

" What will it avail you, sire, to have lifted so high the glory of your country, unless you direct your mind to works which are of estimation in the sight of God, and which are to be recorded in the book of life ?   Consider the terrors which are to usher in the last day, when the Saviour of the world will appear in tremendous majesty, and send judgment unto victory. Reflect if the stars are then doomed to fall, if the glorious canopy of the heavens is to be rolled together as a scroll, how will those works endure, which are constructed by man ?   Can you, sire, affix any real grandeur to what must one day be blended in the dust ? Elevate then your mind, and fill the page of your life with other records and other annals."

We have often been struck with the manner in which truth is pressed upon the conscience, and the sinner urged to immediate repentance. The following is a single instance from many that might be presented :

* "Pendant que votre majesté regarde en bas de cette élévation," &c., &c.

* " When God transported the prophetic spirit of Ezekiel into the valley of bones, he heard a voice cry out, ' Can these dry bones live ?   Say unto them, Oh ! ye dry bones, hear the word of the Lord.'   The application is obvious ; bring it home to your own bosoms ; enforce it on your own situation.   Let no time be lost ; defer not to a distant period your repentance ; the voice that now whispers to your soul, ' Oh ! ye dry bones, hear the voice of the Lord,' will perhaps never invite you more.   The season of age and weakness will betray you ; when you are arrived within a few steps of the grave, you will find neither time, nor disposition, nor capacity to perform the solemn task which you have so long delayed—your soul will be encumbered with a train of confused, turbid, comfortless thoughts (I have unhappily often witnessed such scenes),—your cold lips will utter a few imperfect prayers that will not reach the heart any more than water gliding over a marble surface will penetrate the substance.   Seize then the present hour—the offered moment. Why will you perish ?   You, my brethren, who have been distinguished by so many blessings, to whom, in your earlier years, the immaculate page of Christianity was unfolded ; who were reared in the hallowed bosom of religion, why will ye perish ? You for whom this roof resounds with the voice of the preacher, for whom that table is spread with celestial food, why will you perish ?   You for whom Jesus died, for whom he rose from the dead—and now, willing your salvation, shows to his Father the sacred wounds he suffered, why will you perish ?

" The best method to raise our thoughts above this speck of earth, is first to contemplate the deceitful and fugitive tenure of terrestrial existence.   May we not compare human life to a road that terminates in a ruinous precipice ?   We are informed of the dangers we incur, but the imperial command is announced, and we must advance.   I would wish to turn back, in order to avoid the ruinous precipice, but the tyrant necessity exclaims, ' advance, advance.'   An irresistible power seems to carry me along. Many inconveniences—many hardships—many untoward accidents occur ; but they would appear trivial, could I withhold

* Quand Dieu transportoit l'esprit prophétique, &c.

my steps from the ruinous precipice. No! no! An irresistible power urges me to proceed, and even impels me to run—such is the rapidity of time. Some pleasant circumstances, however, present themselves; we meet with objects in the course of our journey, which attract attention—limpid streams—groves resounding with harmony—trees loaded with delicious fruit—flowers exhaling their aromatic odour into the passing gale. Here we would be glad to wander, and suspend the progress of our journey; but the voice exclaims, 'advance, advance,'—while all the objects we have passed suddenly vanish, like the materials of a turbid dream. Some wretched consolation still remains—you have gathered some flowers as you have passed by, which, however, wither in the hand that grasps them—you have plucked some fruit, which, however, decays before it reaches the lips. This, this is the enchantment of delusion. In the progress of your destined course, you now approach the tremendous gulf which breathes forth a solemn vapour that discolours every object. Behold the shadowy form of Death rising from the jaws of the fatal gulf, to hail your arrival! Your heart palpitates—your eyes grow dim—your cheeks turn pale—your lips quiver—the final step is taken—and the hideous chasm swallows up your trembling frame."

We make but one more quotation from his sermons, from a discourse on *the Sufferings of the Soul of Jesus*, founded on Isaiah liii. 6. And we do it the more cheerfully, as his sentiments on the doctrine of the Atonement are so correct and scriptural.

* "The most soothing consolation to the man plunged in affliction, is the consciousness of his freedom from guilt, which, like an angel, watches at his side, and whispers comfort to his soul. The holy confidence arising from this source supported the martyrs, and upheld their enduring patience under the pressure of the severest tortures. This consolation acted with a magical influence; it calmed their sufferings; it lulled the exquisite sensation of the flames which consumed their bodies, and diffused over their countenance the expression of a celestial joy.

* La consolation la plus douce pour un homme qui souffert, &c.

But Jesus, the personally innocent Jesus, found no such consolation in his sufferings; what was given to the martyrs was denied to the King of martyrs. Under the ignominy of a most disgraceful death, under the impression of the most agonizing torments, he was not allowed to complain, nor even to think that he was treated with injustice. It is true he was personally innocent; but what did the recollection of an immaculate life avail him? His Heavenly Father, from whom alone he looked for consolation, who from eternity had shed upon his beloved Son the effulgence of his glory, now withdraws his sacred beams, and spreads over his head an angry cloud. Behold the innocent Jesus, the spotless Lamb, suddenly become the goat of abomination, burdened with the sins of men. It is no longer the Jesus who once said, ' Which of you convinceth me of sin!' (John viii. 46),—he presumes to speak no more of his innocence. Oh! Jesus, I view thee bending beneath the weight of human guilt. See, my brethren, see imputed to him the sins of men ; see the turbulent ocean of iniquity ready to engulf him ; wherever he casts his eye, he beholds torrents of sin bursting upon him. By a wonderful commutation, which comprises the mystery of our salvation, one is smitten and others are delivered. God smites his innocent Son for the sake of guilty men ; and pardons guilty men for the sake of his innocent Son. How inadequate is all language to express such mercy ! Let this sanctuary be to every one of us a Calvary, and let us not depart hence, before we have kindled in our bosoms the flame of eternal gratitude for the sublime act of love which is this day recorded through the Christian world."

But it is in his *Funeral Orations* that the eloquence of Bossuet is specially seen. These were prepared in mature life when his taste was chastened, received all the correction which his hand could give them, and by universal consent are the enduring memorials of the loftiest genius. They are not only uncommonly spirited, and animated with the boldest figures, but frequently rise to a degree of the sublime. While celebrating the illustrious dead, he employs them as preachers to the living; while sitting on the tombs of kings and princes, he crushes the pride of all kings, levels them with the meanest of their subjects, and confounds them in the common dust.

His success in this species of eloquence is seen in his *Funeral Oration for Henrietta, Queen of England, wife of Charles 1.* It was a subject worthy of the great talents of Bossuet; a subject most dramatic and eventful—a rebellion crowned with victory —a fugitive queen—a monarch bleeding on the scaffold—all furnishing important materials for such a discourse, and employed in such a manner as to bear the impress of the highest eloquence. While he paints in vivid colours the civil commotions, he shows us God in them all, " setting up one and putting down another," destroying thrones, precipitating revolutions, subduing opposition : and while thus directing our attention to a superintending Providence, he casts a religious awe through the whole scene, which renders it really pathetic, and truly grand.

In adverting to the dignified manliness which accompanied Charles I. in the last scenes of his life, the orator says :

* " Pursued by the unrelenting malignity of fortune, abandoned, betrayed, defeated, he never abandoned himself. His mind rose superior to the victorious standard of the enemy. Humane and magnanimous in the moment of victory, he was great and dignified in the hour of adversity. This is the image which presents itself to my view in his last trial. Oh ! thou august and unfortunate queen ! I know that I gratify thy tender affection, while I consecrate these few words to his memory—that heart which never lived but for him, awakens even under the pall of death, and resumes its palpitating sensibility at the name of so endeared a husband."

Instead of directly saying that Charles died on the scaffold, he represents the queen as adopting the words of Jeremiah, who alone is capable of lamentations equal to his sorrows.

† " Oh ! Lord, behold my afflictions, for the enemy hath magnified himself : the adversary hath spread out his hand upon all my pleasant things ; my children are desolate, because the enemy prevailed. The kingdom is polluted, and the princes

---

* Poursuivi à toute outrance par l'implacable malignité, &c. &c.

† Jérémie lui-même, qui seul, &c. &c.

thereof. For these things I weep; mine eye runneth down with water, because the comforter that should relieve my soul is far from me." (Lam. i. 9, 16.)

In this manner he speaks of the queen's escape from her enemies in England:

* " The queen was at length obliged to leave her kingdom. She sailed out of the English ports in sight of the rebellious navy; it approached so near to her in pursuit, that she almost heard their profane cries and insolent threats. Ah! how different was this voyage from that which she made on the same sea, when, going to take possession of the sceptre of Great Britain, she saw the billows smooth themselves under her, to pay homage to the queen of the seas. Now pursued by implacable enemies, who falsely accused and endeavoured to destroy her—sometimes just escaped, and sometimes just taken—her fortune changing every hour—having no other aid but the Almighty and her invincible courage—no winds nor sails to favour her precipitate flight; but God preserved her and permitted her to live."

The *Oration for Henrietta, Princess of England, and daughter of Charles I.,* has not events so grand and striking; and presents not a picture so vast and magnificent—but it exhibits a pathos, though more soft, yet equally touching. Bousset was evidently much affected when he composed this discourse and deeply moved when he delivered it. The fate of a young princess, the daughter, sister, and sister-in-law of a king, enjoying all the advantages of grandeur and beauty—dying suddenly at the age of twenty-six, of a frightful accident, with all the marks of poison, was an event calculated to excite the tenderest commiseration, and to make an impression that would settle on the heart. The Christian orator, tenderly affected by the greatness of the calamity, and the painful circumstances connected with it, declares that " in one single woe he will deplore all human calamities, and in one single death, show the death and emptiness of all human grandeur." He has done it—he exhibits the earth under the image of a universal wreck—shows us man con-

* La reine fut obligée à se retirer de son royaume, &c.

tinually striving for elevation, and the divine power hurling him from the eminence. From the experience of her whom he deplores and celebrates, he vividly delineates the uncertainty of life, the frailty of youth, the evanescence of beauty, the emptiness of royalty, and the utter nothingness of all worldly greatness; while sketching these pensive scenes, he continually returns to the princess, and shows us what she once was, and what she now is.

He describes the manner in which she was almost miraculously delivered out of the hands of her enemies.

* "In spite of the storms of the ocean, and the more violent commotions of the earth, God, taking her on his wings, as the eagle does her young, carries her into that kingdom ; places her in the bosom of the queen, her mother, or rather in the bosom of the Christian church."

How terrible must have been the impression, when he spoke of her death ; when, after a sentence unusually calm, he suddenly cried out :

† "Oh ! ever memorable, disastrous, terrific night ! when consternation reigned throughout the palace ; when, like a burst of thunder, a dispairing voice cried out, ' *The princess is dying— the princess is dead !* '"

At this sentence, the orator was obliged to stop—the audience burst into sobs, and the preacher was interrupted by weeping.

Some moments after, having spoken of the greatness of her soul, and the nature and extent of her virtues, he suddenly stops, and, pointing to the tomb in which she is inclosed, exclaims :

‡ "There she lies as death presents her to our view ; yet even these mournful honours with which she is now encircled will soon disappear ; she will be despoiled of this melancholy decoration, and be conveyed into the dark receptacle, the last

---

* Malgré les tempétes de l'ocean, et les agitations encore plus violentes de la terre, &c., &c.

† O ! nuit désastreuse, O ! nuit effroyable, &c., &c.

‡ La voilà que la mort l'a faite, &c., &c.

gloomy habitation, to sleep in tne dust with annihilated kings, among whom it will be difficult to place her, so closely do the ranks press upon each other—so prompt is death in crowding this gloomy vault with departed greatness. Yet even here our imagination deludes us ; for this form, destitute of life, which still retains the human resemblance, the faint similitude which still lingers in the countenance, must undergo a change, and be turned into a terrific something, for which no language has a name ; so true is it that everything dies that belongs to man, even those funeral expressions that designate his remains."

The following is the conclusion :

* " Should we wait until the dead arise before we open our minds to religious instruction ! What this day descends into the grave should be sufficient to awaken and convert us. Could the divine providence bring nearer to our view, or more forcible display the vanity and emptiness of human greatness ?

† " I entreat you to begin from this hour to despise the smiles of fortune, and the favours of this transient world. And when you shall enter those august habitations—those sumptuous palaces, which receive an additional lustre from the person we now lament—when you shall cast your eyes around those splendid apartments, and find their better ornament wanting, then remember that the exalted station she held, that the accomplishments and attractions she was known to possess, augmented the dangers to which she was exposed in this world, and now form the subject of a righteous investigation in the world to come."

We pass over several of his other orations to the one which we have always regarded as his best—that *on the Prince of Condé*. If ever an orator entered into his subject with the highest enthusiasm, and imparted it to his hearers with elevated passion, it was Bossuet on this occasion. He thoroughly comprehends the character and acts of him whom he celebrates ; collects and combines in a manner the most admirable all the particulars which relate to his birth, his life, his death, his private character, and public career. While thus happy in his arrangement, in

---

* Attendons-noues que Dieu ressuscite des morts, &c. &c.

† Commencez audjourd' hul à mépriser, &c. &c.

description he has all the impetuosity of his hero, and details events with the rapidity and force with which his warrior gained battles. He seems to have at his command all incidents, present, past, and future—he vividly paints, and skilfully unites them— he collects together, and presses upon the imagination a multitude of objects the most grand and startling—and hurries us forward with such precipitation that we become almost breathless ; all preparing us for the following conclusion :—

* " Draw near to this mournful solemnity, people of every rank and profession—draw near, ye great, ye humble, ye rich, ye poor, and chiefly ye, Oh ! illustrious progeny of the house of Bourbon, draw near, and behold all that remains of a birth so exalted, of a renown so extensive, of a glory so brilliant. See all that sumptuousness can perform to celebrate the hero! Mark the titles and inscriptions it has flung around—vain indications of an influence not now to be exercised. Mark those sculptured images, that, sorrowfully bending round yon monument, appear to weep: mark those aspiring columns, which magnificently attest our nothingness. Amidst this profusion of honours, nothing is wanting but the person to whom they are dedicated. Let us then lament our frail and fugitive existence, while we perform the rites of a sickly immortality to the memory of our departed hero. I now address myself particularly to those who are advanced in the same career of military glory. Approach and bewail your great commander. I can almost persuade myself that I hear you saying, ' Is he then no more—our intrepid chief, who through the rugged paths of danger led us on to victory ? His name, the only part of him that remains, is all-sufficient to excite us to future exertions ; his departed spirit now whispers to our souls the sacred admonition that if we hope to obtain at death the reward of our labours, we must serve our God in heaven, and not be satisfied with serving our sovereign on earth.' Yes ! serve your heavenly King—enter fully into the service of your God, the great remunerator, who in the prodigality of his mercy will estimate higher one pious act, or a drop of water given in his name, than the sovereigns of the earth will

* Venez, peuple, venez maintenant, &c. &c.

prize the sacrifice of your lives in their service. Shall not they also approach this mournful monument, who are united to him by the sacred bond of friendship? Draw near, ye companions of his social hours; pay homage to the memory of your associate, whose goodness of heart equalled his intrepidity of soul, and let his death be at once the object of your sorrow, your consolation and your example. As for me, if I may be permitted, in my turn, to deliver the sentiments of my affection, I should say, Oh! thou illustrious theme of my encomium and of my regret, thou shalt ever claim a place in my grateful recollection. The image, however, which is there engraved, is not impressed with that daring eye which foretells victory; for I will behold nothing in thee which death effaces; but on this image shall be found the features of immortality. The image presents itself as I beheld thee at the hour of dissolution, when the glories of the heavenly world seemed to burst upon thee. Yes, at that moment, even on the couch of languor, did I behold thee more triumphant than in the plains of Fribourg or Rocroy—so true is what the beloved disciple says: 'This is the victory that overcometh the world, even our faith.' Enjoy, oh prince, this victory, and let it be the object of thy eternal triumph. Indulge these closing accents of a voice which was not unknown to thee. With thee shall terminate all my funeral discourses; instead of deploring the death of others, I will labour to make my own resemble thine; and happy will it be for me, if, taking warning from these gray hairs, I devote myself exclusively to the duties of the ministry, and reserve for my flock, whom I ought to feed with the word of life, the glimmerings of an eye which is almost extinguished, and the faint efforts of a voice that is almost expiring."

Nothing could be finer—nothing more effective to bring down our elevated feelings to calm serenity—nothing better fitted for the closing scene than those "gray hairs," that "feeble voice," that glance into a future state—all well adapted to inspire the heart with the tender sadness becoming such an occasion. Surely Bossuet should be placed in the same rank with men of eloquence, which Milton holds in the class of poets.

After Bossuet had left Paris, to enter upon his other functions to which he had been appointed, BOURDALOUE appeared in 1669; preached the "avent" before the court in 1670, and was chosen one of the preachers "before the king." At his first appearance, his powers as a pulpit orator were highly estimated; multitudes of classes crowded to hear him—his reputation thus early established, never diminished—the lustre increased as he advanced; and to the close of his life he was regarded by all as one of the finest preachers of the age. He had not, it is true, the lofty talents of Bossuet, but he excelled in labour him whom he was incapable of equalling in genius; for forty years he devoted himself almost entirely to the art of preaching; to the preparation of sermons for the instruction of the people. These sermons, instead of sketches on which he enlarged during delivery, are full written discourses, prepared with much care; and on every variety of subjects suited to the pulpit. They are not such as answered only a temporary purpose, like vegetables of a night, or insects of a day; they are read as specimens of oratorical elegance; put into the hands of youth as models; and presented as lessons for the formation of their taste and the improvement of their hearts. No one can read them without perceiving the elevation to which genius may be raised by intense study. In the variety of subjects which are discussed, we see a fulness and luxuriance which leaves nothing further to be said or supposed; an accurate logic which detects and exposes sophistry; an admirable use of the Scriptures, and sometimes of the Fathers; a profound knowledge of the human heart; a continued effort to keep himself out of sight, and an habitual aim at the conversion of his hearers—all expressed in a style simple and nervous, natural and noble.

A clear and proper method is visible in all his writings; to this he devotes much attention; in this he far excels Bossuet; he has the happy talent of arranging his arguments and thoughts, with that order of which the Roman critic speaks, when he compares the merit of an orator who composes a discourse to the skill of a general who commands an army*—everything is found in its proper place.

* "Est velut imperatoria virtus."—QUINT. INSTIT. II.

But Bourdaloue is not more distinguished for the soundness of his judgment, and the strength of his reasoning, than for his power at times in affecting the passions. Not satisfied with impressing the mind with the sense of truth, he rouses the affections of his hearers by the energy and pathos of eloquence—we meet continually with those strokes of passion which penetrate and melt the heart. In his sermons on the *Passion of Christ,* of which he has many, but in which there is no repetition (presenting in each the subject under different views), there are several instances. We quote from one, founded on Luke xxiii. 33, in which is illustrated the truth, that in the death of the Saviour, " righteousness and peace have embraced each other."

I. *Christ died as the victim of Divine Justice.*

II. *As an exhibition of Divine Mercy.*

Under the first head the preacher asks ; * " Who is the victim immolated on the altar erected on Calvery ? None other than the eternal Son of God, in whom dwelleth all the fulness of the Godhead bodily. From the moment of his incarnation, he became the sacrifice, he descended into the world and clothed himself with a mortal body to do homage to the Creator of the universe, and to offer himself a burnt-offering. In the temple of Jerusalem, this sacrifice was continued, when, presented by the hands of Mary, he was placed in the arms of Simeon ; but that was the morning offering—this upon the cross was the evening sacrifice. But why was he exposed to this inexorable justice—this ' Lamb of God without blemish and without spot ? ' Of what crime had he been guilty ? What had he done to draw upon him wrath from on high, and which exposed him to such ignominy and death ? You know that in himself he is the Holy of holies ; that in his celestial abode he received the adoration of the angelic spirits, that he was perfectly blessed, and that he needed no creature to add to his happiness ; that when he appeared on earth as an exile, and deigned to converse with men, he knew sin only to combat and destroy it ; that to him was rendered more than once that illustrious testimony which re-echoed along the banks of Jordan, and resounded upon Tabor

* Car quelle victime lui est immolée sur l'autel, &c., &c.

—'This is my beloved son, in whom I am well pleased.' Yet this Saviour, thus holy in himself, 'took upon him the form of a servant,'—yea, of a sinner ; and though he had never committed sin, and was incapable of committing it, yet 'he bore our sins in his own body upon the tree ;' his holy Father charged our sins upon him, covered, as it were, his whole soul with them—' laid on him the iniquity of us all.' Under an aspect so hideous, so abhorrent to infinite holiness, Heaven considers him on the cross ; under such a weight of sin, the justice of God views him a fit object of its vengeance ; it suffers him not to escape ; it pursues him in a hostile and vindictive manner, and pronounces the sentence of condemnation. Represent to yourselves the victim of which the apostle speaks in his epistle to the Hebrews (xiii. 11)—upon which were placed the iniquities of the people, for expiation, and which 'was burned without the camp.' It is a sensible image of what was accomplished in the person of our Redeemer. They conduct him out of the city— they bring him to Calvary—it is the last place where he is to appear, as the 'man of sorrows ;' and there divine justice stands waiting to exact the whole debt for which he is responsible ; to execute the heavy punishment by the executioners it has chosen. When God drove guilty man from Eden, he sent an angel with a double flaming sword to guard forever the access to the tree of life. By the ministry of an exterminating angel he smote the army of Sennacherib, and for the safety of his people made known his power against the haughty monarch ; but when a sacrifice was to be effected for the salvation of men, no angel was sent to afflict the soul of the Redeemer ; supreme and sovereign justice itself descended, and invisibly presided over the bloody and terrible execution."

In a similar manner the eloquent preacher proceeds, and shows in detail how the executioners of the Saviour are mere instruments in the hands of God of completing his purpose ; and how powerful, and holy, and severe is that justice which crushes a God-man.

The second part, which represents the death of Christ as an *exhibition of the divine mercy*, affords a beautiful instance of antithesis; making, by the contrast, the object stronger and the impression deeper. In the first part, we behold the divine justice citing the Son of God to its tribunal, and sacrificing him, satisfied with nothing but his blood and death; so inflexible as to disregard his dignity and personal innocence; everything, therefore, is awful, and the thoughts terrible. In the second part, all the love and grace of which the Saviour is capable, is presented, and everything is tender and pathetic.

* "The nearer Jesus advances to the close of life, the tenderer is his heart; on the cross he breathes only mercy. He prays, and it is a prayer of mercy; he promises, and it is a promise of mercy; he gives, and it is a gift of mercy.

"1. *He prays, and it is a prayer of mercy*—of the richest mercy, for he prays for his enemies. He prays for the priests and rulers of the synagogue who had formed the conspiracy against him; for the soldiers who had arrested, the people who had insulted, the false witnesses who had calumniated, Pilate who had condemned, and the executioners who had crucified him. It would have been mercy most wonderful, if he had done it on the acknowledgment and repentance of their crime. But he pleads for them, when they are loading him with new outrages; when they are uttering blasphemies and imprecations; when they are shaking their heads with scorn, and saying, 'he saved others—himself he cannot save—if thou be the Son of God, come down from the cross'—when they are deriding his power and holiness, his offices and divinity. In the midst of such insults and execrations, he raises his eyes to heaven, and what does he ask? Is it not that the thunders may descend, that righteous vengeance may follow the commission of such horrid crimes? No! my brethren, mercy leads him to speak, no word is uttered which is not dictated by mercy. 'Father, forgive them, they know not what they do.' He does not say *God*, but *Father*, for that is a name more tender and endearing—more favourable for giving audience to petition, and for averting wrath. He does not plead for this one or that one less guilty than others in the conspiracy against him, but he prays in

* Plus il avance vers la fin de sa carrière, plus son cœur s'attendrit, &c. &c.

general, without excluding any, without excepting those who treated him so cruelly in the court of Caiaphas and Herod; those who scourged and smote him, or those who pierced his temples with thorns, or those who drove the nails into his hands and feet. There is not one whom his arms and bosom are not open to receive—not one for whom he would not be an advocate and intercessor. He more than prays, he extenuates their crime; his love leads him to find something to plead in their behalf— 'they know not what they do'—they are blind, and know not the enormity of the offence which they are committing; they know not whom they revile and torture; they know not that they are crucifying the Lord of glory.

" 2. *He promises, and it is a promise of mercy.* Admire the virtue and efficacy of that prayer which has just ascended to heaven—scarcely is it offered before it is answered by a miracle of grace—scarcely is it offered before an enemy of Christ, a thief and malefactor, is converted and pardoned. He was a wretch, worse probably than Barabbas—a blasphemer who united with the other malefactor in reviling Jesus, for the Evangelist says (referring to them both), they ' cast the same in his teeth.' But behold, by a secret and resistless impression of divine grace, this bold blasphemer and robber changed into an humble penitent, who gives glory to God, who publicly confesses his sins, and acknowledges himself worthy of death, who publishes the innocence of that ' just one' who is crucified, who addresses Jesus as his sovereign, and asks admission into his heavenly kingdom, and who receives from the Son of God that consoling assurance, ' to-day thou shalt be with me in Paradise.'

" 3. *He gives, and it is a gift of mercy.* Do you ask, what is his last will and testament? what the disposition of this dying man's effects? what personal property or landed estate does he bequeath? Ah! my brethren, what riches had he to leave who ' had not where to lay his head'—who in ordinary circumstances was sustained by alms, and in extraordinary cases, by miracles? What then does he give? From that engine of torture to which he is fastened he looks down, and what is before those eyes that begin to be weighed down by the hand of death? His own mother Mary, and his beloved disciple, John—that is the price-less treasure, the precious succession. At this sight, all exhausted as he is, his heart awakens; in his state of suffering, increasing every moment, he is not so occupied as to be regardless of these friends; he cannot leave them without giving them a last proof of his remembrance, and a genuine pledge of his love; he cannot commend his spirit into the hands of his Father without affording them consolation. With serenity, firmness, and ten-derness, he turns to his mother: 'behold thy son—he will discharge the filial office, guard, nourish, and defend thee.' Then saith he to the disciple, 'behold thy mother—regard her as thou wouldst the tenderest of all connexions, as thy mother.' 'And from that hour that disciple took her to his own home.'"

The conclusion, in which the hearers are invited to cultivate love to Christ as the best preparation for death, is urgent and tender—we have, however, no room for it.

We have spoken of the fidelity of Bossuet in addressing his king; we find the same faithfulness in Bourdaloue; the same disposition to remind him of his duty to his God; the same pungent appeals to the conscience, the same, or severer reproofs of vices which were prevalent in the court. Instead of quoting from his addresses, we shall relate a circumstance which is well authenticated, illustrative of this trait in his character, and of the power of divine truth; fully equal to the courage of John the Baptist towards Herod, or to the intrepidity of Paul before Felix.

In one of the sermons which he preached before the monarch, he described with great eloquence the horrors of an adulterous life, its abomination in the sight of God, its scandal to man, and all the evils which attend it; but he managed his discourse with so much address, that he kept the king from suspecting that the thunder was ultimately to fall upon him. In general, Bourdaloue spake in a level tone of voice, with his eyes partly closed. On this occasion, having wound the attention of the monarch and the audience to the highest pitch, he paused. The audience expected something terrible, and seemed to fear the next word. The pause continued for sometime—at length the preacher, fixing his eye directly on his royal hearer, and in a tone of voice equally expressive of horror and concern, cried out in the words of the prophet, "*thou art the man!*" then leaving the words to their effect, he concluded with a general prayer to heaven for the conversion of all sinners. When the service was concluded, the monarch walked slowly from the church, and ordered Bourdaloue into his presence. He reminded him of his general protection of religion, the kindness which he had ever shown to the society of Jesus, his particular attention to himself and his friends. He then sternly asked him, "What could have been your motive for insulting me, thus publicly, in the presence of my subjects?" Bourdaloue fell on his knees; " God is my witness that it was not my wish to insult your majesty; but I am a minister of God, and must not disguise the truth. What I said in my sermon is my morning and evening prayer. May God in his infinite mercy grant me to see the day, when the greatest of monarchs shall be the holiest of kings." The king was affected, and silently dismissed the preacher; but from this time the court began to observe that change which led Louis to a life of greater regularity.

More known and read among us than either of the others of whom we have spoken, is MASSILLON; whose name is almost proverbial as a master of pulpit eloquence. He was transferred to Paris about the year 1690, and was, therefore, contemporary with Bourdaloue. Admiring him who at that time was regarded as the prince of preachers, he determined not to imitate him, but to strike out for himself a new path in the field of pulpit oratory. He was satisfied that profound argumentation is not sufficient for the pulpit; that a preacher must not only instruct the mind, but succeed in affecting the passions; that if some of the hearers are incapable of laying hold of an act of reasoning, all have souls capable of being moved by weighty sentiments. This plan he proposed; and this plan he executed like a man of genius.

None of the French preachers have so much of that *unction*, that tender and affecting manner which interests and allures ; that mild magic, gentle fascination, endearing simplicity which characterizes the Evangelists. This is apparent in almost all his discourses. He has not, it is true, the sublime strains of Bossuet, and does not so often produce violent agitations, yet he succeeds in insinuating himself into the heart, and awakening the tenderest affections ; he lays open the secret recesses of the soul with so delicate a hand, that the hearer, before he is aware, is persuaded and overcome. Instead of wandering in abstract speculation, he has all the liveliness of continued address, and speaks *to* his hearers, *all* his hearers, because he speaks to the *heart*. This is the characteristic of his eloquence—what in others is proof and reason, in him is feeling. For this cause, every one saw himself in the lively picture that was presented ; every one imagined the discourse addressed to him, and supposed the speaker meant him only. Hence the remarkable effects of his preaching. No one after hearing him, stopped to praise or criticise—each retired in a pensive silence, and with a thoughtful air, carrying home the arrow which the preacher had lodged in his heart.

In his funeral orations, he is not so happy; he does not there fully sustain his character as an orator. He who in his sermons made his eloquence seen and felt—at one time gentle and persuasive, at another strong and vehement; who knew so well how to paint religion in all its charms, and sin in all its deformity, who seldom failed in reaching the heart, here disappoints us, and shows that he was better calculated to instruct kings and princes than to celebrate them. We must not, however, overlook his funeral oration at the interment of Louis XIV.—an office to which he was probably designated by the monarch himself ; for we are told that among other arrangements which he made on his death-bed, he gave particular directions about his funeral solemnities. It is a discourse worthy, in many respects, of the grandeur of the occasion ; possessing a majesty of style well becoming such an occasion, and adorned with all the magnificence of imagery—but yet, with all its richness, while it excites the highest admiration, it is scarcely capable of touching

the heart. One excellency, however, must not be overlooked—
it is not an unqualified eulogy—the orator speaks openly of the
follies and vices of him whom he celebrates, and hesitates not to
declare that this reign, so brilliant to the monarch, was most
disastrous to the people; an instance well worthy of being
noted, of the courage and fidelity of a minister of God.

The exordium has often been quoted. To see the propriety
of the language, and to account for the effect, we must consider
the text of the preacher, and the circumstances of his position.
The text was Eccl. i. 16, 17—"I became great,* and got more
wisdom than all they that were before me in Jerusalem; I perceived that this also is vexation of spirit." The circumstances
were peculiar. The church was hung with black; a magnificent mausoleum was raised over the bier, the edifice was filled
with trophies of the monarch's glories, daylight was excluded,
and its place supplied by innumerable tapers; and the ceremony
was attended by the most illustrious persons in the kingdom.
Massillon ascended the pulpit, contemplated for some moments
the scene before him, then raised his arms to heaven, looked
down on the scene beneath, and after a short pause, slowly said
(in allusion to his text, which he had already repeated), in a
solemn, subdued tone, " *God only is great!* " With one impulse,
all the audience rose from their seats, turned to the altar, and
slowly and reverently bowed.

Another instance of the mighty effect of his preaching, is
known to every one, and has been quoted a thousand times—the
instance mentioned by Voltaire, when Massillon preached his
celebrated sermon on "the small number of the righteous."
When the preacher was drawing near to the close, the whole
assembly were moved; by a sort of involuntary motion they
started from their seats, and manifested such indications of surprise and terror as for a time wholly disconcerted the speaker.
We have often read the discourse to inquire what could produce
such a startling effect. Much of it is to be attributed to the
timely and repeated use of that powerful figure, Interrogation;

---

* Though in our version it is, "I am come to great estate," yet in the
French it is, "Je suis devenu grand."

a figure by which Demosthenes aroused the Athenians, and Cicero overwhelmed Cataline; a sure method, when employed at the proper time and place, of startling the hearers, and agitating the heart. The preacher had accurately described the character of the righteous—he had succeeded in separating his hearers from the rest of mankind; they thought of no others, and regarded themselves alone as criminals to be judged. They see the judge descending, ready to make the separation and to pronounce the sentence; they are filled with trembling solicitude to know on whom the thunder will fall; their imaginations are terrified, and their thoughts confused. When the orator has brought his hearers into this state, and sees their countenances reflecting their emotions, then gathering all his strength, and with tones and actions corresponding, he pours forth the sublime apostrophe; "Where! O! my God, where are thy people? Where are you, O! ye righteous—stand forth, and enjoy your reward!" There is a startling surprise in this interrogation, that may well excite sensation. The words increase the consternation which had long been gathering; each hearer answers the repeated questions put to him by personal accusations; he feels that he is the criminal; he hears the irrevocable sentence; and he shrieks and trembles, lest it be immediately executed.*

If Bossuet be compared to the great Athenian orator, Massillon may well be termed the "French Cicero." Like him, he is rich in ornament, pathetic and persuasive; has a diction smooth and elegant, and is capable at times of seizing and captivating the heart.

We shall not present any extracts from his writings, as so many have been translated into English; though it is much to

* This sermon was preached a second time with most powerful, though not perhaps equal effect, in the royal chapel at Versailles, when Louis was deeply affected.

"Une commotion·fut excitée par le même trait de ce sermon dans la chapelle de Versailles. Louis XIV. la partagea devant Massillon qu'on vit aussitôt changer de visage, et couvrir son front de ses tremblantes mains. Les soupirs étouffés de l'assemblée rendirent l'orateur muet pendant quelques instants, et il parut lui-même encore plus consterné que toute la cour."

be regretted that some of these translations are so weak and inaccurate, and fall so far short of the original.*

We cannot take leave of these illustrious preachers without inquiring into their *manner of delivery*. Like the ancients, they regarded it as an essential branch of oratory, paid to it eminent attention, and are said to have carried it to a high degree of perfection. Bossuet (as we have already intimated) seldom wrote all that he said. Retaining in his memory what he had composed in his closet, he filled up the unfinished sketch in the pulpit, and found a readiness of expression, marked with energy and grace. Bourdaloue and Massillon wrote their discourses in full, and preached memoriter; the latter so accurately, that when asked, which he regarded as his best sermons, he replied, " those which are the most exactly remembered."

Bossuet, in his personal appearance, was liberally gifted by nature for an orator ; possessing a fine and majestic figure. He spake with great authority, in a manner which indicated the expectation of success; with a strong, firm, and manly voice; with an air of candour, simplicity, and vehemence, which showed that his object was to convince and persuade, rather than to gratify and please. Bourdaloue, in one respect, was peculiar ; in the delivery of his sermons, especially in the exordium, he partially closed his eyes, and is so represented in all the portraits of him we have seen ; though he was never charged with the want of ease or grace. In his manner he was grave and serious, and had all the dignity of a prophet. His voice was full and clear, and when elevated to the highest pitch, was sufficient to fill the largest house with the volume of the sound, and to produce a deep impression. His eloquence was usually attended with a strong conviction that great as he was as an orator, he was still greater as a Christian and a minister of God. Massillon ap-

---

* His "Le Petit Carême," or Discourses before Louis XIV., and his work on the "Priesthood," have been well translated ; but we cannot say the same of some of his best sermons, translated by Dickson. That work is servilely liberal, retaining the French idioms, expressing the thoughts of the writer most unskilfully, presenting rhetorical and grammatical errors, and giving us very little idea of the elegance of Massillon. If he had been translated, as Saurin has been, by Robinson, how much more would he be read and prized !

proached still nearer to perfection, and had the power of uttering his sentiments with the highest possible skill. His clear and melodious voice was completely under his control—the lowest whisper could be distinctly heard—and some of his tones were so sweet and tender that they went directly to the heart, and at once drew tears from the eyes. And yet, when necessary, his shrill tones penetrated like arrows; he could utter such piercing cries, as would startle his hearers, and bring them upon their feet—and by such instances of the terrible, make his whole audience bow before him. Thus differing from each other, these orators, in one respect, were all alike; in their elocution, they imitated nature, as they had, in composition, followed her directions. They spake with such life and spirit, such freedom and fervency, that (whether Bossuet was speaking extempore, or Massillon repeating what he had committed to memory), all seemed to come fresh from the mind and heart.

Such is the character of that eloquence which once prevailed in France, and such the character of the men who employed it. They exerted a commanding influence, and swayed the minds, and imaginations, and feelings of their auditors, as Demosthenes did the Athenians, and Cicero the Roman senate. Deeply affected themselves, they deeply affected others; strong emotions displayed by words, countenance, tones, gestures, the whole manner, produced, we have seen, effects perfectly overpowering. Is not eloquence like this—the eloquence of warmth and passion —peculiarly suited to the pulpit? Must men be regarded as mere intellectual beings, void of sentiment and feeling? Is not this elevation of soul and style as well adapted to our age and country as to the age of Louis the Great, or the country of France? Would it not produce similar effects? Shall men be allured to our sanctuaries by artificial attractions rather than by the charms of eloquence; by the gorgeousness of architecture rather than by that most attractive of all arts, the art of speaking; by the fascinations even of music, rather than by the enchanting oratory, which, while it expands the understanding, touches the secret springs of the heart? That will please men long after external ornament ceases to gratify; satiated as they will be, in time, by other arts, they will never be weary in their attention to solid thoughts well attired, and well exhibited, in listening to a preacher habitually under the influence of strong passion, and speaking boldly, ardently, and simply.

May the time soon come when there shall be multitudes of such preachers; when great numbers, embracing the whole truth, without any mixture of superstition or error, shall speak in the sublime strains of BOSSUET, with the energy and elevation of BOURDALOUE, and with the insinuating grace and melody of MASSILLON.